Cecil Bling Annul

Theatre

BEHIND
THE
MASQUE

41187

URBAN NAGLE, O. P.

New York

McMULLEN BOOKS, INC.

Imprimi potest:

    JOHN F. RYAN, O.P.
    THOMAS SHANLEY, O.P.

June 14, 1951

Nihil obstat:

    MARTINUS J. HEALY, S.T.D.
    CENSOR LIBRORUM

Imprimatur:

✠ THOMAS EDMUNDUS MOLLOY, S.T.D.
    ARCHIEPISCOPUS-EPISCOPUS BROOKLYNIENSIS

Brooklyni, die II Iulii 1951.

FOREWORD

There is on the fringe of Broadway an organization known as The Blackfriars' Guild. Judging by the number of questions and their variety concerning this unusual venture, perhaps an explanation is in order. At least that is my reason for writing so disorganized and haphazard a book as this promises to be. Its focus will be chronological. If you plunge into a new field and don't know where you're going or exactly where you've been, perhaps chronology is as good a pattern as any. But if you've spent your life in the high discipline of playwriting, and people ask you just what you're doing—or what you think you're doing—perhaps the answer will be as undisciplined as are most accumulations of facts. It may prove nothing, but it will tell who we are and how we got there.

Questions have been asked and that is the best reason I can think of for writing down answers. Those questions will be answered here between whatever interruptions and digressions present themselves.

One of the first questions which forthright people ask, and which cautious people look as though they would like to ask, is: "What are priests doing in the theatre?" Behind that question there are several overtones, depending on the background of the questioner. Some say (with their eyes, of course): "No doubt the Church is making a belated attempt to appear liberal."

Others: "Are you really in good standing and do the authorities really know about this?" (This type has a mischievous look in its collective eyes.) Third group: "I suppose it's pleasant recreation to get away from the work you're supposed to do." There are dozens of categories, but these samples are given merely to indicate that the question is frequently asked, and one likes to note that a question has been asked before setting out to answer it at length.

The second series might be summarized in the blunt form: "How official are you?" Some of these questioners are rather adroit and are accustomed to act under ukase, and they vaguely suspect that Colleges of Cardinals, after careful study, have set us up by mandate and steer our activities by regular proclamation. Other wingers, suspecting just the opposite, would deplore being found dead in connection with a venture which hadn't formal approbation all the way up the line. Theatre is such a human thing—such an individualized thing—that organizations don't do it. People do. No organization wrote the *Lauda Sion* or the *Pange Lingua*. St. Thomas Aquinas wrote them—and perhaps with a broken quill. But adherents of both extremes ask the same questions with the same glint in their eyes.

Then there is the bluff type, whether of the theatre or not, which coughs before the question: "Just what are you trying to do here?" Incidentally, this type loses interest long before the halting answer is finished.

The scholarly type says: "Now, just what is Catholic theatre and what is a Catholic play?" That's going to take some answering.

The oft-repeated question which has a pragmatic sound about it runs in this vein: "I have a nephew (or niece) who showed great talent in high-school dramatics. Would you give him (or her) an opportunity to act with your little group?" To this question we have a formula. The prodigy registers with us and his (or her) name goes in with those of almost ten thousand other nephews or nieces.

Some questions can't be disposed of in so mechanical a fashion. Yet they will be answered here. A simple way would be to describe our present operations—to cut through a twenty-year-old venture at this point in time, explaining its functions and attempting a series of essays on the philosophy behind it. But that might be stuffy, and you wouldn't have seen it grow.

The actor is essentially a masquer—by profession. But the producer-playwright grows or finds or buys a masque in twenty years. It's that simple. He lives in a world of masques and finally he is looking out through slits in papier mache. The chuckles and tears are kept inside because the little ones might be hurt by one or the other. And so, whether he be a tough old commercial producer or a priest who stumbled onto Broadway by a series of accidents, it's your guess whether the mood is comedy or tragedy. He sees much of both and he won't tell you, because he's never sure.

That's my apology for a chronogical story, which is more pleasent to write (if more tedious to read). Though it offers the spectre of autobiographical touches, it may preserve some of the uncertainty, some of the heartache and some of the laughter which have made up The Blackfriars' Guild.

CONTENTS

BEHIND THE MASQUE

1: THE TRAP

W<small>E ARE NOT THEATRE PEOPLE WHO BECAME FRIARS,</small>
Doctor Carey and I. There! It's good to get that said
at the outset. Now I don't have to maintain any pose.
We are not theatre people who became friars; we are
rather friars who knew so little about the theatre that
we walked across a gridiron thinking it was a floor. Of
course, we fell on the stage. And when you shake hands
with the devil you can't let go.

It seems to be my fault that we got up in the fly-
gallery in the first place. I wrote a play. Just like that.
Judging by the number and quality of scripts which
come to Blackfriars, I'm sure there's nothing egregious
about taking a flyer at playwriting, because everybody
dashes off one or two before realizing that it is a highly
specialized business. What does demand explanation is
how that simple act inflicted such consequences on a
number of lives.

My theatrical background was not exactly standard
equipment. In fact, my knowledge of the glamorous
people of the trade in high-school days when most victims are trapped was limited to a doorman and a few
ushers. It happened because of a change in our family
fortunes. My father had been something of a capitalist,
but he suddenly put that title behind him, less because
of his study of Papal Encyclicals on Labor than because
his company was rapidly going broke and he thought

1

it advisable to sell out and look for what, with heads inclined and faces crimsoning, we learned to call a "job."

Providence—the city, in the persons of a good many inhabitants—offered him various partnerships (for a reasonably small investment) in businesses of which he knew very little, but the all-pervading Providence proposed that he salvage what remained from years of hard work and installed him as theatre fireman at the Providence Opera House. When he was established in that neither lucrative nor arduous task, he gathered courage to present me to his new business associates, and to make conversation, in one of the pauses which sprinkled that memorable meeting the doorman asked me if I'd like to see a show or two.

We worked out a formula. I arrived weekly at nineteen minutes after eight (curtain was eight-twenty), handed the doorman nothing which he carefully tore in half, dropping one part in the box and returning me the stub—visible only to such people as see lobblies and pookas. This bit of pantomime was necessary because the company manager was always spying on the house and the local management wouldn't trust archangels. As the lights were dimming, I presented my half of nothing to the head usher, who squinted at it until darkness permitted him to escort me to what he thought would be an inconspicuous seat. Occasionally there were developments because a newcomer offered proof of greater claim to the seat than I could demonstrate. But I handled my invisible stub as a magician palms a coin, accepted the usher's apology for putting me in the wrong place, and picked up the thread of

2

the play from a new vantage point. We had the catastrophe of a full house when Gilpin came with *The Emperor Jones*, so I was retired to a seldom used flight of back stairs which actually enhanced the eeriness of the experience.

Since that process went on for three or four years, and almost every week brought a new play, a twinge of conscience sometimes assails me and I feel partly responsible that so glamorous an institution as the Providence Opera House is now gone. But in estimating my bill, I'm inclined to mark it down a bit because, in the light of greater maturity, I have come to the conclusion that many of the productions which I thought magnificent fall a little short of their advertising. That may be weak ethics, but not too bad criticism. The remainder of the bill goes out the window when I see the retribution being visited on Blackfriars in New York where gate crashing is a fine art and Annie Oakley an army. We're not too hard on gate crashers if they smile as they go by, keep out of cash customers' seats and don't look as though they got away with it. Thus in a roundabout fashion I pay a debt and hope to discover and encourage some of the playwrights of tomorrow.

In 1924, having reached the cataclysmic age of eighteen, I took time out to organize my life. That isn't exactly accurate, because time was called on me. I was taken for a duck by a son of an undertaker and shot at. He didn't miss. And surveying the world from a hospital bed, I decided to live a thoroughly communistic life. So I applied to join the Dominican Order, which has been making a go of that sort of thing for more than seven hundred years. St. Dominic recruited the outfit in 1221 to straighten out some people who were rebuilding God with notions which were creeping in from the East. There is nothing very theatrical about the Order, unless perhaps the striking white habit and black preaching cloak which its members still wear. Intellectually, the Dominicans are about as conservative as they come, priding themselves on purity of dogma.

In the beginning they had more colorful characters, but that is always true of beginnings. Fra Angelico was filling their walls with limpid madonnas; Thomas Aquinas took time from his monumental works on theology to write the songs which are sung more often in this country than anything on any hit parade—*O Salutaris* and *Tantum Ergo;* and Albert the Great developed his experimental laboratories to such an extent that people wagged their heads and whispered stories of black magic.

When that estimable company accepted me, I was very happy and determined to do as the others did, with no thoughts of the make-believe world of theatre. But it seems that in the novitiate in Somerset, Ohio, where I was painstakingly endeavoring to remove mundane things from my mind, a situation arose. We do nothing more enthusiastically than meet situations.

By way of harmless recreation, there was an established custom that the novices prepare a Chrismas play for their own entertainment. Now, the novice master who was busy injecting a semi-military discipline into a group of rugged individualists was new at his end of the business and perhaps not too familiar with its theatrical involvements. Anyway, the play wasn't planned until the day was almost upon us. And a play we'd have, because it was a tradition. Yes, sir! We'd relax from our studies if the relaxing process flattened us. We were not the fickle type to break with a tradition for the trivial reason that we hadn't anything ready.

So the novice master hastened to Columbus, consulted a friend versed in drama, and returned with an impressive pageant concerned with the voyages of one Christopher Columbus. (In those glorious days we had our food and clothes bought in the same impersonal manner.) That much is understandable. But why I was placed on the production committee eludes me, unless my haunting of the Providence Opera House was known to the authorities.

My objections to the pageant were principally technical. It seemed to me that the fabrication of the Nina and the Pinta and the Santa Maria which were part of one scene would be expensive and a little cumbersome. A wiser head than mine computed the cost as infinite, because we'd lose our minds and souls in the process. Incidentally, there were thirty in the class and the cast ran into hundreds.

With trepidation, therefore, the committee reported unfavorably. The novice master was not proud of us. Faced with mere technical difficulties of set building and casting, we had sought an escape! It was a tradition, wasn't it? Not only was our ingenuity impugned, but even our courage. It seemed as though a gauntlet had been flung. I picked it up by volunteering to write a play—a little play cut to fit. If anyone wants one iron glove, I'd be glad to send it prepaid.

The plot was lifted without much feeling of guilt from an unpublished (I hope) script by Vincent McHugh, who later achieved recognition as a novelist. I had a proprietary attitude toward it anyhow, because one of the roles was written for me.

When the writing was finished—a recollection here and a substitution there—there were casting problems. Even the detached souls in a religious novitiate thought that their parts should be fatter. (I am very understanding of that vice when it crops up among professionals.) So, having very little to lose, I obligingly plumped them up until, bad as the play was in its original form, it became hopelessly distorted long before the curtain was drawn. Another small objection I had to padding the minor roles was that it made the lead unimportant by comparison and, as you have guessed, I played the lead.

Far be it from me to countenance the impression that I was more than a cog in a machine. Men who are now famous preachers thundered my hurried lines; men who hold university chairs paraphrased them, too. Due to the array of natural talent with which I was associated in this first venture, it was declared a success. This accolade is hardly a mark of distinction among amateur theatricals, but since this antedated the subsequent bluster of scrapbook and clipping bureau and since I mercifully destroyed the script, we'll have to let it go at that.

One bit of praise I never forgot. The following year, when I had moved on to the House of Philosophy in Chicago and my former novice master was whipping his charges into the proper traditional spirit for their Christmas play, he is reported to have said, "We were very fortunate last year. We had. . . oh, what's his name. . . and he wrote us a play." Much later I learned that the essence of publicity was to get the name right, whatever you said about it, but in those simple bucolic days I was happy in the acknowledgment of achievement. Of course, he might have gone further and said "a good play," but he was a meticulously honest man.

One play led to another as one play is likely to do. Although there isn't much time for such nonsense in the curriculum of a Dominican House of Philosophy, I was challenged by the offer of a prize made by a women's college in the east for a play of a religious nature. The announcement wouldn't have turned the trick, had not a friend said, "I bet you can't write one." Such taunts have been the undoing of many.

The only theatrical venture in my life, comparable to this in sheer folly, was the running of a summer stock company; but of that later. I snapped up the bet and set out to write a play about Biblical events, equipped with an introductory course in Scripture (three days a week), the inadequate library of a new house and a vague recollection of *Ben Hur*.

A ponderous set of tomes bearing the title *Dictionnaire de la Bible* came to light and, after reading columns under *portre, fenetre, maison, chambre* and all the domestic nouns I could recall, I wrote the scene plot with the assurance of a native. The geographical and topographical references were somewhat vague and the resultant picture of a civilization of two thousand years ago superimposed on this shifting foundation was surprising indeed. Worse still, the heroine was sweet, the hero noble and the villain black. There is a forthrightness at twenty-one which is hard to recapture, come twenty-two.

I named the play *Barter* (and being a New Englander never could pronounce the word) and sent it off. There was some consolation in the fact that the judges deemed none of the entrants worthy of a prize. Maybe a few choruses to attract relatives and friends to performances would have helped, but that is an unworthy thought. However, along with the other contestants, whom I shall probably never know, I received the equivalent of my first play rejection slip.

Years passed. A merciful veil of silence may well be drawn over my struggles with philosophy and meditation. Whatever drop of disappointment or bitterness at not having become a sideline playwright might have fallen into my cup was well dried out by the passage of time. But without warning, a judge of the almost forgotten contest wrote to inform me that the Drama League, in conjunction with a publishing house, was offering a bigger prize for similar material and might be more easily satified. The old script was covered with dust, symbolizing oblivion and indicating my qualifications as a monastic housekeeper. The deadline was so near that I had time to do little more than wrap it up.

Because the whole thing was regarded as a lark, I received permission to dispense with the business of official censorship. That item was to be caught up with later in the unlikely event of success. Now, this is noteworthy, because the Dominican Order, special guardian of theology, is nothing if not conservative.

Hoping that the suspense has been properly built up, I will breathlessly announce that *Barter* won the prize. The manner in which it won is probably a better test of its worth. Three different judges chose three different plays for first, second and third, naming nine in all. The upshot of that unparalleled unanimity was that the judges had to meet and I suppose my champion shouted the loudest.

That disputed decision had reverberations. Not a few who read the script under duress and who offered frank opinions of an uncomplimentary nature now decided that it had great merit. Some day that bandwagon is going to tip over with all on board, but there was a week or two of adulation. The staid Order of Preachers made no move toward closing its other departments and setting me up as a playwright. Instead, it promptly collected the prize money and became very touchy about censorship problems. One trivial episode comes to mind. One of my censors (and superior, to boot) questioned me about the mother of Judas, who had a few lines in the play. He found the treatment intriguing, but naturally was interested in my sources. Not being thoroughly purged of the old leaven, I told him glibly that I found Judas in the Bible and thought he had a mother. As I recall, his retort was a bit cutting, but, to the dismay of posterity, it slips my mind at the moment.

Being thus established by a series of accidents, I decided to read some good books to maintain my position. That was a waste of time, too. The critics haven't exactly gotten together in determining what makes a

9

good play and the "How To Write" boys rarely exemplify their guide books. For that matter, I got a little bewildered plowing through the moderns on art in general. So, after a series of pitched battles, I found myself slipping backwards and backwards until I lined up with St. Thomas Aquinas, who once wore the same habit that I was wearing—or one just like it. Thomas wasn't satisfied with the moderns of the thirteenth century so he went back to Aristotle. Every producer on Broadway today knows or suspects that Aristotle is dead and was never fully aware of box-office problems and their ramifications.

However, dead or alive, Aristotle was more comprehensible to me than a few of the first nighters who rush out to meet their deadlines. Among other things, he said that art was the right way of making something. I can understand that. If it is a knife, it is supposed to cut; if it is a chair, it is supposed to hold you up when you are tired standing. Then he broke down art into fine arts and useful arts.

Beauty was the differentiating feature between them. This was, of course, in the days before industrial engineering. Beauty, these real critics thought, was worthy of definition, too. They had the quaint old-fashioned notion that it was pleasant to know what they were talking about, so they defined everything. They'd never hold jobs as political writers today.

So they said that "beauty was that which, being seen [or perceived], pleases." That economical statement opens interesting vistas. Inasmuch as the object of beauty pleases, it has a subjective element. But inasmuch as it is "seen," it has an objective element and can be discussed.

Today we run to subjectivity: I like it; you don't like it. So we slam a mental door in one another's face and talk about something else. But the dispassionate scholars who for hundreds or thousands of years have looked on finite beauty as a dull mirror of Infinite Beauty were not worried about box office, federal taxes or real estate, so they could afford to ask fundamental questions.

They came to the conclusion that beauty required integrity (completeness, oneness), proportion and clarity or effulgence.

I'm sure this is all useless equipment in writing plays for the American stage, but I hung on to it because it was about the only academic advice I could understand. If drama belongs to the fine arts and if these definitions are acceptable, the whole thing makes sense.

First, drama has for its prime object something besides rolling the visiting fireman in the aisles. Everybody accepts that in theory, but the chosen souls who serve up our theatre, usually on an investment basis, are naturally less interested in the integrity or form of the piece than in guaranteeing returns from an entertainment or diversion viewpoint.

Second, there is no clash between Church and theatre. If these rules apply to the drama and are observed, there is no need for censorship. If there is to be proportion or consonance in this art form, it can hardly be designed to harm us. After all, art serves life. If a knife is made to kill, there is in its making a certain disproportion. So a play can hardly conform to the rules of true art, if it is designed to draw us away from our ultimate goal—God.

This requisite rules out irrevocably the "art for art's sake" school. We don't eat for eating's sake or drink for drinking's sake or sleep for sleeping's sake. These are all part of life. Even if seen as a relief from boredom, they serve the greater art of living. So, obviously, those craftsmen who injure their fellow men by denying Divinity, by advocating political slavery or by glorifying lechery are first of all false to their art. It is rather pathetic that churchmen or policemen have to interfere for the safety of the people to teach the experts what their predecessors knew thousands of years ago.

The third requirement is clarity or effulgence. That's the feeling one gets upon coming over the crest of a hill and seeing a breath-taking sunset. It is sometimes caught in a stained-glass-windowed cathedral. It always has to do with light. That's why it is the ineffable aspect of beauty. Strangely enough, it comes more often with tragedy than with comedy. It is not always present in the variants of *Tobacco Road* which fill the coffers of producers at the expense of the people.

These requirements I do not wish to impose on anyone. I merely state that, when people had time to think, they were accepted by Aristotle, Thomas Aquinas and a host of others. The tempo of modern civilization may have made them obsolete. They might not fill theatres on Broadway today. If that be true, then they or the theatres must go. That point has been decided. They went.

But with this quaint and hopelessly outmoded equipment I faced the American theatre.

12

II: MONASTIC SOCKS AND BUSKINS

TIME PASSED AND THE REMOTE PREPARATION FOR MY
as yet unsuspected dabbling in the theatre took a new
turn. While the basic diet was theology, we were allowed to specialize in something more profane that we
might be equipped as teachers, and my part-time venture was psychology.

The wisdom of the choice, though accidental, was
uncanny, because a good grounding in psychiatry
makes a flyer at the theatre much less of a jolt. Of
course, that wasn't the original intention. I simply
thought that in the care of souls it would be helpful
to know what made people tick, and that psychology
(stressing its etymology) would provide the answer.
It wasn't as simple as that.

Empirical psychology is a very young science, and
from time to time stresses certain incidental features.
They tell me that years ago one of our wholesale universities was weighing the soul. Apparently it didn't
weigh enough to justify publishing the results. In another phase, Professor McDougall had everybody in
the trade watching pigeons and mice. So psychologists
turned carpenters to build rat mazes and pigeon cotes.
Wundt's influence leaned toward auditory phenomena,
so we had a collection of organ pipes in our laboratory
which came in very useful for tug-boat sound effects
in our irrepressible Christmas plays.

In my time we did a lot of interesting things such as applying electrodes to frogs" legs to watch the toes twitch, examining the brains of the country's better-known monkeys and giving one another lie-detector tests at the drop of a hat. The stress was on statistics.

Like the woman who swept and garnished her house looking for the lost groat, we were in quest of the G factor. We didn't know what the G factor was, and wouldn't have known even if we found it, but it was an exciting search. The simplest principle to remember about statistics in application to psychology is to take a few dubious premises, give them numbers or letters, whip them into a formula, multiply by twenty and become dogmatic about the answer.

I was a little weak in the formula department, so they set me studying the calculus. Nobody ever told me why it was called *the* calculus, but it isn't very important. My engineer classmates were vitally concerned about the relative speed of falling stars or trains which left stations at different times. I prefer to watch the plunging meteors open-mouthed and I still fall back on the timetable.

In justice, however, much of that diversion concerning what goes on inside people has been helpful. I present it merely as background, incongruous though it was, for my first amateur production.

But to catch up on chronology, first, I had written a play about St. Catherine of Siena. It is utterly inadequate for many reasons, but I can't imagine a playwright doing her justice. According to a recent biographer, Catherine made modern feminism look foolish. But that isn't why her life can't be dramatized prop-

14

erly. It's rather because the saints have a higher "threshold value" than the rest of us laughing, crying, ordinary mortals, and you can't depict for stage purposes the heights of contemplation.

The twenty-fifth child of a wool-dyer, Catherine was untutored, yet she compelled Popes and kings to follow her advice—practically, her commands. Unlike Joan of Arc, she accomplished more through others than by taking command herself, and in that sense is less dramatic, but she was sure of every step of her mission as opposed to the baffling contradictions which biographers find in St. Joan.

She has a haunting power today for those who seek her, and many a night when lights were out and no statistics could keep me awake, I scribbled lines on foolscap with a thick pencil before falling off to sleep.

Ordination came and, like many another, I was ready to change the face of the earth. There was no sign of deviation from the general norm at this point. Two thin published plays are scarcely ominous, especially since both were on religious subjects. I still thought of working in psychology—a normal kind— but that was not to be my portion.

Besides the Dominican House of Studies which is affiliated with Catholic University and which was my home at this period, the Order serves a parish church in southwest Washington. Father Prior of St. Dominic's, for that is its name, asked Father Prior of the House of Studies, and my superior, if I would produce *Barter* for his parish during Lent. My Father Prior said I would. Now we can stop all this formalism right away, but I wanted to get everybody set up properly.

15

If this proves a hurdle to anyone—that one's superior should answer for one—I'd like to forestall any sympathy, by saying that I prefer it that way. It has good precedent. It simplifies life no end. For instance, if I think I need a new hat (and the idea usually comes from someone who has looked at my hat), I ask my superior. If he concurs in the general opinion and wants me to wear a hat in public, he gives me the money to buy one. Otherwise, he doesn't. Maybe I should have chosen a less painful subject for an example, because my hats manage to assume a queer shape about the third or fourth time I wear them. In fact, I feel a kinship with Wouter Van Twiller, one of the first governors of New Amsterdam, of whom Washington Irving said he had a head of such "dimensions that Dame Nature with all her sex's ingenuity, would have been puzzled to construct a neck capable of supporting it; wherefore she wisely declined the attempt, and settled it firmly on the top of his backbone, just between the shoulders." However, lest we digress, there are very few important decisions in a lifetime, and when one gets past these, it is convenient to elect superiors who make all the unimportant ones. So I found myself producing *Barter* at St. Dominic's.

My first, and I hope, last, theatrical act was to visit the parish hall and demand that the proscenium be torn down and the stage space doubled immediately. Now, that venerable stage had served its purpose for about fifty years without anyone having protested, but my demands were met without question. The next visit to the scene found a stage piled high with broken plaster and ancient two-by-fours. The latter looked

16

substantial, and as buildings in old Jerusalem should be of substantial stuff, and as there was nothing nearer at hand, I commandeered them for scenery. Casting ran apace as it generally does. Even in 1932 it was easier to find actors than technicians to work for a cause, and since science (witness the calculus) was hardly my strong point, I turned to friends for help in the matter of building sets.

At this point, there is thrust into the story the engineering genius behind the massive structures in that particular production and, for that matter, behind most of the complicated structure of the subsequent Blackfriars' Guild. I refer, of course, to the ceaseless goad to my lagging steps, the perennial thorn in my side—the man who gathered in the money which I, as producer, spent.

The Reverend Doctor Thomas Fabian Carey of the Order of Preachers was at the time a deacon and a few months away from ordination to the priesthood. His theological and psychological studies had often been interrupted by the renovation of a radio set or the repair of a reluctant doorbell. Naturally, although we hadn't been particularly close in the past, I thought of him to supplement my obvious technical deficiencies. He gathered three associates (now enjoying distinguished careers far from the turmoil of opening nights), and agreed to create from two-by-fours and whatever else looked usable a dungeon, a rooftop and a room in the fortress Antonia.

Known now, of course, as Father Carey (Burns Mantle has referred to our New York company as Father Carey's chickens), known in those days as

17

Brother Fabian, he will be referred to in these pages as "the Doctor." This is no empty title because he picked up that degree in psychology as casually as he picks up a hammer or a breviary. However, my satisfaction in thinking of him as *the* Doctor comes from the fact that he wears the distinction with less self-consciousness than any man I've ever known, and takes all the curse out of the stuffed-shirtism associated with pedants. In fact, if there is any pedantry left in me, after our years of association, it must be attributed to a headache or the weather. It is definitely not a state of mind.

His forthright character is indexed by his terseness and directness of speech. Although much of his formal education came through the medium of Latin, he leans towards the clipped Chaucerian words. I could never think of him saying *aspersorium* since he knows that *stoup* means the same thing. Under pressure, as when, for instance, a set falls down, his speech becomes more pithy. Quick to appraise people, the Doctor invariably expresses his evaluation in understandable language.

He taught psychology for six or seven years at Catholic University, and illustrated the point that, barring fundamentals which have been defined as dogmas, there is amazing freedom in the Church. Of course, the architecture of the institution wherein he spent these days bears out the point, for nearly every building is of a different style and faces in a different direction.

In those days the Doctor was a stumbling block to conventional teachers and preachers because his preparation for a lecture had more to do with walking briskly up and down to stimulate the adrenals than

18

with consulting dusty tomes. To this day, he is a mild source of amazement to the hard-bitten people of the theatrical world, because with a disarming smile he insinuates the idea that he not only knows the score, but also the name of the game and who's playing.

My complaints against him are few and easily counterbalanced by the innumerable times he has saved me from aggressive high pressurers who could readily have taken me in; but, in justice, they must be enumerated. One is the fixed idea seized upon early in our relationship that I was insufferably lazy and that his major task in life was to prevent me from sitting down comfortably. In this questionable cause, his zeal has never flagged. The second complaint I would make has been well couched in the words of one of New York's photogenic ex-mayors. This frequenter of fires is reported to have said about one of his appointments which did a bit of a boomerang, "I don't make a mistake very often, but when I do, it's a beaut."

Many of the incidents which further cemented or threatened to disrupt our strange partnership must wait for their chronological places, so, back to the cold, drizzling day when it began. We gathered in a little pagoda-like summer house (why, I don't remember), and I told the Doctor and his crew all about the rooftop, the dungeon and the fortress, adding blandly that we had the wreckage of a proscenium arch with which to build them. There have been moments when I wished that pagoda at the bottom of the Potomac.

"Fools rush in where angels fear to tread." Well, it's written and may as well stand. But, aside from its triteness, that little apothegm gives me quite a turn now that I see it. Angels certainly tread lightly on the boards of Blackfriars. Were it not for a magnificent treatise on celestial spirits in theology, I might be inclined to deny their existence. Certainly, in the theatrical sense of the word, they have trod or flown elsewhere.

Our enthusiastic, if inexperienced, crew built three sets which for artistry were better than passable, and for solidity and durability made the theatre which housed them look like the neighboring temporary buildings of the first world conflict. One item, for example, was the flight of stairs leading up out of the dungeon. We had to fly it and four men could manage the job, but, on one occasion, when we risked it with three, the stairs came down while the men went up. A scene change always called out block and tackle gear, but with a large crew we achieved the improbable.

Some items were so big we simply couldn't put them any place. One of these, a beam which spanned the stage, was carefully laid behind the footlights. That seems an easy solution were it not for the fact that a respected and venerable member of the cast found it difficult to see without his glasses. By dint of drawing on my extensive knowledge as author, I convinced him that spectacles simply weren't worn in those days, so he agreed to go on blind. You've guessed the rest. He hit that ambushed beam and skated perilously along the footlights. But, being an old trouper, he landed on the right side and turned on the next line without the audience being surprised in the least.

The critics or their deputies said they were duly impressed. So, while the reviews were still damp, I assembled the company and asked them if they'd like to continue as a city-wide drama organization. I'm sure you who sit with the gallery gods at this play within a play realize that I'm slipping towards the centre of the vortex. But eight years of cloistered life hadn't taught me to be wary of the enthusiams of a first night. So judge me not too harshly. The founding of the Blackfriars' Guild had something of the inevitable about it.

The company was enthusiastic. How could they be otherwise? The applause was still ringing in their ears; the make-up was hardly scrubbed off their faces; the little human jealousies were momentarily cast aside in this charged atmosphere. Like old fire horses hearing the bell, like old sailors watching a brig weighing anchor, they were carried outside themselves. The Doctor and I were hypnotized, too. I made a speech and asked them if they would create a theatre submerging personalities. I wanted no stars. I sought a very superior type of play. I'd make it our business to learn more about the drama and discover the right scripts. This was an utterly new idea (I think I said). Looking back at that evening now, I'm inclined to smile. It isn't a cynical smile, either. One doesn't smile at one's lack of knowledge before attempting to learn. But I'm sure my words had been said in effect ten thousand times in the history of the world. And I'm sure that ten thousand times the assembled companies shouted an enthusiastic, "Yes!" And I'm sure that those who said those words in the past were also very young.

Thus was launched the Blackfriars" Guild of Washington. Perhaps it is about time to say something about

21

its rather odd name. It has been subject to misunderstanding. On four or five occasions we have been thought to engage only in work for the Negro. That has come under our scope, but the primary intention was a type of theatre. Again, I was paged in a hotel lobby as the head of the "Flag Flyers." We haven't been conspicuous as flyers of flags. Another time, I wired regrets about a proposed speaking engagement, shrewdly limiting myself to these ten words: "Sorry can't make the second. Am Blackfriaring around the country." The answer was terse. "What do you mean you're backfiring around the country?" So, a word of explanation may be in order.

When St. Dominic dispersed his original band of fourteen throughout Europe, he included England, knowing no doubt that there'd always be one. They arrived with their white habits hidden under black traveling cloaks or cappas. Hence they were called Blackfriars. The English seldom surprise one. A certain amount of confusion arises from the fact that most people encounter friars without their traveling or preaching cloaks. So it baffles them that those who wear white are called Blackfriars; those who wear brown are called Whitefriars; and those who wear black, brown and grey are called Greyfriars. But, very simply, they arrived with their overcoats on and first impressions are lasting.

The Dominicans who came to England enveloped in black finally built a friary near London which was called Blackfriars. The site is now within the city at Printing House Square, near Blackfriars' Bridge and Blackfriars' Railroad Station and the old title is given to the surrounding territory.

Their achievements need not concern us here, but the reforming sixteenth century saw them suppressed along with much that was England. Henry VIII, Defender of the Faith, and Queen Elizabeth would have none of them, so Blackfriars became an empty museum.

At this point in time, William Shakespeare was getting his start. He had scripts and actors, but experienced a little trouble in finding a theatre, which unfortunate situation has been repeated within our memory on Broadway.

It seems that the license commissioner (and that, too, strikes a familiar note) had something against the managers and refused them permission to perform within the city proper. But good old Blackfriars, being just outside the walls, as is Hoboken to New York or Peabody to Boston, offered no technical complications, so Burbage, the company manager, snapped it up.

Now that I've mentioned Burbage, I must admit that I've always considered him a sort of uncle or something. There were two of them who basked in reflected glory of Shakespeare. Uncle James was the leading man for whom the bard wrote *Macbeth, Hamlet, Lear* and *Othello.* Young Cousin Richard, on the other hand, was more manager than actor. My assumption of relationship comes from the fact that my maternal grandmother was a Burbage. I would delve into this genealogical business, had I not been warned by a former teacher, a brother of the Christian Schools, of Erse extraction, who said, "Don't look up your ancestors or you might find that those who didn't hang by their tails were hanged by their necks."

One more historical note might presage some mod-

ern Blackfriar aspirations. Back in 1605, the Red
Bull Theatre appeared in Clerkenwell. Three years
later, the King's Men—Shakespeare's Company—
leased Blackfriars for winter productions. Almost immediately, the Red Bull and other rivals lost their
supremacy and, to remain alive, began to bow to the
clamor of lower-class demands. Those theatre-lovers
who sought something "genteel" transferred their pa-
tronage to Blackfriars. We didn't know all this in
those pioneer Washington days, so it makes a gratifying discovery.

The conclusion of this research is that the word
Blackfriar embodies a Dominican tradition; consequently, a religious tradition. Moreover, it signifies
the best in Elizabethan drama. Even though these
two traditions haven't glided along through the years
in undisturbed tranquility, today they are hinting at
an introduction. Blackfriars is, of course, the name.

III: WASHINGTON ODYSSEY

IN THE FALL OF 1932, I HAD THE GOOD FORTUNE to be assigned to St. Dominic's, the headquarters of the new organization, while I continued to read for a degree in psychology.

A few meetings of the enthusiasts were devoted to assigning jobs, and, although it didn't happen as quickly as it takes to record it, the unavoidable fact soon made itself apparent that just about four of the original company had any intention of assuming the burdens of theatre. Since these were the organization, they were named president, vice-president, secretary and treasurer, respectively, and we settled down to the incidental tasks which might pop up.

There was the problem of plays. I was limited to an odd hundred masterpieces seen ten years previously in the Providence Opera House, and for one reason or another these failed to conform to our standards or our budget. We couldn't keep doing my one accidentally famous opus; in fact, there are those who remain convinced that it wasn't worth doing in the first place.

One of our officers (I'm safe in that statement; we were weak in enlisted personnel) who knew something about the theatre suggested Barry's *Holiday*. We liked the idea, not because every amateur outfit was producing it that year, but because, in a soft way, its thesis appealed to us. That thesis, you remember, is that it isn't important to have too much money; it's enough to have just enough. Unfortunately, we have not always managed the just enough.

Casting came off well, and the Doctor supervised the building of two attractive sets, but delays resulting from the newness of the organization held up production until February, 1933. So, when we opened it was with great expectations. We were all aware that it was a creditable job and we confidently expected to gain immediate recognition as one of the best companies in Washington.

At the end of the first act, I knew we were in. The second act plays itself. I even gave the worriers who always haunt lobbies a little nod indicating that all was well, when I was sent for by the pastor who had seen the play from the last row. All the way down the aisle I smiled because the play was right in there. You feel those things. But when I saw the face of the pastor of the church, the smile wandered away to wherever smiles go.

He said a lot of things in three minutes; among them that those smoking, swearing, drinking women might not be portrayed on the stage of St. Dominic's parish, that he would stop the show immediately if I could not promise a drastic reform in the next two acts.

It was something of a tight spot. The town had turned out for an initial offering. The press was there. The Guild was mortgaged to the hilt, depending on this success to pay its bills. My months of speech-making and theorizing were going to sound pretty silly to all the members. Yet, the problem had to be faced sometime. I'm glad now it came early in the game. At that moment, there wasn't time for dispassionate thinking, but in the two decades which followed there has been.

Are we to be governed by fundamental morality or by local conventions in this project? You might note that we never looked on this as a hobby from 1932 on. It was part of something important. We didn't know where it was going, but most of our thinking was focussed on the future. Was the schism between the Church and the theatre an irremediable one? By that I mean, must drama which is acceptable to Catholics be of a religious nature or on an adolescent level? Might we not grapple with problems which beset people in the world?

Holiday is not a very good test case. I'm afraid it makes my point too strong. It bore the good will of all the Catholic reviewers it had encountered. Certainly, by the first curtain there is only mention of a drink; perhaps one or two characters use the word "hell"; and I guess everybody but the butler smokes. It is a pretty innocuous piece on the whole. But it points up the problem beautifully. If so inoffensive a play was to be halted in mid-air on a night when so much was at stake, where were we to turn in the future?

Is the Church which has built an elaborate school system, teaching millions all they know of secular sciences as well as religion, and which has put a sizeable investment into a press, going to ignore the theatre? Or, is it going to feature only religious plays —the *ecclesiocentric* theatre which some talk about?

Or, if it ventures into a wider field, is it going to focus on smoking, drinking and matters of taste in speech? None of this sounds like the Catholic Church.

The orator who says that the theatre came out of the Church in the tenth century may draw on good sources and be most effective, but he rarely adds that the two institutions are not very close in the twentieth. The implication of that speech, of which we are always hearing variants, is that the drama is a good and useful thing. The point needs no laboring. It is instinctive to all peoples whether for solemn religious services or for relaxation and fun. The Church services themselves partake of the dramatic form.

But if the Church regards the theatre as an enemy, an irredeemable lost child, who can blame the theatre for going its merry way? If the theatre is guilty of excesses or deviations from its own rules and best interest, and the Church knows the answers, then might the Church very well offer positive suggestions as it has in other fields.

The necessary rapprochement will not be effected if the Church limits itself to religious drama. Such a program might have been adequate in the tenth century when there was little competition, but today, when people are amused by a well-established theatre and practically educated by the ubiquitous moving picture, it would not draw them back. They must be spoken to in the medium they have learned to understand and like.

That much is generally admitted, at least in theory. It is when one comes down to cases that the problem arises. The bulk of available scripts which might conceivably draw an audience (and that factor is usually given due consideration) has been doctored or tailored for the New York theatre-goer, or, more accurately, the theatre-goer who comes to New York. That means that while they wouldn't think of offending anybody's sectarian sensibilities, but rather invent a common denominator in dogma, they consequently hit a common denominator in publicly accepted morality and conventions.

The average parochial audience at this point in time in the United States is composed of a scattering of people one or two generations removed from the old world, who have had scant educational opportunities and who in spite of, or perhaps because of, their motion picture education, are justly suspicious of the unorthodoxy of the stage.

The task is to train them to make distinctions or to make distinctions for them. There are very specific norms in the business. Greater conformity to those norms and more flagrant departures from them are both more likely to be discovered in the theatre, with its great diversity coming from small audiences and small investments, than from anything as centralized and formularized as the movies.

There is a place for the parish theatre and it should conform (to a degree) to what its audience wants. It shouldn't be an upsetting, smart thing. Little by little, tastes can be elevated and the superior minds would do the parish a service if they bore with a little banality, knowing that the little ones were reaching up and that better things were to come.

That was a far cry from our dream. We were much

less apologetic in our approach. It was an accident of centuries of slavery and despoliation which caused the breach between the "parochial mind" and the modern theatre. Perhaps the former was the sounder of the two, but it certainly put difficulties in our path, since Puritanism had given paganism its greatest weapon in confusing accidentals with fundamentals.

We believed, and with pretty good authority, too, that a Catholic could discuss religion, politics, sociology, science, sin—anything under the sun—if he weren't led into wrong doing or wrong thinking in the process. We believed he could attend dramatic performances where these subjects were treated, if the regular safeguards were employed. If that be liberalism, it has been enunciated pretty consistently for the past two thousand years. Our particular problem was to spring an adult theatre on people who weren't expecting one. We foresaw more obstacles from those within the Church than from the outside. We were right.

That night I returned backstage and between the warning and the rise on Act Two told the cast to rewrite gently, if any of the objectionable features cropped up. They were up to it, and this isn't rose-colored glasses. The audience applauded long; the press gave glowing notices; we lost only a few dollars; but—we had no home. The Blackfriars' Guild was evicted.

There was a melodramatic touch about the actual expulsion because we moved out the contaminated scenery for storage in a nearby cellar during an unusually heavy Washington snowstorm, and many a

30

"Bless you, Jack Dalton" was uttered by our amused helpers who didn't realize the enormity of the schism. The scene only lacked the burning of the mortgage. We've never achieved that. The irony has never worn off that scene for me. There we stood in the snow, dedicated to bringing back the theatre to fundamentals in art and morality, and we were evicted for perverting public morals a block away from 4½ Street in southwest Washington.

Thus began the Washington Odyssey. It would be dull to enumerate all the famous and obscure places in which we rehearsed and played. Merely to mention Catholic Charities (harboring the harborless), St. Patrick's Parish Hall, Sears Roebuck Art Gallery and the Wardman Park Theatre might indicate something of the restlessness which followed us.

No one ever told me why Sears Roebuck had an art gallery in Washington nor why that institution accepted these wandering troubadours rent free, but such is the case and we were duly grateful. We did a one-acter there on a memorable evening, and I had been asked to secure a shotgun as an essential prop.

The word "Blackfriars" was never mentioned in the common room at St. Dominic's after the big snow, but when I asked permission to be out rather late, everybody knew where I was going. Close to twelve, I tip-toed through the halls carrying my borrowed shotgun and walked smack into the Prior. The conversation was bound to be a bit one-sided, because he could choose his words very carefully and ask as much or as little as he liked, whereas I, borne down by an unreasonable sense of guilt, thought that I should do a lot of talking about the unusual burden I bore. Had it been in a hunting lodge under other circumstances, I might have strolled brashly by. But it was a monastery, where fast talking doesn't get one very far because talking of any sort is discouraged.

The conversation ran, or limped, something like this:

"Good evening, Father." (With a hopeful note.)

"Good evening."

There was a pause. Now had he said, "What are you going to do with that gun?"—had he given me anything to build on, in fact, I might have found some hidden resources, but he merely stared in a sort of fascination. So the onus was mine.

"Oh! This gun. They used it in a show tonight."

"Oh!"

I slithered towards the staircase, feeling as though I were walking on ground glass in sensitive bare feet, then gave a short moronic laugh and said, "Yeah! It was a prop in a play."

Lost encounters like this would have been milestones except that they happened almost every time I turned around. The magnificent obsession cost thousands of small battles, but we always looked to the day of final triumph. It's a pleasant state of mind, but it ages one.

The mention of the Wardman Park Theatre conjures up another episode because of which the Doctor and I nearly came to a parting of the ways. He was carrying on his role of scenic artist and studio-director, while I was directing a completely innocuous play. No one could criticize this offering on moral or conventional grounds and no one would be bothered on any other grounds.

We never probed deeply into this utilitarian division of labor to ascertain whether I was the more qualified as a director or merely would last longer at a task which required a great deal of sitting down. However, that he was more capable at supervising the wielding of hammers was indisputable. So he gathered the better craftsmen of our flock and rented a former bakery in Brookland.

The owners of the bakery (there was much litigation about the title and so many people demanded payment that in the end we paid nobody) were informed of our undertaking. But the rest of the world as it passed along that busy university street must have wondered if, among his many accomplishments, the Doctor was going in for something distinctive in cakes and pastries. Weary of questions, he whitened the windows and went to work in relative seclusion on the construction of a new set.

In his psychological researches, the Doctor came to know quite a little about color, but his approach was rather from the technical than the artistic side. He decided on old rose—at least that's what the color chart said—but when the nightmare was completed, I had a lot to say about the rights of the director in matters pertaining to the artistic ensemble. The argument was shortened because practical matters pushed theoretical ones out of the picture. We had one Sunday morning to clear up the discussion and hang the set in the hotel theatre before giving a dress rehearsal to which an audience had been invited.

33

At high noon, as the job was nearing completion, an inspector walked in, and his walk marked the beginning of many interesting—some pleasant, some unpleasant—encounters with inspectors in the years that followed. This inspector merely asked the Doctor if the scenery was flame-proofed. That seems a simple question, but the Doctor missed the right answer. He said that, while it wasn't exactly flame-proofed, there wasn't anything for the inspector to worry about. This the inspector decided to put to a test, so he struck a match and quietly burned a hole in the nearest flat, putting out the fire with a frosty speech to the effect that no power on earth could raise that curtain until the law had been complied with.

The Doctor has one decidedly unpleasant characteristic. When the going gets rough, he looks at me wordlessly, with an expression which eloquently says, "See what you've done." Although the rational portion of my mind insists that I had nothing to do with the crime, I always wilt under the gaze and assume a guilty responsibility. On this occasion he took advantage of his hypnotic stare and coerced me into approaching the management of the hotel, in which the theatre was situated, to browbeat them into resurrecting their paint crew to flame-proof the scenery before a disappointed audience came and went.

The loss wouldn't have been irreparable if Washington's finest had missed this masterpiece, but curtains for some reason or other must go up. So I scurried from one assistant manager to another, finding, at length, that the painters were buried in the bowels of the massive structure, doing some work in a vegetable cellar. They could be talked into considering our problem, for a price, if the hotel gave permission, but it would take them an hour or so to clean their guns.

Then I was dispatched from drug store to drug store, since nothing else was open on Sunday, to buy the ingredients for flame-proofing material. The finished mixture had a unique aroma. At half-past one, a hastily built staging was completed and the erstwhile beautifiers of a potato cellar were shooting with their almost lethal guns at the Doctor's old rose parlor.

At twenty minutes past two, a good ten minutes before curtain time, these casual gunmen lugged their equipment down the aisle through a nearly filled house, and the audience had a specific odor with which to associate the play, in case they couldn't make up their minds.

The leading lady, who had to do a lot of dusting, due to the script and my lack of inventiveness, was more than busy. In fact, she darted here and there wiping off the fluid which dripped from the teasers on our rented furniture. The walls changed colors during the course of the play. We always had a penchant for achieving effects. However, the venture paid our season's debts and taught us to flame-proof scenery the easy way.

In that winter of discontent between peregrinations around the District of Columbia we came to the conclusion that an extensive educational program was necessary before enough people could be found to supply the financial support to make possible the production of the type of plays we sought to offer, assuming that such plays could be found. An answer took shape in my mind—a short-cut to the solution of the problem. Since the people I knew were more interested in actors than in the ideas expressed in plays, why couldn't I gather together a few of the stars—top-bracket people who might devote some of their talents to such a cause? After all, there were many people of undisputed ability making sacrifices for political ideologies which were admittedly materialistic. There must be as many, given the spiritual roots of America, who would like to acknowledge God as the head of life and art.

This hallucination grew to the point where I envisioned a sort of religious community of actors who began the day by gathering around the altar (not at the crack of dawn, since the day of theatrical people starts late) and who believed that they could help the world through their chosen medium.

There may be. Somebody may find them some day. But those I interviewed or wrote to manifested a consistency of reaction which dimmed the vision. All agreed, in effect, that, if I found a good play with a fat part for them and a producer willing to plunge, they would be delighted to make the sacrifice. In some instances, that sacrifice would have been the substitution of a job for the inactivity of the current depression.

That wasn't such a good idea. If the people of the theatre were trained in a different tradition, it wasn't their fault. If the only cause which inflames the imagination of the youngsters coming into the business is a redistribution of wealth which has had dubious success, perhaps we haven't presented the case for eternity in sufficiently vivid colors. We may have compromised somewhere along the line. So, the short-cut was blocked.

The next move was to talk to people about values first and then teach them to act. It was obviously the hard way. It might be impossible, but it had been done at Oberammagau. Better to try and fail than to bemoan the plight of the world from an arm-chair.

With a deep breath, I forsook the wandering troubadours of imagination and tried to catch up with the very real wandering Blackfriars of Washington. These I found in a state of high excitement, because they had been suddenly invited back to St. Dominic's. Father Prior of the snows was promoted elsewhere and his successor reasoned that a successful dramatic group might pay off some of the debt incurred in the rehabilitation of the auditorium. Most likely he also thought that, with reasonable care, he could control any conspicuous offenses against faith or morals in public productions which might escape my notice.

When that good news came, we gathered from basement and bakery, from cellar and friar's cell, our goods and gear and turned our faces again toward St. Dominic's, where we hoped to grow old and maybe even significant amid the comforts of home.

37

IV : FROM LOAVES TO FISHES

THE GUILD HADN'T SPENT MUCH TIME IN ST. Dominic's, but it was home and we entered softly, looking around like prodigal sons. It was beautiful after our wanderings. Now we'd vindicate anyone who had faith in us. We'd do something big. My play about Catherine of Siena certainly filled that bill and was scheduled for the opener. Whether I wrote good plays or not, I definitely wrote big ones. After that production, the Blackfriars in Washington were inclined to regard as artistic and Catholic only one-set shows with small casts.

Aside from the ever-present inconsequential fact that we had no money, there were further complications. The new Father Prior was so pleased with the refurbished auditorium he inherited that he decreed we should not mar its beauty by building scenery in its sacrosanct confines. There wasn't a cranny in the basement which could be used for such destructive practices as hammering or painting, so, if we were partial to scenery, we must build it elsewhere.

The bakery in Brookland had resumed baking, so that was unavailable. I was given to understand that it was my turn to find a workshop. So, after several excursions in southwest Washington—the quaintest and most picturesque part of the city—I discovered a fish dealer of good will who had a vacant garage.

The now-almost-forgotten depression was enveloping us and tenants were not clamoring for space, so he allowed us to use the upper story. To reach our new quarters we had but to open a massive double door and grope up an immense ramp. I say "grope" because the deal, one-sided as it was, failed to include such incidentals as light, heat and water.

Nor could these niceties of modern civilization be conjured up quickly in spite of the fact that the equipment was present, because thoughtless tenants of former days had paid no bills, and the various Public Utilities' Companies demanded exhorbitant back payment. Finally, the electric company relented.

We amazed the natives by drawing water in pails from a sort of town pump, usually in the dead of night. Washington is quaint in more aspects than politics. Our spray gun was rigged to the motor of a car. I know that we replaced a spark plug by a rubber hose. Further elaboration is too technical for me. However, as the upper windows were high and the hose not overly long, we had to put the power-supplying automobile on the sidewalk, which confused the local constabulary no end. They were satisfied when we explained the contraption and reminded them that there would be no complaints because nobody in the southwest section of the city ever called the police.

The generosity of the owner didn't stop with us. He also befriended a poultry and live-stock farmer who brought his horned and feathered friends to roost, bray, moo and cackle on the floor below. There was an aroma less associated with the theatre than flame-proofing and no more delightful, pervading our work.

The comments of the animals on our endeavors, while difficult to translate accurately, seemed derogatory.

Of heat there was none, and that December seems in retrospect to have been unusually cold. Punctual as usual, we were opening our '33-'34 season in mid-winter. Numbing fingers were warmed on floodlights which cast eerie shadows on the bleak walls. The one little electric stove was always busily melting glue, faintly reminiscent of the business of our new benefactor.

Yet, the beginning of the indoctrination of Black-friars occurred there. There, people began to grasp what we later expressed more articulately. I remember their faces, grotesque over the floodlights which were spread around the floor. And although I don't know why the incident is still so vivid, I remember that a girl banged a finger on a well-manicured hand with an unskillfully wielded hammer. She wasn't aware of it until I noticed the blood, so cold was that loft. I was talking about the things we were going to accomplish. We may succeed some day. At least, there was an investment made.

It was a costume play, and although I have never been regarded by either friends or critics as a sartorial model, I dipped even into that department. On the authority of old prints, Catherine's habit, and especially the veil, were made of soft things. I think that nuns or sisters should dress that way. You see, I'm not worried about the hair shirts. They find those aplenty, in a metaphorical if not a literal sense. I'm merely thinking that, since they are a symbol to the world, their dress should reflect themselves—iron inside, but gentle to the world. I'm not happy about the influence in nuns' habits of French laundresses when starch was in vogue. But that's a digression and possibly not the best way of making friends.

Props were relatively easy. The Doctor lived at the House of Studies (near the bakery) and I lived at St. Dominic's (near the garage). Religious houses are gold mines for dressing up majestic dramas. Pictures of former superiors in expensive frames adorn the walls or are neatly stacked in the cellar. Nobody throws away these images of the living, because in the fortunes of a democratic institution they might be back.

Another department developing in monastic cellars (which are really not filled with prisoners of the inquisition) is the art section. Not that the portraits and photographs are not artistic, but the department in question spells ART in capitals. Visitors to European priories in days gone by took receipts for their donations in surplus paintings. Some grace our walls to this day, to the delight of all. Others, after more mature appraisal, are moved downstairs.

When the Prior of the House of Studies came to *Catherine* and saw the curtain go up on the Palace of the Popes in Avignon, he was very surprised indeed. Not only was his cellar rifled, but many of the best pictures were plucked right from the walls (if one plucks canvases ten by fourteen). The next morning showed the extent of the plunder, as the walls exhibited a surprising two-tone effect and the community became conscious of pictures which had been unnoticed for years. The Doctor generalized when he sought permission for the looting, but it is understandable that a man who adds a major dramatic production to an ordinarily full schedule is liable to slip up in a few of the particulars.

The artistic triumph was somewhat dimmed by a certain amount of financial confusion. The parish took half the gross. The Guild took all the expenses. The arrangement wasn't particularly equitable, but the Guild made seventeen dollars and I wrote three sets of books to make everybody happy. Private donations made all the books accurate.

Ever gentle in their criticism, the members sensed that I was not a good business manager nor even a satisfactory delegate when it came to infighting. There was a great upsurge of democracy and we devoted interminable hours to constitutions and by-laws. Some of the capital's good legal minds addressed themselves to the problem of ensuring the rights of life, liberty and the pursuit of happiness to all members of the organization without discrimination. That sounded like a good idea, because it promised to divide labor. We worked out an apprenticeship period and defined with fulsome minutiae the voting rights of active members. I devoted seven years to making our theatre extremely democratic, only to arrive at the conclusion that it doesn't work.

Members of a group attempting to produce something which falls under the generic term of art aren't defending their rights. They are giving something and one can't confine by legal statute the size of the gift. There are derived rights, of course. Had we banded together to place sandbags along the levee of a rising river, the man with the empty wheelbarrow should

42

get off the plank to make room for the man with the full wheelbarrow. But to allow all actors to vote on the selection of plays and directors can become as chaotic as to allow several painters of various abilities to daub on the same canvas.

In this year when democracy flowered, we decided by popular vote to repeat *Barter,* principally because it was cheaper to dust off the old sets and costumes than to contrive new ones, and it is unlikely that any other play will be written which could use or would use such a collection. At least the play-reading committee found nothing which such obvious pecuniary advantages and, since comprehensive examinations were staring me in the face, I had no opportunity to seek a challenger. Those days were long because, while theatre practice makes for late-to-bed, the monastic rising bell still followed the schedules of the mediaevalists who retired early to save candles.

The second *Barter* was less spectacular than the first. Some of the former scenery had been used for permanent construction or for firewood. We read a book or two on stagecraft and learned with some disillusionment that one had but to create the appearance of buildings not build entire edifices. We substituted one-by-twos for two-by-fours, and the famous staircase was lightened by being written out of the play. This was the "farewell to realism" stage.

During this period a young reporter burst in for a story. He was with the N.C.W.C. News Service which syndicates most of the material for Catholic papers. We interrupted each other excitedly for three or four hours and that day he joined the Guild. I've forgotten whether he got a story or not. But E. Francis Mc-Devitt, for that was his name, wrote us an exclusive in play form called *Eight at Tillumcott*. It received good notices, but its greatest significance lies in the fact that it was the first play cut and tailored for Blackfriars. A local paper noted that the "Guild has reached the point of producing and creating its own material with out the benefit of professional support or aid."

The press usually said nice things about us. Here is a sample of the sophisticated coverage of 1933: "They [Blackfriars] proved that it is possible to combine in a single production good staging, and we mean really good staging; smooth acting, and a set large enough to hold six people without two of them falling over the footlights." See what I mean?

Then came a break. We were offered the use of a building owned by the National Council of Catholic Men. Such a home of our own represented independence from the differences of opinion which successive pastors are likely to bring to their new charges. It further promised us the opportunity of becoming a regular radio company for network broadcasts. It brought hope of permanence—of an institution national in character, well publicized and financially sound. It was just too good to be true. So it wasn't true.

The realization of this opportunity began with organizational work and the physical renovation of the building. Consequently, it fell in the Doctor's department. And the Doctor at this point became seriously ill. I accepted that blow as I slithered into the breach, only to be told that I had ruined his health. Now, there was never a more floundering, inept Simon Legree than I, nor a more strongly opinionated, outspoken victim than the Doctor. But I missed him.

The Guild's treasury—about one hundred and thirty five dollars—was dumped into paint and renovating equipment. We scrubbed floors and washed walls. Furniture was donated. Just as we prepared to celebrate the completion of the first floor, I received an order transferring me to Providence College.

This might suggest a homily on the insecurity of members of religious orders or the modern hair shirt of obedience, but, after all, the technique has thousands of years to its credit and it has stood the test.

The Guild which was becoming more and more involved in debating the constitutional rights of members felt reluctant to make any guarantees, so the new project was abandoned. We didn't suddenly become a sound, independent, national organization. Our hoarded dollars, the result of two years of pinching and scraping, was in paint, varnish and wax on the walls and floors of an empty building which was soon to be torn down.

"Good-Bye to Washington." It was said to the Guild at a little birthday party in the Mayflower Hotel. For all the casualness and gaiety of the affair, I felt depressed, from a very human point of view indeed. I felt that in some way I had let people down, people who had built hopes which might not be realized. To a few friends I confided that feeling and they assured me that in a very short time it would pass. They were wrong. It's almost as acute now as it was that night. So I went back to St. Dominic's and packed for Providence.

E XACTLY TEN YEARS AFTER LEAVING, I RETURNED to Rhode Island and Providence Plantations. More than that, I was retiring from the theatre at the age of twenty-eight, not because of harrowing experiences acquired while at the business, but simply because I was given another job. Washington would go on, I sincerely hoped, but it would go on without me.

When my books on psychology and allied mysteries were unpacked, the dean announced that the English department needed a teacher and that among other things I was to teach drama. That looked like a joke going too far or a lark flying too high. It was obviously a conspiracy to make me read plays. They were read fast and furiously that I might keep ahead of a nimble-witted class of Juniors who had no scruples about embarrassing a young instructor.

The prize at the bottom of the package was my further appointment to take charge of the Pyramid Players, the undergraduate dramatic society. They had been doing Shakespeare with apparent gusto, but I suspected some coercion was employed when my first invitation brought out enough men to cast the male section of *The Glass Menagerie.*

The new job meant that my retirement from theatre was not only brief, but that from now on I was to go at it the hard way. Whether that condition of indifference exists in all schools which have no regular dramatic department, or is indigenous to Providence, I hesitate to say.

It is safe, however, to note here that Providence is not the greatest theatrical city in the world. The late George M. Cohan, who was born about two miles from my birthplace, is reputed to have said, "There are two bad weeks in the theatre; Holy Week and Providence." Other wits have challenged the authorship and other cities have laid claim to the distinction, but my home town could handle all comers. I don't think the inhabitants would come out to see a hurricane. They saw one.

To understand this indifference to spectacles of skill or wit, one must go back to Roger Williams and his boys. They were serious thinkers who wanted no truck with theatrical trifles or competitions that weren't played for keeps. In fact, they didn't want too much outside influence of any sort. The very name "Rhode Island" might well have been wishful thinking, since a good moat might discourage intruders. "College Tom" Hazard, of whose family Oliver Hazard Perry won fame on Lake Erie, said that the creed of the early settlers went something like this: Thou shalt love the Lord, thy God, with thy whole heart and thy whole soul and thy whole mind. Thou shalt regard thy neighbors from Massachusetts with righteous hatred and those from Connecticut with fitting contempt.

They were the first colonists to enshrine toleration as a virtue, and their descendants still think it is one. It is usually one degree above warfare. You are entitled to your opinion, but don't try to inflict it on anyone else, and above all, don't charge for it. So the best medicine shows, fresh from New York, came, starved and went.

Does this sound like a contradiction of my enchanted Opera House days? Well, drama was a novelty then, as baseball had been in the nineties. After a while, the people saw right through it. Later, I learned that Thursday was the best day to buy scenery. Some die-hard producers thought that Providence was still a good dog town. So they opened Monday, the papers got them Tuesday, the sheriff Wednesday, and we bought scenery Thursday.

Against this backdrop, the Pyramid Players gathered enough enthusiasts and coerced enough unenthusiasts to stage a small comedy without the aid of George Spelvin. The authorities, the company and the few who made up the audience considered it quite an accomplishment. We even toured Warren and Bristol.

In Warren, where I had lived as a child, we played the Town Hall. The stage was almost all apron, so we put half the furniture in front of the curtain. The curtain itself was raised by a continuous rope which had become slack over the years, so when our curtain man pulled it the wrong way we had a lot of floating line, which, when he corrected his error, wandered out and snatched a gas fixture from the wall. Our make-up man, standing nearby, casually capped the open gas pipe with a half-filled cold cream jar and went on with his work. I wonder if they ever put the fixture back or raised the gas pressure.

When the crew picked up the sets and furniture,

they met a janitor in grey overalls, sweeping up grey dust with a grey broom. They asked him how he liked the show.

"Not too much," he replied.

"Why not?" they asked.

To which the grey janitor replied evenly, "There wan't enough mirth in it."

There was an air of peace and contentment during that fall and winter. Providence promised a very pleasant life. Its traditions were well established and if one stayed on the beaten path a long if not a great future was assured. I might get back into my own field some day. Or I might even learn something about the new one. Then, like Mr. Chips, I could gaze into an open fire and find solace in the accomplishments of my students. Maybe I'd be asked to write articles on drama for encyclopedias. Let me see, now: "The drama sprang from the imitative or mimetic character-istic of man but at the very dawn of civilization it took on a religious or propitiary significance."

That would be a good life. No broken fingernails, no paint-spattered clothes, no embarrassing publicity, no humiliating begging, no misunderstandings with superiors. Just an oracle who could afford to be a little opinionated because of a few apodictic books with footnotes in foreign languages. Not very exciting, but very orthodox.

Reports came in from Washington announcing that the Guild had taken up quarters in the former church of St. Paul's through the understanding kindness of the late Father Dacey. *The Passing of the Third Floor Back* was the season's opening, and they declared it an artistic success, but a financial failure. It was futile to think of helping at such a distance. If I wrote, I might confuse them. No! I must forget Washington. That was of the past. I must gather my footnotes and look to the future.

What that scholarly life might have offered I never found out. During a brief hospitalization, some old friends came to visit me. Wouldn't I help them form a dramatic organization in Providence? *No! No!* Didn't I believe all the things I had been saying? *Yes, But Providence was a tough theatre town. It wouldn't work.* But if it succeeded in Providence, it would succeed anywhere. Why not make a real test case? *No! I have a very heavy schedule. There aren't enough people interested.* How many are needed? Couldn't five or ten zealots make a reasonable start? *Oh, I don't know.* But you said once . . . .

I had said a lot of things. I said that sixty-five or seventy million weekly movie-goers were getting a questionable diet; that radio, while young, was for the most part intent on selling merchandise; that the New York theatre and the tributaries into which (instead of out of which) it flowed were vague about standards. I did say that we weren't forced to accept all that as an unmixed good; that a few thinking people here and there could change it; that it was futile and somewhat pathetic to complain about current conditions, if one were too indifferent to do something about them. Here were a few people willing to work and I was going to be a scholar. Oh, well! The Providence Chapter of The Blackfriars' Guild was set up early in the year 1935.

Providence College graciously offered its all-purpose auditorium if there were no conflicts by way of debates, undergraduate dramatics, meetings, basketball games or basketball practice. As the latter occurred nearly every free night, we learned to wait until the conflict subsided, take down the portable baskets, open the windows and start from there.

The next sentence kills me, but it really wasn't my fault. The new Guild wanted to start with *Barter*. Prophet in his own city, etc. My reading course hadn't come close enough to contemporary authors to provide acceptable alternatives. There wasn't anything very exciting about the production except that, even now, from the vantage point of wider experience, I think it had a good cast.

The late Mal Kelly, veteran of Broadway from 1900, who played innumerable roles for A. H. Woods and Leo Ditrichstein, came out of retirement and played the patriarch. He didn't appear in the last act, and as its curtain was going up in the fifth performance, he said "Do you mind if I slip out and see how this thing ends? I've heard some good reports about it." Broadway before the Russian drama schools was as baffling as Broadway after them, as evidenced by Mal's repeated, "I don't want the whole script. It's confusing. Give me my sides."

The leading man, Dick Fleck, by a strange series of transfers in his business life, played the role in its premiere in Pittsburgh, did it again for the Washington Blackfriars, and at this point was assigned to Boston, so he commuted and played it again. Originally, he played one scene behind barred doors in a dungeon—the one with the stairs—but, since I wrote the stairs out because of their weight, we chained him to the floor this time. In rehearsal the veteran complained that the chains were obviously inadequate to restrain a man as violent as he was supposed to be. That remark annoyed the stage manager, Bill Stuart, who went around muttering, "I'll fix him. I'll chain him." He did. On opening night, we held a curtain while the best minds available grappled with the problem of removing the towing chain of a wrecking car from the frantic Fleck.

Financially, it was the familiar story. Providence wasn't shaken to its roots. When we paid our rent and settled with the school orchestra, everything else having been cash-in-advance, we had netted $59.47.

The strategists got together then and said, "Give them comedy. Get them in the habit of coming to see us and by and by we can sneak in some serious drama." That theory is for the most part a delusion. Those who are attracted only by the prospect of being rolled in the aisles will continue to skip the heavy offerings. The best reason for doing comedy is because it is a good thing to laugh and to bring some laughter to others. So we went to work on *The Drunkard*.

Don't think that that piece was always regarded as comedy. A few excerpts from the author's preface, while not depicting that person as a shrinking violet, indicate the seriousness with which the 1844 premiere was received. "There could not have been a better time chosen for the production of this most successful and Domestic Drama. No unprejudiced person will attempt to deny that it was the cause of much good, and mate-

52

rially aided the Temperance Movement it was meant to advocate. Mr. Smith's [who incidentally wrote this preface] personation of Edward, evidently the result of accurate and laborious study, and deep knowledge of human frailty was at times terribly real, . . . and universally acknowledged to be the most natural, affecting acting ever seen in this city." Actors haven't changed much in a hundred years.

We played all eighteen scenes, requiring twenty-eight stage hands. For all that it would have gone off as a pleasant season's wind-up were it not for a sudden impulse of mine to put the hero on horseback in one of the early sylvan scenes.

Two nights before opening, I watched a run-through with as much detachment as a director can gather. I thought it needed something. That remark reminds me of Art with a capital A. Then I got it. It needed a horse. To some of my Dominican brethren I proposed the great idea and they said in chorus, "You wouldn't dare put a horse on that stage."

That sounded like an out-and-out challenge. It's one thing to question a director's ability; it's another thing to question his courage. I wasn't afraid of a horse—I didn't think. Furthermore, Hampden played *Cyrano* in Providence and the audience withheld their applause until a pair of jaunty steeds drew a coach across the battle scene. That was proof that they loved animals.

To find a horse, and quickly, was the problem. Such impulses must be acted upon at once. A second thought might have brought too much caution. I recalled seeing an inoffensive-looking creature with a hunted look in his eyes, grazing in a meadow adjoining the House of the Good Shepherd. I phoned the Mother Superior immediately and said, "How about your horse?"

"Haven't you heard?" was the reply.

Of course I hadn't heard, so I said as much.

"Well—last Thursday—he died."

That announcement I accepted philosophically. If his time was up, I'd rather have him slip away at home than on my stage. That would have been overdoing it. But Mother knew a milkman who had a very healthy horse and no doubt he would oblige.

Impetuously, I phoned the milkman and blurted my proposal. I got the equivalent of a lecture.

Yes, they had a horse, but he was a respectable animal who toiled the early morning hours bringing milk around for children and he'd have no truck with theatre people. Why, the only theatre people he ever met were roistering home at an hour when good folk were in bed. Who would deliver the milk?

Passing up the rhetorical questions, I asked in a small voice if he knew any no-good horses who would associate with anybody for a program notice. He relented. Yes, come to think of it, a local brewery had retired a rather profligate animal, and if we'd mention their product, something might be arranged.

Why couldn't he atone for his ill-spent life by appearing in a Temperance play? The brewery expressed delight to co-operate, insinuating the popular thesis that there is always a heart of gold in the unregenerate. His name was Rainbow and he was a little outsize. He would be at the stage door at six-thirty on opening night for last-minute instructions.

He appeared on schedule. In fact he came from the west, cresting a slight rise, and blotted out the setting sun. His manager looked like an elephant trainer by comparison. He was the biggest horse I've ever seen on the loose. There was a comparable beast at the San Francisco World Fair, but it cost ten cents to go into a tent and gasp at him. I had a spectacle on my hands and was not adequately prepared to handle it.

Fascinated, I went to meet him. I shook hands with his manager, still unbelieving. We looked each other over, Rainbow and I, and I detected the ghost of a sneer on his impressive face. We New Englanders, except for the plutocrats, are usually either horsey or boatey. We are seldom both. I was boatey. Rainbow knew I was not his master.

The cast and crew were assembling. Trouble was in the air. Stars of the dress rehearsal were reduced to feature players. Rainbow dwarfed everything. Carpenters, grips, props developed a mutinous look in their eyes. It was as though someone had sneaked in a carnival on them and they resented the quick shift from technician to animal handler.

Action was needed to break the ominous silence, so I pointed to five or six cement steps leading down to the stage door level, and blithely said, "Take him down there."

The manager said apologetically, "Sorry, but he doesn't go down steps."

"He doesn't go down steps?" I echoed.

One of my assistants, in an effort to be helpful, ventured, "Horses don't like steps. . . . He's a horse."

That I took unblinking, but thought fast. I couldn't

win in the realm of horsedom. Theatrical talk was much safer. So I snapped, "Bribe him."

After a stony silence, someone said, "What with?"

Remembering that policeman's horses nibbled at sugar and apples, I suggested those delicacies. So, someone got an apple and held it out at arm's length halfway down the steps.

Rainbow affected a little annoyed smile, indicating that since he had retired he had plenty to eat and had no intention of relinquishing habits of a lifetime for a miserable apple.

Twenty-eight stage hands looked at me—as though that were any help—so, to save face, I blurted, "Let's fool him. He doesn't mind declivities, does he?" They exchanged glances uncertainly and the neophytes probably expected to see Rainbow lowered with mirrors. I hurried on with the plot. "Lead him around the building and take his mind off the whole thing. Talk to him about other famous horses. When you come back we'll have it filled in and he'll think it's a little hill."

We hadn't much fill, but did our best with planks, branches and dirt. Rainbow sauntered back after his instructive and perhaps entertaining walk with what the French are supposed to call *deja vu*—that vague recollection of having been there before. He said, in effect, "No!"

The management refused to yield. His name was on the program and he was going to appear. As a last resort I shouted, "Gentlemen, push him down." The "Gentlemen" got them. The little men looked at their equine Gulliver and then back at the desperate little man who said, "Push him down." But they manifested ingenuity. Dozens would rush in flying wedge formation at a narrow section like a knee which looked more vulnerable than the towering solid bulk above. Sometimes he got out of shape, bunching up in the middle as too many feet got on the same step, or stretching out perilously as hind legs failed to keep pace with forelegs. But with the help of some utterly silly talk from his manager about being a "nice horsey," he yielded to the determined efforts of the Lilliputians.

He was not a nice horsey when he reached the bottom. In fact, he laid back his ears and curled his lips so ominously that those who knew something about horses gave him a wide berth.

The next problem was to get him through a door. He had no aversion to doors, but this was a very ordinary door and Rainbow was a very large horse. Furthermore, I wanted my hero on board so I called my equestrian over to discuss the problem.

"Paul," I said, when he arrived, "here is your mount." That little speech wasn't exactly necessary, because Paul was well aware of the fact and gave evidence by turning a little green. This descendant of a long line of pirates was decidedly boatey, having been a purser on the old Fall River Line, and he thought horses were something to put two dollars on the nose of. There was no problem of fitting a saddle or stirrups. A howdah or morris-chair would have been more practical. So I went on, "Paul, if that animal has enough sense to lower his head and get through that door, you do the same thing."

The Domestic Drama began and the crucial scene came up. The galumping and thumping of that steed

57

on the wooden floor brought nightmarish speculations. Would the floor hold him? Would he jump out into the audience? Too late now. Paul was aboard, riding more like cargo than master. True, he held a rope leading from a halter, but it was used more for hanging on than for guiding. Rainbow ducked his head and emerged through the door, but I looked for Paul in vain.

He got his head down all right, but in doing that his legs spread out and he was swept over the stern as they hit the sides of the door. A swarming crew got the rider established again and the ensemble clumped out onstage. The heroine, who had been picking imaginary flowers from the wood-wings, crept outside the tormentor and teetered perilously over the bass drum. The high-hatted, moustachioed, black-cloaked villain, who was hiding behind a stump, picked the stump up and sidled off the stage, his heretofore arrogant laughter resembling the cry of a frightened bird.

Had Rainbow been an old trouper he would have thrilled to the lights, the music, the applause. But he was not of the theatre. These little things unnerved him. From this point on, the reports of eye-witnesses differ. Paul thinks he reared. That is patently impossible, because he would have gone through the grid. I think he raised his head to get his bearings. Paul pulled on the halter rope hard and Rainbow backed up. A good thing in itself was this backing up, but it crumpled the wood-wings like paper.

Twenty-seven stage hands (the electrician was over with me) tried to push the reversing brute forward, but were helpless. But Paul came through. He slithered, dropped and unclimbed the distance from Rainbow's deck to the stage, turned the beast around, slapped his ample flank and improvised the fitting phrase, "Go, noble steed, and graze on yon bounteous beauteous grasses."

Rainbow went, comet-like, through the mob, through the door and up the stairs which had so annoyed him previously. He even threw a shoe in the process and then clumped into the night, with his manager in frenzied pursuit. They got together a few thousand yards away and a stage hand followed with the shoe, thinking he might need it in the morning. As the stagehand approached the two, he was surprised to hear the manager saying in a petulant disappointed tone, "Rainbow, you let me down."

Thus rang down the curtain on the '34-'35 season. I went on retreat the next day to take inventory of my spiritual assets, and maybe that was just as well.

Washington reported good public relations. It was called by the press the best outfit in town and this was surprising because of its youth. The chapter won more favorable nods by its production of *Cradle Song*. A little anti-clericalism flared because of my being transplanted, but the Doctor recovered, rallied his breaking lines and ploughed on.

In fact, scattering us far and wide (if my going to Providence could be called a far-and-wide scattering) tended to spread the idea—like stepping on quicksilver. It had good precedent, too, in our own ranks, since St. Dominic sent his first fourteen in twos all over Europe, and they certainly got his ideas talked about.

VI: WORLD PLUS FLESH

WITH AN INTREPIDITY DERIVED, NO DOUBT, FROM handling horses, the Providence Chapter blandly scheduled ten events for the '35-'36 season. These ever-flowing spectacles were offered to hard-headed customers for the grand total of five dollars, thereby underselling everything offered the public north of the Rio Grande. Without giving away dishes or real estate, we managed to ensnare about twenty-five subscribers, and resumed the nightly melee in competition with the basketeers and my undergraduate dramateers for the use of the auditorium. As though that wasn't trouble enough, we took two of the full-length shows on the road.

Catherine the Valiant was the opening. If you are smiling at that, it has served another good purpose. Providence had to get it out of its system because Washington had done it so well. The advantage of competition was already showing. Then, too, I knew how to move people about in it and had only to copy the sets previously designed. But, since we did five full-length plays that season, I had to read four more.

Competition for roles was keen, and competition in amateur theatricals has a way of ruining beautiful friendships. In fact, competition in professional theatricals has a way of ruining beautiful friendships. I guess competition just has a way of ruining beautiful friendships.

60

No school auditorium for this production. We were going into a commercial theatre to clean up or bust. The disjunction is obviously not complete. Nobody cleans up in Providence and we hadn't the good fortune to bust.

Partly because the brothers Fay (of Providence, not of the Abbey in Dublin) were kind souls, partly because the theatre was dark, and partly because of a few dollars, we secured the Carleton. If you don't remember it by that name and think you should (though why you should, I can't imagine) it's had a number of designations. Most theatres in that town change their names every time they're painted. It makes them feel less self-conscious for being there.

This venture into the realms where commercialism rears its ugly head served to acquaint us with some of the interesting regulations of the stagehands' union— and that is something to know.

The mere knowledge has put producers out of business.

The department heads were particularly helpful.

"Props," for instance, said, "Don't lug in no furniture. I can pick it up and save you money. What do you need?"

"Well," I faltered, "we actually have our furniture, but maybe you could get better. We want mostly fourteenth-century tables and chairs."

"Fourteenth century! Oh no! There ain't none of that left."

It was then that I suspected some of our pieces weren't genuine.

But when we backed the truck to the canonized distance from the stage door, they really went into action. To show their enthusiasm for the job they dropped a bookcase smartly on the sidewalk. Since it had no similarity to a volley ball and was not designed for strenuous sport, all the fabricated stained glass fell out of its doors. This occurred a few hours before curtain time, as we couldn't afford their invaluable services for dress rehearsal. However, my enthusiastic amateurs stepped up to repair the damage, only to be told that no non-union man could raise a hand on that stage.

The rules said nothing about voices being raised, and when I threatened a dozen individual and collective law suits they agreed that this might be a state of emergency. Since none of their members could repair the damage, we might be permitted to put the fragments together if we were watched.

Apparently it wasn't, because we carted our five-set monster to New Haven and tackled even more stage-hands in the Shubert theatre. Things which amused us or caused a bit of indignation then have been forgotten, so many fantastic situations have we encountered since, but one episode comes to mind. The carpenter couldn't find his hammer during one of his minor crises, and my eager assistants—anxious to see the show go on that day—offered him one of ours. It was curtly declined with some mutterings about non-union equipment.

In both cities the press was favorable, except that one reviewer in New Haven objected to "the preposterous wig" worn by the father of the Pope. Our mild resentment was occasioned by the fact that Tim Dwyer who played the role had been wearing that preposterous "wig" for about eighty years.

An unofficial comment from a cleric attached to Yale University, who knew that I wrote and directed the piece, was reported to me as follows: "It was badly written and badly directed, but the Pope was a wow."

Besides the five full-length productions, we attempted five lectures each in conjunction with one or two one-act plays. The first lecturer was Padraic Colum, famed Irish story teller and poet, and one of his own works, *The Betrayal*, was the accompanying stage piece. To warm his heart in critical New England we put our top-flight actors of Erse extraction into the show—by name Hanley, Connolly, Feeley and Fitzpatrick. The director was Harry Nugent, heralded by the press on his arrival some years before as "poet, scholar and soldier of Ireland." But Mr. Colum and Mr. Nugent must have lived in different parishes or else Dublin's famous must have a secret vow not to agree on anything in public.

Colum arrived a few hours before his lecture and we gave him a dress rehearsal of *The Betrayal*, asking for criticism but expecting praise. When the rehearsal ran its course, we looked expectantly at the distinguished author, who cleared his throat and said, "That decanter isn't authentic."

Mr. Nugent, at that point, stuck his head from the wings and, disdaining the words of the author, shouted, "That carafe came from my mother's in Dublin."

The two had the same lilt in their speech, but that was as close as they came to agreement on anything that night. Mr. Colum did warm my heart by giving major credit in the formation of the Abbey Players to the Fay brothers (this time of Dublin) of whom he said, "one was an organizer and the other had a great respect for words." I pondered that statement and thought we might make a go of this Blackfriars yet, if the Doctor would organize it, because I was inclined to have a respect for words.

After the lecture and play in which the decanter or carafe played its role faultlessly, we adjourned for a repast, and Mr. Colum said to me, "Since you made such a fuss about the sword-stick, why did you finally have him killed with the dagger?" My mouth hung open because we hadn't dared to tamper with a comma of the script, knowing the author would be with us, so I gasped, "But you wrote it that way. We followed every least direction."

Mr. Colum silenced me for the evening by saying, "Oh, I didn't write the stage directions. I only wrote the words."

Word got around that two theatre groups were getting very definite about moral and artistic standards and were surviving against more than the usual odds in spite of their quaint ideas. That struck a spark in others. One that promised to kindle quickly into flame was headed by Father E. Lawrence O'Connell of Pittsburgh. With a dynamic enthusiasm which made the hurdling of obstacles seem a thing that anyone could do, he had established an enviable reputation in his city as producer and director. With customary directness, Father Larry listened to my story of what the Blackfriars' Guild hoped to do and immediately talked his Newman Players into coming into the fold.

The Pittsburgh Chapter promised to cause us to look to our laurels, when suddenly Father Larry was killed in an automobile accident. Although his passing was of inestimably greater loss to many who knew and loved him, it was a blow to the work which we had planned together. For, as in the case of many capable leaders, most of his plans were in his head and the new foundation melted away.

The ripples from the pebble dropped a few years before went south as far as Louisville and a group headed by Father Celestine Rooney wrote for constitutions. We had progressed so far through our endless arguments in Washington and Providence that we were actually sending out literature.

The Providence Chapter played fifty-nine people in one hundred and fifteen roles in five full-length plays and five one-acters. Barry's *The Joyous Season* and Pollock's *The House Beautiful* came off very well. Although an epigrammatiste has said "The House Beautiful is the play lousy," we are not always in accord with phrase-turning critics. I little thought during those relatively quiet days as a schoolmaster in Providence that I would be working with Channing Pollock just before his death for the cause of American democracy against the strange attack on God which was creeping in from the East.

Some of the survivors of the Pittsburgh Chapter invited me for a lecture to see if they could rebuild. They thought that St. Patrick's Day—the 17th of March— would bring good luck. So it brought a flood. I talked to a huddled handful that came by raft and clinging vine. When I phoned for reservations to return to my not-too-desolate classes, a weary voice assured me that there was plenty of space but that the train was under water. The Pittsburgh-to-Providence jaunt became a minor Odyssey. The trip to the airport (which isn't too close to Pittsburgh to terrify the natives) was made by automobile. The plane even took off in a normal fashion. But, finding no ceiling in Newark, it wandered to Camden. Taxicabs, provided by the airlines, took the passengers to Philadelphia, only my cab caught fire half way there. Another cab finally finished the job and we reached New York via the Pennsylvania Railroad. At that point the exchequer wouldn't stand train fare to Providence, so I made the last leg by bus. The item in a local paper that I parachuted onto the campus was a slight exaggeration.

Though the cards were stacked against Pittsburgh becoming number three link in the chain, there were rumblings—some of them from afar. A Philadelphia group wrote for constitutions, a Cleveland outfit was invited to join, and from Vallejo in the far west came requests for information.

You may be sure that Washington, which now casually referred to itself as "the parent Chapter," was not idle. Washington wasn't of an idle temperament, and with an entire building—theatre upstairs and workshop and clubrooms down—it was making the most of this unprecedented opportunity. Robinson's *The White Headed Boy* and Lavery's *The First Legion* were, as usual, approved in town.

But if that energetic chapter even thought of being idle, it would have had to cope with the pinwheel-like energy of the Doctor, who always sought bigger things to organize. One of these ideas was a big play-writing contest. Its genesis was logical enough. With a hundred people in two cities on the lookout for plays, one of three situations should prevail: (1) we should have found a great many—the catalogues say they're all good; or (2) our ideas about plays must be ridiculous; or (3) there must be a dearth of Blackfriar material. Well, we didn't find a great many; our ideas about plays still suit us; so, the conclusion is that people aren't writing Blackfriar plays.

The American theatre has twisted an art form into a business—a sharp business and a big business. If people want it that way, that's their privilege. We happen to be dissatisfied.

Every other art form in the country can be presented to the people without the necessity of going through a distorting commercial bottleneck. (I regard the moving pictures as merely an aspect of an art form and popular music as a subdivision of a field.) But, if one paints a picture, it can be exhibited at home or in a small gallery first. Quality will eventually be discovered. If one writes a symphony, it can be played first by an unknown orchestra. If one designs a building, it can be erected in Walla-Walla. But by a convention which we have moronically accepted, no theatre piece is worth considering unless it has gone through the play doctors of Broadway.

I will agree with the repetitious critics that a better quality of technique is manifested in Broadway playwrights than among the non-commercials. But I am not convinced that Broadway is an unmixed good because some of its material has good form, while its standards in moral and aesthetic fields which affect the entire life and happiness of man are very much confused. I can't help thinking that the ultimates of eternal truth and enduring beauty come first, and that technique in making something comes second.

Broadway very simply asks: "How much will it cost?" and "How much will it make?" What producer can afford to upset the smug complacency of his visiting fireman audience when fifty thousand dollars is involved? What producer can fling to the world the burning convictions of an author's soul, if his customers prefer *the* American art form as represented by a plump chorus and a thin book.

There are producers who know right from wrong and who have a finely developed sense of the beautiful, but economic pressure corrupts the vision of beauty until it is synonymous with "beautiful critical raves" and the sweet sound of paper money in the box office.

Broadway knows that vicarious wickedness pays. People who would not place themselves in questionable circumstances—whether because of conviction or convention—can step outside the routine pattern of their everyday lives through the transference of theatre. So that big business which is the American theatre must steal a few customers from the house next door, by adroit advertising, press-agenting, reviews, etc., and keep the police away in the process. This represents one weakness of commercial theatre—the weakness of flesh.

Another is, of course, the world. The old categories change slowly. You can't offend a customer. God isn't a customer. You must be careful of the sensibilities of Republicans and Democrats, although if the average audience filled out a questionnaire, the various "parties" would look, as they are, alike. You can't offend evangelical Protestants, "liberal" Catholics or any category of Jews—but you can water them all down until what remain have very few convictions or principles. The average American for whom the best minds must write is such a complex of compromises that he is definitely not worth writing for.

He takes divorce for granted because divorce is legal —therefore, conventional. He may accept God (at least he may use stock unimaginative blasphemy) because God is traditional; but he can likewise reject God, because the rejection of God is smart. Therefore, he mustn't push God too far. Let God rather hover in the distance. Those who can take, let them take; don't embarrass the others. He can go so far toward moralizing as to laugh at the common frailties of humanity— but the overtone must remain in the realm of laughter. Don't try to solve anything, because that's where you get mixed up.

I don't wish to imply that these unwritten laws haven't been broken from time to time. But I assure you they haven't been broken often and they won't be broken even as much in the future. Because to break them you have to spend as much money as to keep them, and if you break them you haven't too good a chance of getting your money back. To break (or keep them) you have to meet the curious demands of the Stagehands' Union, the Teamsters' Union, the Treasurers' and Ticket-sellers' Ulnion, the Press Agents' and Managers' Union, the Scenic Artists' Union, the Musicians' Union, the Wardrobe Mistresses sub-union, the theatre owners' apparently unified non-union, and a ring of organizations too numerous to mention.

A producer can risk dropping that much money down the drain on a non-sure thing, but the results are so disheartening that few risk it a second time.

Aren't the audiences getting what they want? That's what the producer claims when he rationalizes his position and becomes a successful business man. Up to a point, yes. Up to a point only? Then why don't audiences support the brave departures? Because American audiences regard their theatre as a mixed thing. It is partially a descendant of minstrels and medicine shows —so it must amuse. Or it must have the approbation of the current "intellectual" fad. That means the critics— who are caught by the current tradition—or a bloc with a thesis have to save and sell a show during its first week. Playgoers, like book readers, are followers. But, whereas a book can linger for a month or two on a bookshelf, a show can't.

Furthermore, audiences are inarticulate. I know that producers and drama editors are going to question that statement and back up their stand with floods of letters. But, I repeat, the few who are articulate are practically ineffective. You may notice a few people steaming out of theatres and writing vitriolic letters to the press. And these may discourage some customers. But their next venture onto Broadway is conditioned by the critics, the advertisements, a few theatre-going friends, a date, a couple of passes.

A book can be taken down from the shelf and popularized after a year or twenty have passed. But a play must be seen on the appointed nights when its producers are able to meet salaries.

The so-called tributary theatre might have saved it

had the streams flowed into Broadway instead of backing out, but the little theatre was sick at birth.

We were not satisfied with the theatre in general and there was no indication that the octopus of Broadway had within itself the possibilities of a return to health. So the Doctor decided to run a play-writing contest. If we got the plays and managed to keep them running in many cities throughout the country, we could later determine if audiences could be found for them. Remember, we are not interested in destructive criticism. If you like the present system and its product, well, you've got it. But there may be a few who'd like to see what we had in mind.

Now, the important thing about the Doctor's play-writing contest was a lot of money. He wanted really attractive prizes, because playwrights eat. The only way to prevent them from being lured into the commercial machine is to offer them comparable rewards. That little item of money seemed to be the catch in his scheme and our perpetual mirage.

We conferred frequently, rushing to meet between classes (the Doctor was then teaching psychology at Catholic University) and wrote innumerable sets of rules and publicity schedules. Then we popped the idea to various national Catholic organizations, thinking it to be irresistible—but I guess it wasn't.

Today, there has been launched the sort of play-writing contest which we failed to realize in 1935. I salute Father Keller and the vision of The Christophers. And I salute them for having achieved what I failed to accomplish, even though the cynics may say I'd better salute them, having garnered one of their fat prizes.

U NDAUNTED BY DEFEAT, WHICH HAD BECOME A habit, the Doctor took a few minutes from correcting papers to conjure up something bigger to tackle. The idea which finally took shape grew out of a flurry of official correspondence. The young Dominicans involved in Blackfriar work were thought in some circles to be wasting their time and more specific regulations were laid down as to the amount of time and the precise hours which might be alloted to theatricals.

The Doctor knitted his receding brow and realized that in the shifting fortunes of the religious life we might both be assigned to other tasks, because the will of the superior is the law we must follow. There might even by superiors in the future who would regard the work as a hobby—a bit of recreation.

It must have some sort of permanence. We are expendable, but somebody must do it or it won't be done. Perhaps the Doctor was a bit grim about the "somebody must do it" part. He meant me. If Blackfriars and all reasonably exact facsimiles departed from the face of the earth, there might still be no more than the normal quota of wars and rumors of wars, but, when an instrument is being sharpened for a task, it becomes impatient if it possesses the capabilities of thinking or feeling.

The idea in the Doctor's mind grew bigger and bigger. Why not attach the work to a University? And what better spot than Catholic University, of which he was a staff member? When he got that far, it was practically an accomplished fact. The means to the end were filed under "trivia" or "routine."

The Washington Chapter was doing *Smilin' Through*. They didn't tell me why, so I assumed it was because it was written in my adopted Block Island. Various dramatic organizations had been invited to bring productions to the Sylvan Theatre on the Washington Monument Grounds. This open-air quasi-natural amphitheatre with its eighty-foot proscenium opening (which ran the legs off the actors who rehearsed on a smaller stage) lent itself to the bucolic idyll and that was the production they entered.

If you think I've abruptly changed the subject, you don't know what mental gymnastics are required to follow the devious mind of the Doctor. This is going to blossom in quick and easy stages into The Catholic University School of Speech and Drama, but at this point you're not expected to suspect it.

The regular electrician who installed the sound equipment or the lights—I've forgotten which—for these Sylvan Theatre productions had a rival lurking outside, and this rival went secretly to the Doctor, asking him to bring him in and put the regular man out. Sniffing a possible trade, my erstwhile partner said he couldn't think of putting a good man out of work, especially since he hadn't seen the product of the challenger. Said challenger offered a demonstration, anywhere, anytime, of his amplifying or illuminating prowess, and the Doctor arranged a dress rehearsal on the campus of Catholic University "for the Sisters who didn't get to see many shows."

It worked. The Sisters had to be home early, so the production began in twilight against the setting sun, and as the darkness came on the lights took hold. The Sisters, who apparently had a pleasant evening, told their respective professors and deans that what the University needed was good theatre.

Of course, there had been a bit of dickering before, but this turned the trick. Immediate consultation with the Doctor found him with all the answers.

"Who'll finance it?" asked the University.

"We will," replied the Doctor without dropping dead.

Lest I create a false impression, it must be stated that the University is perfectly willing in regular session to make sacrifices, but since the summer session is a help to students, every course has to pull its own weight. This was to be a summer venture in 1937.

"Who'll staff it?" asked the University.

"Blackfriars will take care of that."

"Who'll head it?"

"Dr. Nagle." It was done just like that. Nobody remembered that a few years before I had gone out of those hallowed precincts as a psychologist. Nobody was surprised that I was returning as a dramatic authority. I guess nobody would have been surprised if I returned as a jinni.

But I was surprised. I was surprised by the fact and by the manner in which I learned it. The telegram read:

You're running a drama school next summer.
Learn something about one. T. F. Carey.

I suppose it is a difficult task to run a drama school.
At least, I have met directors who made it look hard. I
concede it is even more of a challenge when you are
unexpectedly handed one over the telegraph. It's something like winning the sweepstakes and getting the
horse instead of the money. But I assure you, to set one
up, while you're five hundred miles away from the
scene, with the Doctor as your obedient and servile
aide, is taxing the strength, ingenuity and—above all—
the endurance of mortal man.

My "thank you" note to his telegram was proper but
guarded. That was before I knew the details about
financing and publicizing the undertaking, but I sniffed
trouble from the message. The fact that he used eleven
words indicated that he was shooting over his head. He
never before had the price of ten.

The Doctor was nettled by my lack of enthusiasm.
Here, at last, he was making me head of something and
I wasn't jumping up and down. That was precisely because I didn't know just what he was making me head
of. Neither did he, but he'd think up something. And I
was more afraid of that.

My meagre opportunities for visiting drama schools
brought unpromising results. The head of one established and respected university workshop told me
bluntly that actors couldn't be taught in a graduate
course. He modified the statement by saying that you
might teach them something, but you couldn't grade
them, because some would fall into leads and others

75

into bit parts. The test, he concluded, was not a diploma, granted for attendance and endurance, but the student's job-finding ability in later life. So, when I asked the Doctor should I run a graduate or an undergraduate school, he told me to stop quibbling.

When I ruled out certain features of the racket-schools, his patience was sorely tried, but he grudgingly approved my diligence in investigating them.

Then came that looked-for addition to American letters, known to posterity as the *Carey-Nagle Correspondence*. The tragedy which brought us together broke off this invaluable piece of Americana during the turbulent thirties. Since it will doubtless be published in its entirety in due time, I shall limit my excerpts to a few general types, all penned by the dynamic Washington partner.

His lengthy epistles literally blew out of his typewriter three or four times a week, and they contained more instructions, graciously called "suggestions," than a field army could carry out.

When I protested meekly that my undergraduate schedule carried three times as many class hours as his graduate teaching, with papers to correct, to boot; that my superiors had made me faculty advisor to two or three time-consuming student groups; that I had very little secretarial help and no equipped Guild hall such as he, but merely a semi-public gymnasium that we battled for, he dismissed it all in a sentence. "You're wasting your time." That is filed under "The-trouble-with-you-is" type.

An illustration of the "builder-upper" type begins: "Now since you are to head this new department, perhaps you ought to draw up a program." Whereupon he laid down a three-page singled-spaced outline for the program that I should draw up, which covered everything except whether the windows of the classrooms should be open or shut.

One clear sharp fall morning when I arose to greet my birthday and revel in New England autumn, the Doctor's letter began: "Your procrastination just happened to hit me at the wrong time." Then, under seven headings (numbered) he recounts his own incredible activities, which subtly indicate freedom from the vice of procrastination. Then follow eight (numbered) paragraphs of "suggestions." I'm to write a 3,000-word pamphlet, hire five staff members, prepare a new playwriting contest, contact a number of theatrical celebrities and so forth. The last sentence reads (and it's still my birthday): "And in conclusion, don't you know it's bad policy ever to desert a sinking ship!" I never understood the exclamation point.

Perhaps the "typical type," to borrow a famous phrase from another trusty Blackfriar, was the Doctor's advice to eight of us who attended a theatre conference. He couldn't make it himself because he was launching some enormous project and anyhow couldn't risk taking his finger off the aortic pulse of his ventures. A general ukase directed to the eight had, under Rule 2: "Attend in as large numbers as possible."

Though I faithfully answered the Doctor's letters, serving thereby as a foil for the great correspondence, I did have a few other things to do. There still was the Providence Chapter to run. And that Chapter, tired of taking down a movable basket (if the word "movable" extends to something which can be moved only by nine men), sought and found a home of its own. Well, that's what all Blackfriars Chapters finally sought. They could discover or invent enough internal troubles without getting involved with hosts or sponsors who had another complete set of problems.

That little independent streak in the Blackfriar plan was not always understood by our well-wishers, who thought we wanted to find a place to put on plays. Very few got the idea that we wanted to do something very radical to the theatre—bring it back to objective standards. Very few do yet.

Pastors thought it would be a good adjunct to their parishes; colleges asked to set up Blackfriars to occupy the time of their students. They all wanted it on their own terms. The clergy and teaching religious required enlightenment nearly as much as the potential actors. The former were preoccupied with social or educational programs; the latter with the urge to exploit their abilities with someone else doing the preparing and the promoting. The ones we needed most were not really listening.

They knew the theatre. Some approved it as it was and sought no change. Others deplored, but took it for granted as they took rain for granted, and never dreamed of changing it. Washington had its own plant on 15th Street, so Providence had to strike out on its own. One of the littlest theatres I've ever seen was found on Hope Street. Perhaps the name of the street was symbolic, but you can't live on hope. Now, strictly speaking it wasn't exactly on Hope Street; it was in back of a house on Hope Street.

However, it was tiny. A former gymnasium, it consisted of a high-ceilinged one-story room, with a stage raised about two feet and a flimsy little proscenium arch. The basement provided a furnace room, a little workshop, and what the actors pretentiously called the "green room."

This 1936-1937 season saw four full-length plays (some of which were duly trucked to Taunton and New Haven where the scenery had to be rebuilt as the stages were three times as large), four evenings of one-act plays and four public lectures. One of these lectures was given by Constance Mary Rowe, the English painter, who is now tucked away in a convent, painting and writing challenging books on art. Thomas Crosby of The Players, the senior dramatic organization in town, gave another, swapping "pulpits" with me. Some of our actors grew restive under Blackfriar treatment and switched to The Players. At least, this organization did orthodox little theatre in the traditional manner and didn't get mixed up discussing standards.

Backstage was so small that we did sound effects in the basement and sent them up over a public address system. This required something rather complicated in signals.

One night we had a veritable evening of surf crashing or swirling outside. *Riders to the Sea* and *Men Folk* were on, I remember. So, a stagehand rubbed a stiff scrubbing brush over a piece of sized canvas and an open mike brought the waves thus produced to where the waves should be—backstage and, incidentally, upstairs.

About the third night of this run, when the novelty

79

had worn off for the backstage gang and when the operator was left alone to his tiresome task, an affluent subscriber arrived in a chauffeur-driven car. Now there was no place for a chauffeur to go on Hope Street except asleep and, as the weather was hovering around zero, this chauffeur unobtrusively came in the basement, where he saw light and suspected heat.

Seeing the man ceaselessly drawing the dry brush across the flat, he ventured, "What's the pitch, bud?"

Solemnly and in slight annoyance, the technician pointed to the open mike—on account of "What's the pitch, bud?" wasn't supposed to be wafted in through a window on the west coast of Ireland.

The chauffeur, noticing no mike in the junk-heaped room, persisted: "What?"

This was too much for the surf-maker, who couldn't talk either, so with one hand he made frantic gestures, never losing the beat of the waves with the other. A strange light grew in the chauffeur's eyes as he backed toward the door, saying, "I get it, bud; it's O. K. G'Night."

I slipped in a little piece written in what I thought was the comedy genre that year, more or less for the fun of it. It previously had been submitted anonymously to the Washington Chapter and the play-reading committee turned it down with snorts. It was pretty well received in Providence and New York.

The most ambitious and most daring thing we attempted was O'Neill's *Days Without End*. The author permitted us to play it without royalties, which was for us an unusually nice gesture.

Although known as "the O'Neill play that has the

priest in it" by many people, it isn't particularly Catholic for that reason, any more than *The Joyous Season* is Catholic because it has a nun in it. The reasons for such classification are deeper than that. But, except for a few minor objectionable spots which were circumvented, it does solve its problem in the proper manner, even though it discusses sin. Since we were trying to break Providence into an adult theatre and since this seemed like a good test case, we put it on and reasonably well.

The reverberations nearly shook New England loose from the Atlantic Coast. Customers said they weren't coming back and the cautious grew more afraid of us. It began to look as though the process of teaching people the difference between fundamentals and accidentals—between morality and conventions—was going to be a difficult one.

It was at this period that my superiors used to get anonymous letters, pointing out the menace I was to the New England which bred me. Fortunately, they passed the letters on to me for my scrapbook. I had always expected a little opposition from the entrenched interests in the theatre in achieving our plan, but we didn't dream of the extent of the beating we'd have to take from within.

Washington's program ran along similar lines. Who copied whom doesn't seem as important now as it did then. However, instead of closing with the controvertible piece of O'Neill, the Washingtonians did a rollicking comedy and made everybody happy.

Louisville, Number Three Chapter, waxed and waned that year. The Louisvillains began with a class in make-up and rather overshadowed the two older units by promising plays in Italian, French and Spanish, throwing in, I presume, a few in English if time permitted. They did open auspiciously, presenting Lavery's *Monsignor's Hour* to an invitation audience. Then a two-fold blow struck. Father Rooney, who was still the spearhead, was transferred to Madison, Wisconsin, and the flood of '37 came and destroyed the sets they had so carefully built. When the floods come and the spirit goes, even Blackfriars close their doors.

Ideas don't die, however, and before the season was over Madison, which had just met Father Rooney, was chartered as Chapter Number Four. Correspondence concerning affiliation of existing drama groups or the foundation of others was under way with Cleveland, Trenton, Auburn (N.Y.), Grand Rapids, Great Bend (Kansas), Canton (Ohio), Springfield (Ill.), Dayton, Ottawa, Chicago, Brooklyn, Greenfield (Mass.), New Orleans, Los Angeles, Minneapolis and St. Paul, Rochester, Lowell (Mass.), Cincinnati, and Pittsburgh again. The idea was getting around.

VIII: A CONFERENCE IS BORN

THE FOUNDATION OF THE CATHOLIC THEATRE
Conference came along at this point and it came along
with a rush. Mr. Emmet Lavery thought that there
ought to be a better organized Catholic theatre. Knowing a little about Blackfriars', he sent me a copy of an
article he was preparing for *America* in which he
called for action from any or all who were interested.

That same Mr. Lavery seems to have upset people
along the line from the days of his affiliation with the
Federal Theatre Project through his appearance before
an investigating committee in Washington. Perhaps the
friends of Russian communism have influenced his tim-
ing. They instinctively realize that, since the rewards
are so small—material redistribution in this world—
they must be secured within the lifetime of the workers or they'll never come at all. The Church, with
its eye on eternity and its complete acceptance of suf-
fering, sacrifice and apparent defeat in the earthly
sojourn of its members, can move slowly and on un-
equivocal principles.

. So, as Emmet invades camps of friends and enemies—calling the rest of us to hurry up and get things
done—he will always be suspected of compromises.
Thought I haven't seen much of him lately because
of geographical reasons, I have at hand a sheaf of
letters from this period which show him an enthu-

siastic, sincere, intolerant-of-delay planner and leader of Catholic theatre.

His article prompted me to contact Catholic University to propose a meeting or convention of some sort, and the University agreed. So I prepared an article for *America*, accepting the challenge, but the late Father Dineen, S.J., of the Loyola Community Theatre in Chicago got his bid in first and I was very much in the middle.

We straightened out the ensuing snarl in the best way possible. We had two meetings—the first in Chicago where we got to know the others in the field, and the second at the end of the summer session in Washington where we crystallized our ideas. These meetings set up the Catholic Theatre Conference. Its accomplishments are better appraised in the light of fourteen years of service, so I'll catch up with it further on.

The Doctor didn't come to the Chicago meeting, even though it was held in his old home town, because he had a lot of planning to do to build and equip a drama school, but he did send us rather explicit directions. I think he'd try to organize a riot.

To begin with, the University gave him the gymnasium as the scene of operations. Its proportions were a trackman's dream; you could travel out of sight of the coach. How to harness that enormous covered stadium to make it function as a theatre and school might have taxed the ingenuity of many. The prospect jolted me, coming from the littlest theatre I had ever seen to the biggest. The Doctor's budget was a cool zero. We had to equip those vasty spaces and pay salaries out of tuitions of students whose coming we had to promote. That was all. But working on nothing was an old story. I think we'd be embarrassed if we had fifteen dollars.

No more appealing to men of vision. We had tried that, too, and realized we weren't going to live long enough to see results. So the Doctor went to New York and dropped in backstage of theatre after theatre. He engaged stagehands in conversation. Those who manifested that they didn't like him and all he stood for got a cheery "Good day." Those who indicated by the absence of a glare that they didn't mind pausing in their arduous labors to pass the time of day were subjected to a patter of questions such as: "Who makes this stuff?" "What do you do with it when you're through with it?" etc., and in a week of such wandering and poking he had all but organized a club. Its members were dedicated to directing equipment that they would otherwise burn or destroy to Washington for the Doctor's rather mad venture. The "boys" steered him to a well-known set builder—Martin ("Barney") Turner—and pretty soon truckloads of flats and drapes, not to omit a switchboard or two, were on their way southward.

Classrooms were built of flats, lashed and braced in the conventional manner. A proscenium on the gigantic platform stage offered the greatest challenge. So he laid out sixteen or seventeen big flats on the floor, cut off the tops in a huge semi-circle to fit the rounded roof, bolted them together, and hauled them up as a unit, using forty-five hundred feet of line on a four-wheel-pulley arrangement. Then he merely coiled and tied off the loose ends so that the gymnasts could easily take it down when football pushed the theatre out where football thought the theatre belonged.

We gathered sixty-nine students and an enthusiastic staff. I had met Josephine Callan at the Chicago convention and now signed her for the staff, where she has remained all these years. Father Gilbert Hartke, O.P., was a new instructor, giving a course on directing the high-school theatre. A dozen or more bishops wrote us, wishing us well, and so we launched the Blackfriar Institute of Dramatic Arts at Catholic University. A little pretentious in sound, perhaps, but it saved the face of the University if we failed or didn't make expenses and it gave us pretty nearly complete control of the idea behind the work.

We were not thinking in terms of just one more drama school. I'd not like to face death with that as my contribution in life. We were not thinking in terms of sending musicals to Broadway. We were training Blackfriars, first in standards and secondly in technique, that a theatre of the people based on Catholic philosophical norms might be palatable in the provinces. At least that's what I told them a few hundred times, but perhaps I didn't say it loudly enough.

To manage six public productions, the Washington and Providence Chapters offered their services for the first two weeks. The Providence offering was the more notable because of the distance the troupe travelled and because they chose Claudel's *The Tidings Brought to Mary*. In spite of the fact that it was a pretty good job, it indicated the need of education for theatre-goers, because for days afterwards priests and Sisters managed to digress in their English and philosophy classes, asking what it was all about.

That our audiences and students might better understand what we were saying, we descended to what I believe is classically catalogued as "high tripe" and did McCarthy's *If I Were King*—the old Francois Villon vehicle—and vehicle is the word.

It used up most of the older students, taxed the costume department, and caused us to look to the highways and byways for a few guest actors. The armies of France and Burgundy gave me some concern until I remembered that the football team was hanging around and looked quite formidable. So I asked them whether they would consent to walk on as an army, with no more mental taxation than the making of a few ferocious grimaces if they felt up to it. They looked sheepishly at one another as though they were finding themselves in some sort of compromising position, but, swayed by the presence of the pulchritude which drama schools always gather, they said they would.

Except that they were costume shy, they made a formidable host. Patient explanation to the effect that they would look very un-Burgundian and unmilitaristic in sweat shirts and track pants broke one or two down and the resistance of the others followed. In fact, I shot too far in asking one of them if he could pick up poor little Huguette in the third act. It's very sad, you know. An ambushed villain stabs the poor little thing and she lies there dead, offering a problem to the director, who finds her a distraction

87

when the Burgundian herald dashes in and has a big scene with Louis, the Spider King. Nobody mentions the corpse, but it is there and I don't think France was ever quite that callous. So, to repeat, I asked one compact giant if he would pick her up and gently carry her off. Gallantly, he agreed. So we tried a run through. Putting his feet together, he got her about a foot off the ground and then fell on top of her.

We blackboarded that play and threw in some signals, so, finally, by dint of putting one foot out in front of the other, he managed to do tolerably well. But on the night of the first performance, one of his brother fifteenth-century GIs sidled up to me and said,

"Hey, Father, you know the guy that's supposed to pick up the girl."

I said, "Yes."

"Well, he usually faints, an' he thinks he's gonna faint tonight."

"Oh, he does?" I murmured. "At about what time does he think he's going to faint tonight?"

"Jus' about the time he picks her up."

"Thanks for the tip. Get me the whole French army and tell them to walk lightly. The third act is on."

So the French army in chain mail came across creaking boards. And when the motley host with pikes and halberds lined up I asked, "Can any of you all-Americans pick up a one-hundred-twenty pound girl and carry her eight feet without falling on your face and without fainting?" One thought he could—and the show went on without further crisis in that department.

The trial balloon—and that expression is a quote from the Head of the Summer School—was a success. We had sixty-nine students, plenty of enthusiasm and the help of the Washington Blackfriars, without which little would have been done. Salaries were paid out of tuitions, audiences were satisfied and the venture was launched. Subsequent historians of the Catholic University venture—and there have been many—have conspicuously failed to note that the difference between success and failure was due to the Doctor, who got so much material for nothing and set it up himself. But, then, subsequent historians couldn't know that this was for us a means to an end and not an end in itself.

A word might be in order here about the foundation of the Catholic Theatre Conference. That grew out of Emmet Lavery's letter and Father Dineen's invitation. We assembled in Chicago and sized one another up. That is a privilege of Catholics, since there are so many of us and since we have to agree only on defined dogmas of which there are very few.

Emmet Lavery and Father Daniel Lord, S.J., ran the public show in the theatre and I know of no team which could run a show better. I stayed upstairs to grapple with the building of an executive board.

We were so diverse in our expressions of what Catholic Theatre was, so confused in our speeches, that we decided to appoint committees to examine the problems and to reconvene in Washington after the summer session. So it became a convention with two meetings and if it has made any sense over the years it is probably due to this bit of caution. We didn't know one another, each other's abilities or even each other's views on what should be done, and the six weeks before voting time taught us a great deal.

Lavery took for granted a theatre in every school and dreamed of one in every parish. I had taught in two colleges and helped many a Sunday in various parishes, so I had no such illusions. But we all agreed that where there was a physical set-up and some enthusiasm, the great need was direction in the choice of scripts—in other words, we needed to agree on norms and standards and then get this information circulated.

My own mail in those early days was interesting. "Can you send me some scripts suitable for six Eskimos?" "Do you know any plays in which we could use the entire student body of our school?"

Some of the advisors, in all good faith, were stressing the unobjectionable aspects of their recommendations. This might well be the lesser of evils, but it wasn't making for a strong competitive drama. Although we maintained that an artistic play could not be an immoral play, for the sake of those who had been too confused to follow such simple reasoning we set out to prepare evaluations of all the extant material from the viewpoint of its acceptability to Catholics and also from an artistic viewpoint. A dangerous procedure, you may think, but then we weren't settling that last knotty problem but merely offering the opinions of those who had some right to have an opinion for the guidance of those who hadn't time to make such private investigations.

By this time, Blackfriars had five or six affiliated chapters and were negotiating with others, so there was certainly no conflict between our producing units and the proposed service bureau. When they finally elected the Doctor secretary of the Conference in his absence, the subsequent amicable relations between Blackfriars and the Conference were soundly established.

At the Washington meeting, which was keynoted by the then Monsignor Fulton Sheen, we adopted a constitution and set up committees. The Catholic Theatre Conference was launched and has justified its existence over the years.

The press helped and hurt that first summer session, as the press so casually can. The Doctor interested a Washington paper to do a picture spread, and the young photographer found nothing of interest but Sisters in their religious habits building scenery. This indelicacy drew an immediate protest from some circles.

Actually, that the Sisters learned how to build and paint flats was a good thing. With some elemental knowledge of the physical side of theatre, many good teachers who are put in charge of drama in their schools will no longer be dependent on the artistry of the janitor for their productions.

Two men who contributed largely to the success of that first summer venture were classmates of the Doctor, Father James J. McLarney and Father Walter A. Murtaugh. The former made the curtain speech (without a curtain) at the outdoor performance which launched the entire business and stood by to make speeches or write a few thousand kind words before even a hat was dropped. The latter came to the University to watch model airplanes in wind tunnels, but our need of mechanics took away his air-mindedness-in-miniature, so he installed switchboards, tested circuits, rebuilt amplifiers and even stooped to building flats for illusions which his scientific mind thought ridiculous.

With the end of the summer school and the Washington session of the Catholic Theatre Convention, another milestone was passed. New buttresses were flung out for the edifice to come. Word came from Providence that my mother had fallen and broken her arm, apparently the result of a slight stroke, so I hurried home, realizing that for her this was the beginning of the inevitable slowing-up process which age brings with its accompanying disabilities. I left the Doctor to put the props back and they were sizeable things to tuck away.

The foundation which the Doctor laid so carefully has grown into The Catholic University School of Speech and Drama, but I hardly think that its subsequent achievement, now that it has become formalized and respectable, could be quite as exciting as its pioneer days.

Back to Providence in the rented car which served as the brain-trusters' office. Back to Providence to settle down to the relative humdrum of teaching, of running the Pyramid Players and the Providence Chapter of Blackfriars. Back to Providence with the hope that the new foundation at Catholic University would be the spawning ground of Catholic theatres throughout the country.

IX: STRAW FOR BRICKS

THE NEXT TWO YEARS WERE ALMOST MONOT-
onous from a theatre-building point of view, although
they included speeches in more than fifty cities from
coast to coast, two Blackfriar conventions, the second
summer session at Catholic University and a great
many other exciting specific happenings.

The pattern had a sameness—a pattern which began in a burst of enthusiasm, cost a tremendous amount
of energy, and in most cases ended in failure or in ces-
sation of activities which is a sort of failure. Actually,
the suspension of activities in most Blackfriar Chapters was attributed to the fact that the war took most
of the men away. But men came back from that war as
from all wars and resumed where they had left off.

Perhaps the very mention of war and dramatics in
the same paragraph suggests an incongruity. Men who
face death on battle fields and the women who wait
for them can hardly be bothered with the trivialities
of a make-believe world. But if the theatre were regarded as a teaching medium and if it could be made
worthy of that role, more than likely fewer men would
die on battle fields. It is not so incongruous to speak
of truth as a means of opposing wars.

There were internal problems—problems indigenous
to the theatre and the parish or school, problems indigenous to the mind of American youth—which made

the enduring of Blackfriar Chapters difficult. The war accelerated a focusing of these problems and finally convinced the zealots that a groundwork was to be laid.

These two years, from the summer of 1937 to the summer of 1939, marked the building of the Blackfriar string, or road or empire, with its strengths and weaknesses. Perhaps an analysis of these will serve to encourage or to deter those who are rushing into the arena in this new generation. Wars make for cleavages between generations which peace finds unnecessary.

The Washington Chapter, now five years old, did four full-length plays (one an original), an evening of one-acters and five lectures in the '37-'38 season. Of course, it had numerous social evenings and the prescribed day of retreat. This religious feature was part of all Blackfriars Chapters. It consisted of Mass and Communion and three or four talks during a quiet and recollected day by a priest who knew something about the spiritual problems of young thespians.

In our capital city, a wise drama group schedules its productions within twenty-four hours of government workers' pay days. Resident Washington is social and aloof; that means it attends the functions which do it most good in maintaining its *status quo*. It doesn't want progress but it does want to hold on. Student Washington and government working Washington is (a) not invited to mix with social Washington, (b) ambitious for self improvement, and (c) horribly bored. That becomes, then, the field in which the too many dramatic groups compete.

Providence did five plays, including Claudel's *The Tidings Brought to Mary*, some one-act plays and a few lectures in its tiny theatre which was rarely taxed to capacity. Resident Providence isn't going to be softened by new ideas, there are no government workers and the students, if they do anything, must study.

Louisville attempted a Blackfriar Chapter in a medium-sized city which already had a Catholic theatre. The argument advanced was that they hoped to do a better job. Perhaps there wasn't room for two. Perhaps there isn't a demand for one. Perhaps the pioneers of today and tomorrow should try co-operation before they go into competition. In any case, the Louisville Blackfriar report will never be complete because when the flood waters closed over the daring souls they uttered a final "Glub Glub."

Madison got off to an impressive start with the advantages and disadvantages of being sponsored by a parish. The chapter declared its city-wide character and did some plays in a new central Catholic auditorium, but met and rehearsed in the parish hall. Yet, reports indicated that other parishes were slow to push the work officially, regarding it as the project of a rival. This is very understandable and is the biggest difficulty in accepting parochial sponsorship.

In my peregrinations I managed to attend a few meetings in Madison. Unlike their effete eastern brothers, these Blackfriars in a preponderantly German community cut the discussion of constitutions a little short and tapped a keg of beer to wash down some substantial sandwiches including—believe this or not— "Blackfriar" limburger cheese. Despite changes in clerical advisors and clerical attitudes, despite theatre problems, Madison kept going until there were but four men left after the draft. It resumed operations immediately after the war. So, to Madison an orchid or, perhaps, a keg of mead.

The fifth formally accepted Chapter was Rochester, New York, and for a while it was the most impressive unit in the circuit. Msgr. John S. Randall, with whom I had corresponded when he was an assistant in Auburn, was transferred to a diocesan post in Rochester and his appetite for a Catholic theatre was whetted by the opportunities of the larger city.

He had no theatre in parish or school to incubate the idea as had the older chapters. But with more organizational ability per pound than his predecessors, Msgr. Randall secured the active co-operation of the Bishop and started a subscription drive. Dinners, speeches, organized teams of solicitors netted 1,800 season subscribers and 120 active members.

This was obviously the proper way to operate. Rochester Blackfriars leased a workshop and rented a big theatre for productions. They had a full-time secretary, a paid director and imported such guest stars as Bert Lytell for *The First Legion* and Helen Menken for *The Late Christopher Bean*. They threw in concerts by such artists as Roland Hayes as bonuses.

This was the pattern we all hoped to achieve. Our problems had more to do with lack of official backing and lack of money than with inability to turn out plays. Here we had a formula which provided for our greatest deficiencies. If this failed, what could succeed? At the risk of getting ahead of my story, I will remark that after four years of heady success, the only Chapter with money in the bank went bankrupt. The chronology and the sense of achievement which was ours is not as important as the opportunity to point out pitfalls which may beset future organizers.

Fundamentally, the chapter grew too fast in old little-theatre patterns—and Blackfriars has a different set of ideals. What they accomplished became desirable in itself. The authority and power of a board member became something worth seeking. They argued about the rights of members and the indoctrination of what Blackfriars meant gave way under the pressure of big productions. In brief, they achieved external maturity in a flash and didn't grow inside. The resultant confusion between standard little-theatre practice and the Blackfriar purpose led to dissension. The uncertain heart couldn't pump enough blood to the magnificent body.

The collapse of Rochester finally shattered my faith in "democracy" as applied to artists. Theatre can be frankly ambitious, inviting commercialism, compromise and catering, or it must be completely selfless. The modes won't mix.

Yet, Rochester is filled with pleasant memories. I set out once for that sedate city for a curtain speech on an opening night. My class schedule made trains unavailable, so I took a bus from Providence to Albany. Upon arrival, I opened my distinctive traveling bag and found it was filled with plumber's tools. The unhappy plumber who picked up the bag I started with found a white habit and a few clean clerical collars. But I couldn't wear his pipe wrenches. We swapped through proper channels a week later.

Lowell, Philadelphia and the Twin Cities of Minneapolis and Saint Paul made up the rest of the roster of full-fledged Chapters by the convention of 1938.

Lowell is divided by the Merrimack River and is divided among the French and "Irish" or non-French. Blackfriars there blithely ignored that "situation" by asking Father Leon Loranger, O.M.I., to be their moderator, while recruiting most members from the Irish and others who must have been surprised to find themselves in that category.

Philadelphia took another tack. It began with an executive board staffed with the traditional Philadelphia lawyers and in no time had adopted an air-tight constitution. The matter of local approbation, actors, scripts, theatre and workshop was to come later. It was a worthy struggle, lasting for some years, and in the process I saw some artistic productions under our auspices. Maybe the clue to its ultimate demise came in the informal speech of a director at a post-mortem or after-the-show snack. He said, in effect, that Philadelphia resembled less a big city than a collection of little villages, a bunch of carrots tied together by a piece of string. The strain on a few was too great to maintain life until the many natural and artificial boundaries were crossed or until the life blood flowed from one carrot to the others.

The "Twin City" Chapter was perhaps the only chapter which sprung directly from Catholic University. To the normal problems of finance, approbation, parochialism and general *status quo* these hardy thespians added a geographical one. From one corner of Minneapolis to the farthest corner of Saint Paul, there are a lot of miles to trudge and the snow falls early and stays deep, once summer is gone. Then, they had to play each show in both cities, doubling production problems. But they survived until the war and kept up a ceaseless string of social activities to stimulate and maintain interest in the work. They had the right ingredients in many instances, but lack of capital and lack of sponsorship or acceptance by established organizations in its stead made that country seem even colder than the thermometer indicated.

The Catholic Theatre Guild of Pittsburgh hovered around the brink of Blackfriars for some time, but decided to stay out of the fold. There were letters expressing fear of "Dominican domination." There need have been little fear on that score, as I suggested and could suggest again. Dominicans are individualists and are not the most famous organizers in the Church. Another unclarified point of contention was that our plays weren't Catholic enough. It's an aspect of the old discussion of whether we should do exclusively ecclesiocentric plays or acceptable theatre of all sorts.

The principles involved were simple and not matters of controversy. It was merely a matter of what a production group wanted to do and could get audiences to accept. Most of our members in all the chapters had their interests for theatre whetted first of all through school plays or various little-theatre groups. Some were confused by the selections made by their own organizations; others merely saw a chance to act. Our indoctrination process began by pointing out to the play-reading committees some of the obvious dangers in many current successes.

We hoped to build good taste based on sound moral

values and right reasoning. Most membership discussions at this point brought out the fact that they weren't quite ready (if they would ever be so disposed) to get the reputation of being preachy. Don't think there can't be good art in expository drama. Some of the mystery and morality plays are ingenuous enough to be captivating today. But, since we were competing with the sort of theatre and moving pictures which had long been dedicated mainly to entertainment, we thought it advisable to prepare a general diet. It would be a step in the right direction to remove the objectionable diet to which our neighbors and ourselves had been exposed. And in most cities there was some hope of getting audiences for this sort of theatre. Remember, no Blackfriar chapters were ever endowed. The funds actually necessary for operation came through the box-office. So, without attempting to define a Catholic play, either narrowly or broadly, we declared that any play which solved the problems it raised in accordance with Catholic principles and which gave no scandal (in the strict theological meaning of the word) was grist for our mills.

Chapters were required to submit their coming play selections for approval on this basis and we approved our share of innocuous comedies as in-betweens. We were accused of compromise, but it was rather adherence to a principle. We were told frequently that audiences in time would prefer serious thought-provoking plays which made them think of eternal verities, but the matter was never proved. We only knew that the chapters did the plays they wanted to do and thought they could sell to their communities.

The Blackfriar convention which followed the second summer session at Catholic University thrashed these things out and tried to work out a system by which we could check the production and acting standards of chapters as a norm in accepting them into the Guild.

Dayton came in next and, due to the unflagging zeal of Mr. John C. Weaver, is the only one of the pioneer chapters which never suspended production.

It would be repetitious to outline the vicissitudes of the other chapters. Boston came in with Father John Bonn, S.J.; Troy added some splendid productions; Albany and New Haven were active.

Among the affiliates were the Cathespians of Chicago, the Tracomian Players of Cleveland, the Mission Players of San Antonio. When I expressed surprise at the short season in this charming city, I was told that it's too hot in the summer and that fall and spring are good riding and hunting weather so there isn't much time left for the luxury of theatre.

There was activity toward a Blackfriar chapter in Cincinnati, New Orleans, Altoona, Dunkirk, Brooklyn, Worcester, Trenton and a dozen other cities, but I'm running away with the chronology again.

The purpose of this parade was to enumerate the problems in establishing city-wide theatre centres dedicated to the work which Blackfriars had more or less clarified. So, here is a summary of the obstacles which should be surmounted before a few people can come to realize a Catholic Theatre.

Authorization. The absence of authority and at least of moral backing by church authority (other than parochial, except in a one-parish town) is not in itself the greatest handicap, but it is the one which causes more discouragement and which serves as a scapegoat for all others. Obviously, there could be found enthusiasts who in the beginning of such a venture would never think of the need of ecclesiastical approval.

But this omission becomes a weapon to the apathetic who will make up a large part of future audiences. It becomes a hazard to any priest who is asked to become advisor to the organization. It dampens the enthusiasm of pastors whose Sunday announcements might be a good medium of publicity and it prevents the fearless presentation of adult plays which might offend some convention or other.

This doesn't mean that the Bishop or his vicar is expected to take an active interest. He has other things to do. But his approval should be secured and made public and through a representative he can see that the scripts are in line with Catholic doctrine. This is a right if the venture is called Catholic, and the Church has found such a safeguard feasible for two thousand years. In spite of the protests of critics and playwrights, it still seems likely that the episcopal mind is more capable of determining right from wrong than the writers of play catalogues, the play doctors and others who cluster around Broadway.

Discipline. We spent ten years writing constitutions and by-laws in order to compel people to share responsibility intelligently. Amateur actors gravitate toward a fatal mistake which professionals and dabblers in other fields get knocked out of them. It was most pithily expressed by a speaker at Providence who came from The Players. I think it was Thomas Crosby, but that's a little vague to me now. Whether he assumed credit for the nugget of wisdom or quoted someone else is also obscure by now. However, he said: "If you sing in the shower, you don't immediately expect a contract from the Metropolitan Opera Company; if you doodle on a telephone pad, you don't demand a hanging in an art gallery; but if you recite before the class and get away with it, you think Katherine Cornell got a break." Let me add that, even if you were worth paying to see, you don't constitute theatre. Even Miss Skinner and Miss Draper have to get tickets sold. It is a group activity, this theatre business.

In the professional field, some actors have manifested that they are able to bring in a creditable sum of money. Any amateur who has the notion he is valuable to an organization from a commercial point of view is wasting his time. He should go right into the commercial theatre and see what happens.

Even the arty tributary theatre is hurt by the star system, where social prestige or artistic affectation can coerce people into forming a back-drop. It is fatal.

All the other art forms are more or less the work of individuals. The painter, the sculptor, the poet, the writer—all work alone. The various cells in the body have various functions and the body doesn't operate properly unless all—or nearly all—of these cells are functioning as they should.

If you grant that incontrovertible premise, the next step is to assign the duties of the various cells. While

103

some of it falls to natural aptitudes, much is learned and more is a matter of discipline. The stagehand is not born with a hammer or broom in his hand any more than the leading lady is born with a star on her brow.

The greatest adjunct to maintaining discipline is a person who can assign tasks intelligently and get them done. He or she needs tact and technique—and the patience of Job. The completely democratic theatre so often attempted by selfish, movie-warped youngsters who haven't even technique as an excuse for their attempts to exploit others is doomed to failure.

If I haven't begun with theatre technique, it isn't because I don't regard it as important. It's rather that you don't find it in the same proportion that you find enthusiasm, and it is a secondary thing—a necessary means to the ends—so it comes under discipline. This is no doubt heresy to the dramatic schools, but the good ones admit it quietly and the racket schools have to maintain a pose to keep in business at the expense of those who haven't a grain of natural talent.

I simply mean that the theatre can go back to the thousands of communities throughout the country without those communities having at the outset a galaxy of great actors. If this humble approach to theatre is accepted and an honest and capable director or guiding spirit has the time and patience, he can point out the lack of technique which is hurting productions and much can be picked up by a little application. This is not a sure formula for professional theatre, but it works in the less polished but basically more healthy community theatre.

Physical Facilities. It is difficult to say anything definitive on this point because our educational process hasn't gone on long enough to have provided the answers. If I strive to distinguish this new theatre of ideas from the parochial theatre, it is merely because I believe the parish theatre isn't ready for the job yet. They may merge sometime in the future.

The parish should have a theatre if it wants one. That's a moderate statement. But I'm presuming to advise theatres, not parishes. Naturally, I think that if there is an equipped parish or school hall it should be used for more than bazaars, basketball and bingo. The social, educational and moral values of a parish theatre need no defense. One can even be a source of income, it is said, but I wouldn't guarantee that. But usually in keeping with its aims (and nothing can be condemned or dismissed lightly for succeeding in doing what it tries to do), the plays are not stimulating enough for those who are hoping for a theatre of ideas. Old Broadway successes, gently expurgated, and admittedly pietistic offerings written by teachers with a view to edification will interest and affect those who have the least need of antidotes against a questionable theatre diet.

It is not to be expected that many artists will happen to live in the same parish and prefer the pleasant but relatively dull life of amateurs. It is not likely that a qualified professional Catholic theatre—made up of people who are household names—is going to spring into being by itself. The idea has been suggested, but there are certain foundations to be built. It is possible, however, to strike a middle course in populous cities

105

and establish a city-wide group which on merit has the right to draw audiences such as the "little theatres" throughout the country have been drawing for years. This can fulfill a particular need for the community and so be a good thing in itself. It can be a means to further ends such as developing new scripts and people of all branches of theatre, who will have the right slant on the problem.

If this type of foundation can be independent of parishes, the work is immeasurably furthered. This is not an anti-parochial streak in me, but is rather based on these conclusions: the individual parish should not be expected to swing this larger community venture; it invariably cramps the activity of the work; changes of attitudes toward the work, due often to changes in personnel, have peremptorily closed theatre organizations which promised progress. The parish just is not geared to build radio stations, publish books, make movies or run competitive theatre.

Where to find these independent homes is not always easy. It can hardly be left to the youngsters who offer most enthusiasm. But, if co-operation of the established members of the community can be found, there is a much greater hope of success.

Accepted techniques, varying from place to place, may be borrowed from successful little theatres as to production, promotion, casting, membership and the rest. But the prime purpose of justifying any of this bother is that we get better plays—the plays we deserve and have been waiting for.

X: SUMMER STOCK

Back at Catholic University for the summer of 1938, I discovered that some of the fun had gone out of it. One decision became crystallized; I'd never teach acting and classes in playwriting were unrewarding. The latter isn't a production-line subject and the former is just a mode—a way of doing things—and there is so much more satisfaction in dealing with ideas.

Even the satisfaction of pleasing audiences with productions has a note of futility when the show closes and the sets are struck. The work involved in preparation, the moments of elation when it lived its brief existence become a fast-dimming memory and what seemed so substantial has vanished somehow into thin air.

When a production opens there is a straining for the next one. To get something said is exciting enough, but let the specialists set the type and bind the book. Watching people read it is boring if not actually humiliating. So the sustaining drive for all this activity is to prove that sound ideas can be expressed through theatre. If that fact must be demonstrated, the least one can do is to offer as many years as are required for the demonstration.

The first Blackfriar convention was held in Washington in the summer of 1938. Father Ignatius Smith,

O.P., did a stirring key-note stint and Msgr. Randall of Rochester became assistant director of the whole Guild. A good deal of constructive thinking was done (since it was a small convention) and great hopes were held for the future.

Rochester held the second convention in the summer of 1939 and our ranks had noticeably increased. But the main topic of this convention was a proposed summer experimental theatre—a real attempt to try out Blackfriar material with good casts. Rochester thought of swinging the deal on the lake front, but the Lowell Chapter finally came up with what looked like the best setting.

I will not lightly consider summer theatre again while a semblance of sanity persists, without a lot of iron-bound provisos. But I would not want to have missed this maddest chapter of Blackfriar history.

The Lowell Chapter, which was really in its formative stages, stumbled on a barn theatre looking for a tenant. There is a horrible fascination about sturdy old barns which most of us find irresistible. We see the darkened timbers, the ease of building an adequate stage (for an unguessed sum), the sunny days, the lakes or ocean, the trees, the "guaranteed" audiences. It is a dangerous delusion. We close our eyes to the fact that summer stock requires more organization than routine theatre because the management is more or less stuck with the personnel all the time. The actors can't be sent home when rehearsals are over, because they live there. They have to be fed and housed. So many people double in more than brass to keep expenses down that the machine is undermanned if anything unusual turns up and, if anything unusual is going to turn up, it's likely to do it in a summer theatre.

But the Lowellites couldn't be expected to know all this. They wanted a theatre in which to begin operations, and a land-development outfit wanted a company (having lost a couple in the past), so it looked more than interesting. That same land-development company put out posters and folders that clinched the matter. They not only promised that Nabnassett Lake Shore and Country Club, "the ideal spot for your dreams," would secure "your future health, happiness or investments," but they offered to provide dramatic productions free to resident members. It seems there's always a catch in things.

The Lowell Chapter believed that it wasn't quite up to a production a week, since most of its people were respectable members of society and held daytime jobs, so its officers asked me if I could help. There were really two barns. Couldn't we do plays sufficiently commercial to attract the denizens of twenty-eight miles from Boston (that should be a selective audience) and pursue our grim experiments in the smaller barn?

There were obviously no financial problems. The rent was free; the audiences in the neighborhood were hungry for theatre and flocked to productions; and the inn beside the theatre would take care of the company for a less than nominal cost. All I had to do was get a cast of good actors from the various Blackfriar Chapters, a director or two, some set designers and builders. Lowell Blackfriars would take care of management and publicity. It couldn't fail and wouldn't cost anything.

Then—and this was the bait—if our experimental or second theatre turned out anything good, we could plan to take it around the Blackfriar circuit. So I bought it.

Circulars went out throughout the organization and highly recommended people liked the idea. It became coast-to-coast, as one of our accepted applicants came from British Columbia. Boston and Providence provided most of the personnel, but Pittsburgh, Rochester, New York, Philadelphia, Toronto and Lowell contributed, too.

As applicants began to sign up and get final instructions and as new equipment was being shipped, an unsuspected angle developed about the inn. It seemed we could buy it for $7,500. This included a kitchen which had a meat block, but dishes, silverware, beds and mattresses had to be purshased separately. "Club liquor license may be secured for $200 if new owner so desires." We didn't need the meat block, and couldn't afford the inn—so it didn't open.

So, the company arrived with no place to stay unless we hired a sort of guest house and took three cabins connected with the theatre. Father Peter Reilly, then of Providence College, came along for a few weeks, but when he saw my plight he stayed on all summer. The food problem would be solved by the Chelmsford diner some two miles away, as long as our money held out. The local management (Lowell Blackfriars) was pretty busy at the moment and turned most of the problems back to us invaders; the publicity department has some trouble with the local papers, so we assumed that little item, too. I rented a car for the summer and named it

110

Dymphna. St. Dymphna is the patroness of the insane. To pronounce the name properly you have to wrinkle your nose like a rabbit or like the customers at our productions.

That's really metaphorical. Those who came were properly impressed by all accounts and we were becoming more critical over the years. But so few bothered coming, we began to realize that northern Massachusetts wasn't in imminent danger of revolution because of our sojourn there.

Perhaps I smiled at the word "Nabnassett" as I struggled with spelling it, thinking it resembled a toothpaste name. But good old Nab was an Indian chief somewhere way back and he had revenge by scaring customers away. In spite of signs and arrows put on trees and electric poles (which the electric company immediately discovered and tore down), very few paying customers found the "ideal spot of your dreams."

When we hadn't enough money to continue at Chelmsford's diner, we set up our own kitchen. One enthusiast, whose family owned three grocery stores and who came with us as stage manager because he loathed buying and selling food, found himself in the early morning markets that we might eat. The commissar saw little of the stage.

I summoned the cast and told them that it would be a good idea if we had a telephone. They shook out their pockets and purses and we got a telephone—and I think they really shook them out because none of them had enough money for the rest of the summer to buy a package of cigarettes.

If we opened with *Stage Door* (in the big barn) it's

111

because we had a cast of thirty to begin with and never would have a cast of thirty again. Food bills were realities. The handwriting was——No! That's a cliche. If you'd prefer a factual statement, I'd never manage to feed thirty for long. In fact, by the third week, the commissar got heavy-handed with tomatoes and peanut butter. All declaimers know that a craw full of peanut butter is a bad preparation for uttering imperishable lines and tomatoes have always had rather unpleasant theatrical associations.

Just to prove that we could do summer theatre in a grimmer fashion than recorded history indicates it to have been done before, I tacked on a weekly road show a mere 260 miles away. Before the company was assembled but after the contract had been signed, I met Monsignor Michael J. Splaine of Boston, quite casually, and he said that he had been looking for me for three years. Monsignor thought that The Catholic Summer School of America of which he was president should have a summer theatre. The enthusiasm with which enlightened Catholics would jump at such an opportunity (and anyone who went on vacation to a place called a "school" must be dangerously enlightened) would guarantee shekels in amount to compensate for any lack of comparable enthusiasm on the part of the dwellers of forests and lakes twenty-eight miles from Boston.

We had to appear at Cliff Haven (the unpedantic name of the Summer School) for one performance a week. Nabnassett thought it needed us three or four nights, but most of the seats were occupied by the ghosts of Indians. Even the residents who were invited free of charge frequently couldn't find the theatre.

112

The regular program was to load flats on top of *Dymphna* every Friday at midnight, assign actors, spots, costumes, etc., to the other cars, and go in caravan over the road. The actors usually ran lines for next week's production. I don't remember that the spots and costumes did anything worth recording. We went through part of Massachusetts, diagonaled New Hampshire and Vermont, and although I'm reluctant to say this as a New Englander, finally struck roads in New York which didn't turn to the right or to the left or up or down every hundred feet or so. If topographical references help this heretofore geographical treatise, we hit the White Mountains, the Green Mountains and part of the Adirondack Mountains. Beautiful country from all reports, but, driving lead horse into the dawn, you don't notice that aspect as fully as might be expected. The caravan usually stuck together because we counted noses at both the all-night restaurants in Vermont and New Hampshire and even spent money recklessly on coffee for those who weren't receiving Communion the next morning. It was starvation to get far away from *Dymphna*.

We usually hit our destination when the sun was well up, had Mass for the company, and then the actors went to bed while the crew set up. These stout fellows who tripled as drivers and stage hands snatched a few hours' sleep in the evening and started back Saturday night to avoid the Sunday traffic. Possibly, the pace was a bit stiff for frail humanity. One night, a pair of overworked drivers fell asleep and disappeared over an edge of the White Mountains. I received a phone call to the effect that they were quite all right, but that

Dymphna was no more. We had a party to honor *Dymphna,* whose spirit departed on a non-show night without cracking a single flat of her amazing load. I was offered fifteen dollars for her remains, so she even paid for the farewell party, too.

Financial matters became really serious, so we began to cut the company. That meant that all went on K.P. and washed dishes. What with a radio program in Lowell designedly for publcity, the pace grew so warm that on occasion the leads drew the dishwashing assignment on opening night. Not strictly Stanislavsky, but then we were backtracking from some of the by-roads which the theatre had followed.

The hope of the little experimental theatre died as we stacked the scripts on one side of my desk and the food bills on the other. We had to do small-cast productions in the big barn and fulfill our contract unless money was forthcoming from somewhere. The take from Nabnassett was incredibly below the estimate, (this time, someone else's estimate) and the percentage from Cliff Haven did little more than transport and feed the company on their weekly jaunt. We were quite broke and in debt. Lowell was sorry (in fact, as its members were in some cases our creditors, I might say Lowell was very sorry), Nabnassett was sorry, and as we had half the summer to go under contract, we were a little sorry, too.

One day at Cliff Haven I hadn't enough money to take care of gas to get back to Nabnassett. The company didn't know it as they blithely rehearsed the next show under the pines. I went down to the lake (which was Lake Champlain) to think. It hasn't been my custom

114

to think myself into any money before or since, but it is a more accepted attitude than that of not caring. And I picked the end of a bench which had an elderly priest on the other. I didn't think he'd help me much in my thinking, but I knew he'd respect my privacy. If priests are drawn to one another's company in trains and the like, it's not so much community spirit as to get away from the inevitable gas-bag who whips up besides you and says "What do you think about the Spanish Inquisition?"—when what is pressing most on your mind is the fact that the train is two hours late.

As I recall, I think we agreed on the fact that it was a nice day or some such unusual conversational take-off and he asked me what I was doing at Cliff Haven. I told him not very well, and why. He was a confidence winner. I told him I didn't have enough money to transport the troupe which he might have or might not have seen perform the night before.

He said "That's strange." Not a remarkable statement to make of anything in connection with most of my clerico-theatrical activities, but being schooled in restraint—or busy thinking—I let him go on. So he did, saying, "I was given this and nobody around here can change it, so I presume it was meant for you."

And I had in my hand a fifty-dollar bill. And the hand that relinquished it, which had been hidden, had a big episcopal ring on one finger. I know that you smart people are saying that they usually are worn on one finger, but I couldn't speak. I couldn't say "Thanks." The old glittering lake swam in front of my eyes. And just for that, I'm not going to tell you who he was, because later he asked me not to. But I went back

115

to the rehearsal and told the kids what happened and they cheered very weakly and walked away alone or in twos—because they caught something of what was sticking in my throat. It's too hard to define. We had hit the bottom and somebody who didn't want a stained-glass window erected in his memory gave us money to buy gas and a meal on the trip back. So we all understood without another word being said about the matter.

Sufficient for the day was that, but it wasn't the answer to the month to come. I put that problem up to Monsignor Splaine, whose name I may as well mention, as I mentioned it before, and although he couldn't adjust the financial arrangements of my Summer School contract, since the people didn't come to the shows, he could change our base, take us to Cliff Haven, and feed us. I don't think any of us were actually hungry—I hate mock heroics—but I do know that we dreamed of steak and trimmin's which we hadn't had for a long time. And for that—and that I might buy our way out to Nabnassett, returning only one night a week—he gave me five hundred dollars. Sometimes I hope I always live so close to elementals that five hundred dollars can make me so happy. No philanthropist, no pseudo-Santa Claus, no Lady Bountiful could have felt happier than I when I had the chance—through someone else, of course—to take that company whom I had come to respect and to love and feed them.

This isn't exactly maudlin, either. You don't build such an attitude from a particular happening or two. It grows. One morning I rehearsed my charges until three or four and told them that Mass would be at ten.

We couldn't afford too many cars spilling over mountains. Maybe later drivers wouldn't be so fortunate. And as I went to the chapel a few minutes before ten with much of the brood, a gentle old lady, knitting on her porch, rasped with an audibility range which a carnival loudspeaker might envy, "Well, it's about time."

I don't think I resented the personal affront intended. I've been immunized to that. The speaker was no doubt an early-to-bedder and early-to-riser, which, since it makes one healthy, wealthy and wise, is a good thing if it isn't worshipped. I'll venture to say that she was sleeping the sleep of the just while we were still beating the first act. Perhaps I wanted to defend my flock which I thought should get some sleep to compensate for the lack of food during the first month. But more, I think it was a cold evaluation without resentment, although it must have rankled or I wouldn't have remembered it.

Father Reilly and I discussed it with some amusement. He, by the way, has not tangled much with the theatre world, but pitched in to help with my problems, especially in the unpredictable world of publicity. His own tastes run to international relations, with dipping into China and the like, which he seemed to find more soothing than running the railroad which was Blackfriars in the mountains.

I rather feared that the charming old lady with the well-developed vocal chords—a theatrical asset, mind you—was of a school which might well take down its flag. She believed in the *status quo*. I don't. There! I've antagonized a lot of good people and I'm sorry. Sheerly for the antagonism—not for the convictions. As a palliative that their indignation may be lessened, may I openly subscribe to the power in the sight of God of a few contemplatives who will no doubt do more than the United Nations, to the sacramental system which must accomplish more than the dull copies which contain but the husks and which make up our text-books on sociology, and to the parish which was the heart beat of life—in any meaningful interpretation of the term—from mediaevalism until the pre-movie and the pre-jukebox era. That unqualified statement should induce thousands of sound thinkers to sheathe the weapons they just whipped out.

But—you must have expected a "but"—I prefer my sleepy-eyed company to the raucous-voiced porch knitter. I'm not trying to make her sinister. I've never met her. She merely represents something which I'm trying to surmount. In the Blackfriar company which commuted from Nabnassett to Cliff Haven I met something which gave the expression "Catholic Action" some meaning. That amazing term is almost regarded as a new idea. It is defined as "a participation of the laity in the work of the hierarchy." It is rather safe to presume that the people in the catacombs who crept out of warm beds and went into holes under the ground were impelled by a belief stronger than any little dichotomy between the hierarchy and the laity. They thought that the command to teach all nations was universal.

My little company had a destination in their theatre which was in some cases close to a destiny. That's what we need first in all art forms—in all art thinking. As for technique: enough had some and most wanted more. Just a minute! I know what that sentence means so I'll explain it. I don't mean that they were the best or the worst or the most average summer stock company in the world from the point of technique. If I put them in any of those classes, I'd be offering an opinion based on either knowledge or ignorance. Or if I took the opinion of critics, I'd be offering a few more opinions based on a host of things. I thought they turned out some good productions, but I know they were the sort of company on which an acceptable American theatre could be built.

They wanted to act—most of them, at least—but they didn't want to hurt themselves in living in the process or to hurt anyone else. If that becomes the standard of actor, playwright and the rest of this misunderstood business, we might have an exciting American theatre which will be good for us.

I mentioned "Catholic Action" some lines back. That thought is trying to get finished. This was one case where it hadn't deteriorated into talk and criticism. These people got first things first in their own minds and then didn't talk any more about them, but went to work at something they loved doing—from gathering at morning Mass to rehearsing far into the night. These Blackfriars worked too hard and too long to have time for platitudes. They discussed everything under the sun, they did one another a lot of good, and they were one of the maddest collections that chance or Divine Providence ever assembled together.

But an enthusiastic company doesn't make a theatre. You might begin with such an important ingredient that may have taken years to find—but you need a great many more. The audiences didn't care about what

119

the actors were trying to do. The audiences had been brought up on a very ordinary fare and when a new idea came along they thought it was a questionable imitation. It so often is, they might well have been right. That they happened to be wrong is merely one of those little tragedies that holds off success when it is so near at hand.

Elliott Norton of the Boston *Post* came up to see us, listened to our story, and said in print (which occasionally impresses me because it may mean a man's job) that we were the most important event in the American theatre in fifty years.

There isn't much more to say about Nabnassett and Cliff Haven except in the factual realm, and everybody in the business has a host of stories. We did a melodrama, on which to eat, and took it into town because there were some 50,000 soldiers of the State Guard and National Guard encamped within a few miles of Plattsburg. With radio announcements, pulpit announcements, posters, camp notices, newspaper plugs—in short, everything that a publicity man could wish—we got eleven soldiers and eighteen civilians interested enough to attend this waste of our time.

On driving back we found that the dining hall of the Summer School was on fire. Anything to ward off monotony. There were forty or more waitresses who slept over the dining room, and the flames had made some headway. Someone whose identity I forget—you don't check on names at fires or panics—climbed the porch roof and ran from room to room to rout the sleepers. This incident I recall because I got half way up and couldn't make the last two feet—an indication of the

120

tragedy of the lovely expression, "falling into flesh." The energy was wasted, however, for the girls were out having a picnic or a roast or something and all were safely out of their beds.

The building went up in flames and fell down in a roar. The local hose cart was rolled out with proper ceremony and from its snake-like back a hundred little geysers watered the grass. A stream almost as large as these dribbles came out the nozzle, too. Meanwhile, the military fire-fighters from the camp in Plattsburg thundered in. For lack of something to do I was breaking the door of the administration building which was next in the line of fire. The commanding officer saw me finish the indelicate job and asked who was in charge. I peered into the night, saw nobody who looked like an official, and told him that I'd do until someone better came along. So, on my questionable authority, the army put typewriters and official papers all over the lawn over a radius that really amazed us in the morning.

The next building—the Brooklyn House where the Blackfriars were quartered—was the scene of hectic activity. Actors who returned earlier manifested the famed *esprit de corps* by hurling the few possessions of their fellow thespians out third-story windows and carrying their own carefully down the stairs. The blaze was five- or six-hundred feet away and was confined to the one doomed building.

We were very wet and the company was generally regarded as the heroes of the night, although our accomplishments were on the chaotic side. And I never even held a court-martial to see if one of us set the fire, because everybody was playing to the eleven soldiers in Plattsburg and the one place they wouldn't burn down is the place where they got their only square meals in five weeks.

The summer drew to a close and we occasionally took stock. It would be good to take something besides debts away with us—debts and memories. The audience reaction was not world-shattering—not even up to the expectations of Elliott Norton. The most succinct instance is the reply of one of the consequential people of the colony who had seen the melodrama, Obey's *Noah,* and the one really experimental play we managed to slip in. We had worked very hard on the last-mentioned item because it symbolized what we believed in, but the audience knew that George Kaufman should write the plays for America. This lady said: "The melodrama was terrific; that thing about Noah was awful; and all I remember about that other play is that you borrowed the divan from the Washington House."

The summer proved that the right people could be found. Now, if the other factors could be gathered together—scripts, audiences, etc., the goal was not impossible of achievement.

We said good-bye to Cliff Haven and Nabnassett, marking it down as a memorable experience. My superiors permitted me to divert my lecture honoraria to paying the debt, so everybody was finally either happy or reconciled. That is not said facetiously or by way of indication that they were willing to hold the lantern while the aging grandmother chopped wood. I got into the difficulty and had a chance to get out of it keeping credit good. And that is all that can be expected in modern theatre.

Back in Providence I found that my mother's health was failing fast. I hurried back from an unfinished lecture tour to be with her at the end. And during her last week when she was rarely conscious I thought about a great many things. And when one thinks thus emotionally toned, the thoughts are inclined to stick or recur.

I thought that it was a good thing she had been so understanding over the years. We did have a very easy understanding which didn't require many words, although both of us could be loquacious about trivial matters. I thought that this attempt to set up a flag in the theatre had been a demanding task and that there were many slights and omissions on my part because of its unreasonableness. There were opportunities to visit, there were anniversaries to remember, there were places to be seen, which I had blandly ignored—and this for years—because a rehearsal or a meeting got in the way. In fact, it seemed that something got in the way every time the right opportunity came up. And she didn't complain. But she didn't enthusiastically approve either, because like the rest of the world she couldn't see any tangible results.

Her whole attitude grew clearer to me in that last week when it was too late for me to do anything about it. She was interested only in heaven, while I, full of self-recrimination, was interested in changing my ways. It became clear that she didn't bother feeling aggrieved. She wanted to work with me even though she wasn't too sure what we were doing. The fear was that I would estrange all my friends, ignore all the normal obligations and wind up chasing a phantom. That phantom loomed large during those long nights.

But when I remembered her enthusiasm over the small successes that I reported and the distant smile when I determined to keep at it, it looked a lot better. And when one night she left us for better things and I tried to piece the tumbled thoughts together, I was more or less resigned that I'd never manage to do the normal things, never be quite fair to my friends, never do the things I wanted to do—because somebody somewhere ought to give this notion of a theatre a try in this our day and I think she'd like me to have a fair fling at it.

And in a few months all the reasons why I was so important at Providence College faded into thin air. I guess it was a defense mechanism at work after all. I guess I was just happy that I could be near her at the end. And when my superiors suggested that I come to New York and work on *The Holy Name Journal,* I wasn't surprised because I had a hand in the conniving.

XI: MANHATTAN MIRAGE

NEW YORK! I HAD NEVER BELIEVED IT TO BE QUITE real. My first recollection was a vivid and haunting memory of wriggling snakes which Mother attributed to a visit to the Bronx Zoo in childhood. There is no connection between the nightmares following that visit and my subsequent appraisal of the teeming island, unless they be of the insidious subconscious sort.

The next visit better sets the background which has persisted. I was seventeen or eighteen. We New Englanders don't go gadding about. We have an insidious smugness—never brashly expressed, of course—which regards as incontrovertible the fact that we have all we need. Some wit has summed it up in the story of a Boston woman who was asked where she and her sister bird-walkers got their hats. Her reply was, "We have our hats." Gothamites don't understand us and perhaps that's what makes them Gothamites.

You see, I'm not a Gothamite. If I correctly interpreted what I read and heard, my cultural ancestors— the Rhode Islanders who manned the privateers— were closer to London, Singapore, Port au Prince and the African coast than to Manhattan. My lineal forebears were shaped and influenced by Cork, Dublin and Rome rather than by the patrons of Niew Amsterdam.

There is a softening process at work and the Christian concept of one world may grow out of the apparent shrinking of that sphere. That may mean that New York will get on the New Englander's mental map with a few more years of radio and television and another war or two.

The remembered trip—at seventeen—was made by boat, if those monstrous and somewhat ludicrous water beetles which paddled along the coast under the flag of the Colonial Line or Providence Line could be called such. At least, they were symbols of an era which is fading too rapidly. I don't disparage the airplane or fast train; I merely mean that most old things pass gradually, while those old tubs just stopped and we weren't prepared for their stopping.

They had few advantages, I suppose, if you had to travel to New York quickly and often—so often that you didn't notice it any more. But if you came for the first time at seventeen and got up early in the morning —whether from excitement or sea-sickness—you saw New York as you'd never see it again. Such a vision of terrestrial beauty—and what, then, must heaven be like—justified the building and maintenance of those ugly, splashing monsters.

Down the East River, round the Battery and up the North River we waddled, hooting occasionally at indifferent tugs—and over the starboard rail I gazed at the mirage. The word is "gazed" and in this instance, it isn't jungle prose. I don't think I've ever gazed before or since. I've looked or stared or gaped—but at this I gazed, trying to hold it there because it was so unreal it was liable to vanish. Much of it did.

The morning mist was low and fuzzy and the spires and towers were suspended in space against the brighter sky above. The movies have caught something of it in color photography to backdrop lesser tragedies; Disney has suggested it a few times. It's been seen before and since—but I saw it once, and that vision was for me New York.

I called it a mirage. I still think so. The word was fresh in my vocabulary, carefully culled from Junior English. Travelers saw towers and spires, entire cities, which weren't there because of reflections in varying densities of desert air. That's New York! More subtle than the crazed visions of dying desert wanderers. It floats across the sky in the morning, part clear, part misty, and when you try to seize it—use it—it isn't there. More inexplicable than the desert delusions, because the stones are real, piled one upon another with a hint of eternity—but the dreams behind the stones, the plans, the hopes, have been eaten by the termites of this island of fluctuation so that nothing but the floating superstructure is left.

I undersand the people of Warren or Wakefield. Their rugged little houses sheltered rugged individualistic souls following a community pattern by way of courtesy. Of course, conventions hurt sometimes and conventions aren't always right—but they are understandable. At supper time—which was six o'clock— the lights went on, the men came home, the children ended their games and everybody talked about the same things. Not so, Manhattan! Canyons of hotels and apartments with blinking windows housed disparate spirits who neither knew nor seemed to care who lived or died a three-inch wall away. And when one crept along the canyon bottoms, breathing subway air, shrinking from the clangor which never ceased, jostling the busy crowds, the skyline which had beckoned was gone. It was difficult to see the sky.

To a born New Yorker, all this is just so much talk. He catches the reality first—his fronts steps, a baby carriage, a neighbor who has the courage to speak to a child, a district leader, a new bus. Only on a picnic or a voyage does he see the mysterious city of the clouds, and his pride is simple as is that of the country lad who has been told that George Washington slept in his town.

Legend has it that those who are born outside New York are the ones who take it by storm. Of course, that is too general a statement to be true, but the outsiders are the ones who are most surprised and so most challenged by the process. We outsiders never quite lose the wonder of the skyscrapers, the bridges, the subways. We still face the city alive and expectant.

There have been natives who kept the breathlessness —outsiders born within the confines of the city—like Al Smith, who never stopped being a little amazed that they'd let a fish clerk make laws to help people. But those who know that their city is real and ordinary will never feel its throbbing as do those who have caught a glimpse of the unreal city of the clouds, and, for the same obscure reason, they'll never quite master it because they never learn that there is anything extraordinary to master.

Well, whatever dreams of mastery I had at seventeen were confined to self-mastery when I returned at just twice that age. My debts were paid and I was to take up the quiet life of an editor, living in a tiny cell in St. Vincent Ferrer's Priory, attached to one of the

128

most beautiful churches in the country at 66th Street and Lexington Avenue. There was magic there, too, as the white-clad friars chanted Prime and Terce when the sun came up outside our stained-glass windows. There was peace in the vortex of a maelstrom. Perhaps that's no more part of this theatre story than fresh air and cool water are part of anyone's story. But they help one to sleep at night.

The first assignment was merely to write, and that offered no hardship if the readers didn't mind a few parentheses. Later, a much less pleasant chore called "editorial work" was slipped in, and before long the editorship was slapped on, if ships so impressive are thus slappable.

The Holy Name Journal, a sedate monthly, had been the official organ of the Holy Name Society for forty years. Perhaps it had become a little stereotyped or, at least, had acquired that settled fortyish outlook. Whatever it was, I decided to limber it up, although a sage adviser warned me that I was supposed to put out a magazine for people who don't read.

There are some problems in religious journalism which the fact-gatherers of the fourth estate need not face. To begin with, it is regarded by those who labor in the field as an essential part of a balanced diet, while most potential readers are bored by its lack of sensationalism.

The reason why millions of people in New York alone hurry to get the paper on which the ink is scarcely dry is due to a completely false value placed on the immediacy or newness of news. This desire to know what is happening at the moment came out of the town-crier days. If he shouted "The Redcoats are coming up the bay," or "The Redskins are coming out of trees," our ancestors gathered up their muskets and powder horns and made an attempt to stop that foolishness. When the Redcoats and Redskins had come and gone, there was time for editorializing. But the mass appeal was in the fact rather than in the reasons behind the fact. The subjects which got top-billing from the town crier were concerned with personal safety and personal economy. Heaven could wait.

In the advance of civilization (I've read that phrase somewhere) there are few things which actually impel us into action. Yet the sort of superstition remains that if we know precisely what is going on all over the world we'll do something about it—something prompt and proper. We are impatient to catch the gist of political rumblings in the Near or Far East, the latest cold or hot war spat on the globe, honestly believing that with a fragment of information we will be equipped for intelligent action. We do act. Frequently, two or three years afterwards we vote for the wrong people because of some ulterior motive having nothing to do with the salvation of what we like to call our way of life.

This "nowness" has spread into less vital departments. Millions who have snatched these still limp papers find themselves gravely concerned with the latest featured divorce or with the astounding fact that a cat got stuck in a tree and had to be rescued by the fire department. No one seems to care that in the passage of time a great many people have sought another husband or wife and that a legion of cats happened to get stuck in a forest of trees. The hypnotism is in the "now."

The religious journalist—especially of the clerical breed—isn't as interested in the fact as in its interpretation, its place in the larger scheme. He follows a mediaeval pattern in which ideas and principles are important. The thirteenth-century man of affairs hadn't the remotest notion of what was happening on the other side of the world within the past twenty-four hours. If he gave the matter any thought at all, it was in terms of what might be happening—based on deductive (and sometimes inductive) reasoning. Today's avalanche of facts stifles reasoning with us. St. Albert the Great reasoned that the earth was spherical, flattened somewhat at the poles, and that if there were animals in these necessarily cold places, they most likely wore thick white coats.

The mediaevalist figured out what should be done morally, politically, socially—and when, perhaps a year after its occurrence, he learned what had been done—he dropped that bit of information right into its slot. He didn't reserve his opinion until he read all the columnists on the following day. If the Soviets were difficult to deal with and a mediaevalist out of due time got wind of the fact, he would have an immediate opinion or judgment and base it on principle. We suspend judgment to see what they might do tomorrow. The passion for facts chokes off thought; the editorial writers think for us—some worthily and some for ulterior motives—so we go through life as individuals and peoples learning very little.

Take this mediaevalist's approach to temporalities and place it upon a supernatural substructure which is the only important thing—and then try to build a circulation. It isn't exciting if the Pope or a Bishop makes a declaration, because we knew what he was going to say all the time. Bishops and Popes have said the same things for the last two thousand years. They got most of it from the Sermon on the Mount. True, it may be well said, but we can read it next week or next month. It doesn't impel us to rush out to buy an extra.

It's also true that religious editors frequently haven't impressive news-gathering facilities or much money for top writers and so they get caught in a lot of trivia. It isn't breath-taking news to learn that the Bishop confirmed a class in St. Aidan's. The children knew he was coming because they have been hard at learning their catechism for the event; the Sisters knew he was coming because they taught the children their catechism; the priests of the parish knew he was coming because they asked the Sisters to teach the children their catechism; and the parents knew he was coming because they had to buy the blue suits and white dresses. It would be news only if the Bishop didn't show up.

The business of adjusting to an editor's chair offered a challenge throughout the day's working hours, but when our (editorial) day came to an end; we slipped back into the first person singular and thought that something could be done about the church's "oldest and rustiest weapon"—the theatre.

New York should be the place. Maybe it was a sort of last stand, last chance. Our little theatrical empire, so difficult to build, so difficult to maintain, so difficult to indoctrinate, was shaky. The audiences seemed to think a play was good only if it packed them in on Broadway. Why not see how that was done? It was al-

132

together a weird business, this conspiracy to commercialize a group art. There was no prospect of changing the system, but one might move in among the inveterate theatre-goers and ask for a hearing. Gotham didn't give you its towers and steeples, but it did let you walk the streets and talk to people. It was worth a try.

The Blackfriars' Guild had given a charter to a youthful group in New York which produced one full-length play at the Heckscher Theatre. But these enthusiasts were concerned with acting rather than with organizing, managing, indoctrinating, so they graciously put the business of the New York Chapter in my hands.

First, I went looking for a theatre—not one of the palaces with their gilded nymphs and crystal chandeliers, because I knew we couldn't afford one. That in itself is some progress since Nabnassett. The loft over a drugstore in the Village, a small dance studio on 72nd St., a garage on the East Side, these and more were investigated. However, they offered the uniform disadvantage that we couldn't convert them and couldn't afford them.

Then, one day, light seeped from somewhere—not a blinding flash which might have been disconcerting, but a pervading thing like dawn. A note from the Doctor intimated that he was a little tired of his work in psychology at Catholic University but didn't know what he was going to do about it. I knew. There was the man to organize the *Journal* and the New York Blackfriars. He might try to organize me in the process, but I'd have to take that chance, and, anyhow, I'd developed great resistance over the years. The superiors were agreeable that he'd be an asset to the Holy Name

Society, so one day the Doctor arrived with a questioning look on his face.

It was a great moment. This was the payoff for his having handed me (and by telegraph at that) a drama school at Catholic University. So I said with a smirk, "You have a job. After your day's work on the magazine is over, you can putter around the New York Blackfriars. I'll look for plays and do the casting and directing, if necessary. All you have to do is find and equip a theatre, take care of sets and promotion and sort of run the whole thing." I almost added "Goody Goody!" by way of postscript, but something in his expression stopped me. I've seen that expression on occasion since.

Thus, an old partnership, strange enough to deceive even the elect, carried on from points 500 miles apart and threatened by many a strain or twist during six years, was given a new lease by our assignment to the same house—and that day I felt that something would come out of the Blackfriars in New York.

We put our heads together, figuratively of course, and decided that this time it would be a good idea to begin with money. Since the Doctor was doing the photography for the magazine insofar as possible, and popping up with plans to reorganize everything that had gone before, and since I dashed off letters easily, he suggested that I dash off a few. His suggestions often have a metallic ring about them. This time I was to address myself and our project to a few hundred cause-minded Catholics in the metropolitan area and pick up the money with which he would equip the theatre.

No trouble at all! With the volunteer typing of a few enthusiasts of the inherited Chapter, I set forth a very

134

compelling letter. We thought it particularly charming, because it offered the recipients so many outs. They could dismiss the matter with a cheque or they might drop in for lunch and seek further information. And its appeal to such as they seemed irresistible. Just in case some might miss the point, we made the list extensive, casting the net in the direction of nearly everybody who had been caught by anything before. Nobody answered the letter.

Weeks became months; no money appeared; the original New York Blackfriars seemed to melt away. Still no theatre. Then one day we were told that the old West Side "Y" on 57th Street was unoccupied and that the owners and agent might listen to our story. On Thanksgiving Day, 1940, we inspected the desolate ghost-filled theatre. It had no proscenium, no switchboard, in fact, not much of anything except uncomfortable seats in various degrees of repair and a most inadequate stage in front of an old-fashioned concert shell. Perhaps the feature which dated it most accurately was a dimmer board for gas lights. Henry Hudson must have dropped anchor when he saw that majestic building. Yet we were very much in tune with the spirit of that Thanksgiving Day.

We made footprints in the dust of the floor as we walked around. Harry Huberth, the agent, was reasonable about the rent. Reasonable in our parlance at that time meant pretty nice. At least he reasoned that it wouldn't be fair to lease it as a theatre until we had time to make it look something like one.

The Doctor said he'd take on that little matter— which was becoming routine for him anyway—while I did something about getting a play. We'd be as badly off as Broadway if we had a theatre and nothing to put in it except people.

In New York, one can find all the answers—most of them wrong—but certainly offering opportunities for the eclectic. In fact, there are organizations for almost all the endeavors and rackets in the world, and since there was one for playwrights, I approached the Dramatists' Guild. Co-operation was immediate. Playwrights like to see their wares on exhibition. The secretary or some official agreed to mail announcements of our quest for material to the then 2,200 members. (We're great letter writers.) We weren't given the names of the members, who among others include the leading dramatists of the country, because names have a habit of getting strung together in some sort of list. But we were to supply the letter and pay the costs.

While the Doctor was scurrying and burrowing for equipment for our new toy, I addressed myself to the task of inviting all and sundry playwrights to send in a sample of their wares. I didn't think this letter as good as the preceding one, but it brought results. I almost lost my office on the head of it and definitely lost all peace of mind for succeeding months while I read heaped-up scripts.

The letter merely announced that the Blackfriars' Guild—new to New York—would be happy to read and consider for production plays which for "some reason or other" had not been chosen for the commercial theatre. Every author has five glib reasons why his play was not done by the top producers in town. Nobody had told me that.

It said nothing about religion which cautious people such as public relations men say is a controversial matter—but simply bore the heading "Blackfriars' Guild" (innocuous enough) and was signed "Urban Nagle, O. P." Those who didn't associate "O.P." with *Office of the Producer* thought it meant *Out of Print.* It really means *Order of Preachers,* the official title of the Dominicans, but you may take your choice.

Not having seen the addresses, how were we to know that half of those 2,200 playwrights lived in New York and just waited for letters like mine? Never dreaming that the response would be so overwhelming, I suggested that scripts be mailed or brought to 141 East 65th Street, which was the austere editorial office of *The Holy Name Journal.* Until then, I had thought of playwrights as gentle souls, timid and sensitive, who hoped that by some inexplicable series of fortunate accidents their plays would be produced. But when they descend en masse on a very inexperienced producer, they resemble locusts—with, of course, individual differences. I suppose locusts have individual differences, too, but that is really a problem for entomologists.

Dressed in a white habit seven-hundred-years old— the model, not the garment—I sat before a statue of St. Thomas Aquinas who was garbed the same way, as I met the horde. The setting seemed to be rather unexpected, judging by the experssions on the authors' faces. In point of fact, much of the flood of cartoons in recent years, depicting monks utterly surprised by modern situations, is slightly inaccurate. Usually, everybody is surprised except the monk.

In this instance, some laughed aloud at the door,

some apologized (for what wasn't too clear), some became suddenly pious, some employed a little high pressure, some fled. One stately woman in a huge picture hat stopped cold at the door, stared at me in a sort of terror and blurted, "Oh! Oh! You don't want my plays. They're much too dirty." She fled without giving me her name, which I should like to have to check my hunch that she has made a lot of money in the art of playwriting. Maybe not—because she at least knew right from wrong.

The stacks of scripts which pyramided around my desk promised a great deal of after-school work for a very new editor. And to get out of the way of the traditionalists who were startled by the rather unusual influx, we opened Blackfriars' office nights.

The next chapter, which lasted for some months, really should be focused on the Doctor, for I was engaged in the dismal task of reading plays which had already been rejected by downtown producers. Our organization has done a lot of that over the years, hoping to find something inherently honest or outrageously courageous which the commercials didn't grasp or couldn't risk.

One day I was snatched from the unadulterated pleasure of reading the worst plays in the world to help him carry in a few items which were left on the sidewalk outside our door, marring thereby, I presume, the beauty of New York's street of pianos and paintings. The items in question were three thirty-two-foot planks, a foot wide and about three inches thick. His occasional helpers were not available at the moment and he had a growing fear that representatives of the building trades

138

would begin to snoop if they saw lumber—or anything —in such large pieces. The first plank gave us some trouble, as it wouldn't bend and wasn't hinged to make the turn in our front stairs. As he hurried me down for the second, he urged me to try to be inconspicuous, as there might be union spotters across the street. To my shame, I flared up a bit and told him that I was likely to be conspicuous just walking along 57th Street. I was likely to be more conspicuous on the front end of a thirty-two-foot plank. He could be forgiven, however, because he didn't know that I had just rejected a seventy-six-scene play—Blackfriars' all-time high.

Those three planks were—and are—the proscenium; two the uprights and one the top. Since he hadn't the heart to cut the plastered ceiling which probably antedates Pompeii and Herculaneum, the Doctor merely stood the uprights and bolted the other across the top. Try it someday. A dozen engineers said it couldn't be done. He doubtless used mirrors and magic. But after a hard day's work at his appointed task, he summoned a friend or two night after night and the proscenium, the gridiron, the switchboard and the rest fell into place, or seemed to fall. They were really put there.

Lest I have weakened the faith of future audiences and actors as to the solidity of his construction, let me allay all fears. No particular item is likely to fall on that stage, but, like the One Hoss Shay, when it goes it will go as a unit. The stage will be found somewhere on 56th Street. And if it lasts for a hundred years and a day, it will be about time.

Drapes in ungainly bundles were piled up, electrical equipment moved in, and even desks and chairs began to take their places in our little office on the fifth floor. Aware of his penchant for doing things the best way instead of the legally approved way, I asked the Doctor if he was using legitimate and approved equipment. He told me tersely enough that the drapes were brought from Gypsy Rose Lee's show at the World's Fair, that his mentor in building the switchboard had been with *Tobacco Road* for six years and that his choice for stage manager had worked recently with Sally Rand. That seemed legitimate and approved by the American public—and if I didn't like what he was doing I could go home and read plays. And, by the way, how was I doing?

In justice to the response which came from the Dramatists' Guild, out of the hundreds of plays which arrived, some were good. A few were exceptionally good, but these had production demands which at the time we couldn't meet. Most of the scripts worth considering which weren't out of our reach because of physical requirements had the obvious taint of Broadway. Some authors told me that they had "spiced them up" to make them salable and that they would gladly spice them down or whatever the reverse process is.

It was so difficult to explain that we weren't concerned with how close to a line we might walk, but rather that we wanted a theatre with a spiritual lift. We weren't merely trying to get by the Watch and Ward Society or plotting to escape being closed by the police. We were starting from the other end and wanted to give people a good theatre—good in the sense that Aristotle and Thomas Aquinas meant when

140

they talked about art. I'm afraid that it will take years for that thesis to filter down to the capable playwrights in this country, because they have had the wrong ideas drilled into them for so long.

The obvious question at this point is why didn't we do revivals. But we thought there was little point in doing a play which had been better done down the street ten years ago or in Greece 2,500 years ago. Life was moving on, and new plays were either reflecting patterns or determining new norms. That was our business if we could justify this theatrical side-line at all.

Since the right script wasn't found in response to our appeal, we'd have to create one. From this horrible necessity we were saved by the arrival of Father Brendan Larnen on the scene.

Like the man who rode off in all directions or like the jacks-of-all-trades whose role was becoming our portion, we—at the Holy Name Office—had undertaken the distribution of over a million copies of the New Testament. We won't digress on whether Catholics read the Bible or not. If they don't read it, I don't know why they bought a million copies. But we worked the promotion rather simply. The Doctor was the chief clerical promoter; I put his material into English; and Father Larnen was appointed to the staff to correct my English.

The Reverend Brendan Larnen of the Order of Preachers is a sly insidious Irishman from Sligo who harassed and badgered me through five years of editorial work. He joined the Doctor in a cheap and obvious plot to keep me working when I most wanted

141

to talk about leprechauns and sail-boats. Between them they straightened up my chair every time I tilted it back and they drove me to mock heroics every time a deadline came around.

Educated like a rolling stone in Boston, New York, San Francisco and way stations—before joining the Order—he gathered no moss, but acquired instead a great deal of guile along with a seraphic expression of guilelessness. Cynical to the core, he thought up ways of torturing me. I'd ask simply "Can you reach that manuscript over there?" And he'd say, "Yes, I can reach it." Then I'd have to ask for it or—worse still—get up and get it. It's been a searing process and I still bear the marks of the struggle.

As a minor occupation, he whipped off a play about "the Trouble." The Trouble, as I'm sure you know, is a variable expresion among the Irish. The sons of kings have always in mind the latest trouble. Throughout the nineteenth century they would use the word to describe "the ninety-eight," but Easter Week, 1916, has held precedence in our time. The institution will never become extinct. Ireland will always manage a new one as memory dulls.

Father Larnen thought there was an ironic twist to the fact that in a short twenty-five years many of the patriots had reversed their roles both in relation to the divergent factions in Ireland and toward England. So, he wrote a wry, sardonic comedy of the people he knew well and we pounced on it. *Up the Rebels* was its title and it may have been symbolic of the less grim struggle in which we were engaged.

142

XII: STANDARDS—AND APPEALS

Now that we had a play and a theatre, we thought it time to announce the fact, and that presupposed the precaution of approbation from the city of New York. At least, we felt vaguely that someone should be told about it. That vague feeling changed into certainty as we investigated the little matter in question. It seems that in opening a theatre in this city the problems of actors and scripts and location are utterly incidental. One must get permission from what are called "departments." A subdivision of the problem is to find out the names and addresses of these departments from which one must get permission. I used to think that the seven million or more people in New York worked in Wall Street, the garment district, the police force, the Stork Club or drove taxis. Now I know that most of them must work in the city's departments.

A fire in Boston, a crashing snow-laden roof in Washington, a backstage murder in Chicago—all these serve as the occasion for new laws in New York, which in turn create departments. And the mind-your-own-business principle which makes Gotham so delightful to outsiders is carried to the extreme that nobody tells you anything until you've hung out your sign. Then you learn about several hundred reasons why you can't open. In fact, you'd better get permission to take the sign down.

I've forgotten the precise chronology, but since my father was a fireman in his youth and a theatre fireman in middle life, I knew that the Fire Department looked into theatres. Reasoning that New York was probably as advanced as Providence in this matter, I thought that the Fire Department should be consulted. Another ember of memory kindled into flame with the recollection that my father—a practical man—always went to a fire station when he was stuck in a strange city. When one has a single idea, one makes the most of it, so, instead of stopping the first fireman I met, I sailed into the sanctum of the Chief and Commissioner. Start at the top. No appeal. That was our motto.

Chief and Commissioner or Commissioner-Chief Walsh might be expected to have a soft spot in his heart for Dominicans, since he had two sons in the Order.

When I managed to take my eyes off his startlingly red telephone, I told the chief that we had a theatre and did he mind. He weighed the question, feeling a little happy that his sons weren't mixed up in any such foolishness, and finally disposed of the problem by saying. "You're in the jurisdiction of Chief O'Donohue. He's in charge of Public Assemblies." And with that non-committal solution he picked up the red telephone and announced my impending visit to his subaltern, adding, I might say, a good word.

Chief of Fires in Public Assemblies! I suppose that isn't the full official title, but it sounded like that to me, and as I sought his office, I wondered if you had to get his permission to start a little fire in the Polo Grounds or in a parade. He accepted the idea of a theatre as simply as though he firmly believed that every priest should have one. He also knew the building well. It amazed me to learn how much the Fire Department knew about practically every building in New York. And he'd send a man up to look it over and advise me if there were any violations.

As I was getting through this first skirmish rather successfully, Chief O'Donohue tossed in a few disconcerting remarks like, "Of course, you must get a certificate of occupancy from the Department of Housing and Building, and if you make any changes you must apply to the Department of Standards and Appeals, and I'm sure you have seen the Commissioner of Licenses."

That was the first intimation that I would spend months visiting departments explaining why we wanted to open a theatre in New York. Of course, we had no certificate of occupancy. We were given a key and started from there. As for changes, we had built a proscenium wall along with other things. Would the Fire Department like this wall or would they call it too fragile? Would the Department of Standards and Appeals say the wall was too substantial to pass as scenery and would they refuse authorization to install it? And would we have to be licensed and—worse— would it cost anything?

The Department of Licenses seemed the proper one to tackle first. If we weren't going to open, there was no need to bother about prosceniums. Besides, the

title had a familiar ring. It was a commissioner of
licenses who compelled Shakespeare's company (under the aegis of my "uncle" Burbage) to get out of
London proper and ,seek the confiscated Blackfriar
monastery.

The incumbent in New York in the year 1940 was
Mr. Paul Moss and he seemed a very busy man. He
also seemed to pass out licenses for everything except
automobiles and marriages. I may be wrong about
that one way or the other. His office, the scene of
innumerable visits, was a combination special ses-
sions court, advice bureau, department of correction,
stage for action and incredibly ordered chaos. Everybody seemed to be appealing at once and the maestro
could bark a refusal at one suppliant and in the
same breath speak in soft reassuring tones to another.

Two blind men preceded me into his office and
that day they certainly were blind. They fell over
everything. They got renewals. The next case (which
threaded its testimony through mine) had to do with
an Irish woman who operated a newspaper kiosk in
Brooklyn. She was compelled to handle a certain
number of copies of *PM* through block booking, but
retarded the sale of Mr. Field's curious experiment
by leaning over them as they lay stacked on the counter and amply hiding the entire shipment. From here,
the Commissioner and his inevitable audience gathered that a spotter for the publisher or distributor
was opposed to this manner in which the lady took
a load off her feet. The testimony differed widely.
One side seemed to remember that the spotter uttered a few unpleasant words about the sons and

146

daughters of the kings of Ireland, 'and was promptly conked on the head with one of the weights used to keep papers from blowing away. The other side averred that for his abuse the spotter was merely advised to return to Manhattan—because Brooklyn would determine what papers it would sell in spite of the racket of block booking. Like Solomon, the Commissioner told the woman to throw her weight on other papers lest she be accused of prejudice, and he warned the spotter to spot with his mouth shut or the case would crop up next in a felony court. My amazement grew out of the fact that in subsequent meetings Mr. Moss remembered that I came to discuss a theatre and not a news-stand in Brooklyn.

He listened to my case, disposing of a few tavern problems with the greatest of ease, and agreed that, since our charter from the State of New York (the one Department we knew about) described us as a charitable and educational organization, we needed no license. We merely had to post in the box-office— or someplace, since we had no box-office—an affidavit setting forth our non-profit status. I said good-bye gratefully, little realizing that I'd be back again and again, playing the rolling stone in response to his mimeographed subpoenas until I knew every knick-knack on his impressive desk and could have easily taken over the job.

The Housing and Building Department greeted me cordially, burrowed through its voluminous files, and discovered in the somewhat dim past a certificate of occupancy for a drama school. So, (all I had to do was return uptown, run a little drama school, and they'd dust off the certificate and make it valid, while they went back to their serious work of running the biggest housing and building problems in the world.

"But" I said softly, "we don't want to run a school."

They looked at me patiently. "But you see the certificate of occupancy says a 'school.' "

"But we want to run a theatre and charge admissions."

"Oh! You don't want to run a school?"

"That's right. Nothing even resembling a school."

I held fast and was on the way to getting a new certificate of occupancy which would absolve me from relapsing into teaching when some adroit questioning caught me off guard and I mentioned the Doctor's proscenium wall.

"Aha!" That's all the D of H & B wanted. I was out of their jurisdiction. Changes had been made or were contemplated. So I was a natural for the Department of Standards and Appeals. It wasn't a problem for the Department of Housing and Building at all.

Standards and Appeals! The two words didn't seem to belong in the same series. But there they were—sitting together. Once you get on the Manhattan merry-go-round you can't get off. You either get the brass ring or you fall on your face. And I didn't want to fall in the face of the Doctor's success. He had thrown together a theatre out of chaos and very little money. (Those two nouns are in the same series, but it would take too long to explain just how.) I had merely secured an unfinished script. The least I could do was get us by the departments. I'm sure they all liked us, but for some obscure reason they dismissed my helpful suggestions about forgetting the red tape.

We'll get to a production if you are patient, but if you are thinking of opening a theatre in New York, you shouldn't miss a single step. Whether you should or not, you won't. They'll see to that. I no longer marvel at the ability of commercial managers in getting plays, actors, publicity and the like. I merely admire their success in getting by the departments.

Standards and Appeals were (or was) as courteous and charming as rival departments. I went through the now memorized story about the proposed theatre on West 57th Street. Ah yes! They knew all about it. It was a YMCA building. They always begin with a standard. Tight-lipped, I breathed that it had been a drama school since. They looked up some appeals and found that the change had been approved. You add an appeal to a standard and—presto!—you have something else. Good, so far! Now we would like to convert it to a theatre—not, mind you, a drama school —and we would like to make a few changes. Easy! That was just what they were being paid for. If I would bring in twelve sets of blueprints of both floors and indicate the changes, they would pass on the appeal. I thought I heard "twelve," but couldn't quite believe it. The Soviet plan for world domination hardly needs twelve sets of blueprints. The office was getting a bit stuffy. I said, "How many sets?" And a smiling S & A official said "twelve" with the same expression that a presidential budget message requests "a billion."

As I reached for my battered hat, I was wondering how long it would take us to knock down the Doctor's

149

painfully built proscenium and I wondered what he'd say as we carried the thirty-two-foot planks down to the street.

At the door, I asked "Where does one get blueprints made?" To which my courteous informant said that it wasn't the policy of a city department to recommend individuals for work, but I must have many friends in architecture and the initial cost is the only one to worry about; duplicates are very inexpensive. By that time I knew most of the elevator men in the Municipal Building and one of my favorites remarked that it was a nice day.

Back to the Department of Public Assemblies of the Fire Department I went to see what Chief O'Donohue's investigator had to say. By this time I was getting the casual greeting of a regular who was reporting for his day's assignments. We had a pleasant and lengthy chat—the chief and I—so pleasant and lengthy and on so many topics other than Blackfriars' that I felt it becoming ominous. Finally, when the Church, politics, recent fires, old fires and the weather had been disposed of, Chief O'Donohue cleared his throat and said that one of his boys had dropped in the theatre—unofficially, of course—and made a few notes which might help us in our desires to conform to City regulations.

You must get the nice distinction between official and unofficial visits from departments. When an application for a license comes through, these watchdogs who have been straining at the leash leap into action and what they write is written. But prior to the official stamp and seal business, they may drop in

150

looking as unconcerned as detectives. The Doctor wasn't half as impressed by my stories of wearily shuttling from department to department as he was by the steady procession of visitors who "just dropped in"—not to buy tickets or even to be considered for acting roles, but "just to look around." Don't underestimate New York. Nobody cares what you do, they say. Well, just as in Atlanta, Nebraska, a great many people find out and, if they withhold approval, you'll have trouble finishing the job.

Chief O'Donohue was not an evasive man. If anything, he was direct. But he hemmed and hawed over the dossier on his desk so long that I knew problems were coming. "You lack certain equipment," he finally said, not in condemnation but in sympathy, "to conform with the statutes. This list is unofficial and I'm sure it will prove helpful." Which meant that when the same man went back, the same list would suddenly become official and into our next conversation there might creep a steely tone.

The first page was a report, in letter form, single-spaced. The next two pages contained an inventory, single-spaced, of things we didn't have. There were so many items on those two pages that, if we dreamed them into the theatre, there wouldn't be room for an audience. I read it twice and the second time it blurred. The chief breathed heavily as though he were wishing that I stuck to preaching and visiting the sick instead of putting him in such a position.

One of the fifty-odd recommendations was a fifty-gallon fire extinguisher. It doesn't seem real in retrospect, but I remember talking about it. I've spent most of my life in the company of two- and three-gallon extinguishers and I presume that a fifty-gallon one would resemble an old time fire engine. I had no idea where we'd put it if one were found.

I dropped the list gently on Chief O'Donohue's desk and its pages settled like falling leaves. There was no point in taking it home. There simply wasn't enough money in sight. We weren't going to open on schedule. I'm sure my smile resembled that of an actor or actress who reaches the finals in our auditions, only to be told that the casting board by a split vote chose that creature over there for the lead.

Where might we buy those interesting, and I'm sure, useful articles, I queried. Even Chief O'Donohue prattled that it wasn't the policy of a city department to recommend individuals. They must learn it from a record. So I cut in rather rudely, "You don't have to recommend anybody. I never heard of most of those things. Haven't you a list of where they might be found?"

He must have enjoyed the show of spirit more than my defenseless and pained look. At least, he smiled. That finished me and I wilted, saying, "Never mind. We can't afford them, anyway." And then, merely as a conversational afterthought I added, "Did I tell you that Mr. Moss said we're not to be licensed?"

Chief O'Donohue's face became illuminated. Wrinkles flattened out one by one. The clouds disappeared. "You're not to be licensed?" he shouted. "Then why didn't you say so in the first place? That means you're not under my jurisdiction. You can ignore the whole thing. You're now in the jurisdiction of the Department of Fire Prevention—Chief Reidy. Come on down with me and meet him."

Chief Reidy—we had no difficulty getting in because we approached the goal like a tornado—was what I might designate as the other type or Erse. Like a shorter edition of DeValera, he looked at me and through me.

Chief O'Donohue told him briefly, precipitously, volubly, that by a remark of Mr. Moss the Blackfriars' Guild (you know, that old YMCA on 57th St.) had leaped out of the jurisdiction of the Department of Public Assembly and right smack into the Department of Fire Prevention. The next non-stop paragraph depicted the over-conscientiousness of the unofficial, and at this point, unfortunate inspector and his lengthy report, "most of which you can cross off."

There was a pause. We were all standing. Chief Reidy said in a soft voice, "May I read what I'm supposed to cross off." Chief O'Donohue said it would be a waste of time, so Chief Reidy slowly read every word of the report as we shifted from one foot to the other. When that ordeal was over, he asked quietly, "Now what am I supposed to do?"

Chief O'Donohue inhaled deeply and spoke patiently, but there was smoke in his eyes, "You're to tell the Father what he has to buy and install to make a non-licensed theatre conform to whatever regulations you have down here."

"Doesn't this report from your department tell him quite a bit?"

"If it was a licensed house, yes. But the situation has changed. This is unofficial and it's much too complete. Just cross off the things he doesn't need. Where could he buy a fifty-gallon extinguisher?"

"Where did your department think he could buy a fifty-gallon extinguisher?"

Chief O'Donohue was not easily beaten. He tried a new attack in a conciliating tone. "Can't you do something to help the priest?"

"Not a thing. I have two sons priests, so I know all about them."

During the next few minutes the Department of Fire Prevention settled for ordinary fire extinguishers and various gadgets which could be purchased by the Guild and found in the City of New York.

I was back to the various branches of the Fire Department many a time since and gathered many more experiences, but the uncertainty of that day stands out in memory. Harrowing as it was, I'm very proud of the representatives of the New York Fire Department who crossed my path. Chief Walsh and Chief O'Donohue have put aside their helmets and gone, I'm sure, to where there are no fires to fight. And I'm sure my fireman father would have liked these men, too.

The Doctor gave but qualified approval to what I thought was success. He was harassed by electrical inspectors, insurance inspectors, not to mention inspectors from all my newly discovered departments. He thought I had kicked too many sleeping dogs at once for him to muzzle or leash while he explained his proscenium in so many ways it began to take on a note of unreality. And I'm not even sure that he ever got the twelve sets of blueprints.

XIII: A MAN WITH ONE SHOE

SUMMER CAME IN 1941 AND WHILE YOU WERE thinking about a host of other things, we were growing aware that we had a theatre almost fit for the presentation of plays. We also had an office with desks, file cases and a telephone. But we had nobody to put in either theatre or office.

There was no temptation to organize on the pattern of the other Blackfriar Guilds. We were not going to debate constitutional rights with actors whose sole object was to play a fat part. They had contributed nothing to the tedious building and play reading, so they weren't going to vote on anything. They were to be given, rather, an opportunity to display their acting ability. The Doctor and I thought we could make this go if people didn't try to confuse us. We had been called communists and fascists before in our efforts to keep groups together. Now, with our pitifully small assets, we'd probably be called capitalists, but we'd have a try at it our way.

A director and a cast would be a step in the right direction. The Doctor was sinking his teeth into a set designed by Ed Rutyna—the spark-plug of the Lowell Chapter—so it was up to me to find the personnel. Father Brendan's opus wasn't actor-proof either.

We interviewed directors—at least a dozen. By and large, they were enthusiastic. An experimental theatre,

155

the backing (implicit, assumed or alleged) of the Catholic Church, a long-range program—all these were attractive; but when I said in my softest and most winning tones that at present, of course, there would be no salary, they all said they'd think it over and let me know Thursday.

It looked as though I'd have to direct. My uncritical friends said there could be worse, but I knew there could be better. A certain amount of pride and humility might have been chasing one another around in my mind during that discussion, but it was solved on the basis of practicality. Basically, I didn't want to devote any substantial part of my life to telling people when to stand up and when (not to mention how) to sit down. The Dominican tradition dealt in ideas rather than modes.

Besides, my training was in psychology rather than histrionics. Opportunity to use that training had been limited enough in spite of years in laboratories and clinics. Someone, however, had to keep the people happy by throwing water on emotional outbursts and offering a word of encouragement to those who were slinking in corners. A director was too busy inventing reasons to get his characters away from doorways and out of picket-fence formations. Note the advanced technique. We had two psychologists on the staff before we had a staff.

Into this heady maelstrom there walked one day a man with one shoe. Soft-spoken, literate, with a partially corrected British accent, he said this name was Dennis Gurney. He didn't care whether we spelled the first name with one or two "n's". Obviously an ap-

156

peaser. He went further, told us haltingly that he had directed stock in Buffalo and way stations, managed a cinema in England, played in the better Broadway plays which lasted less than three nights, and strangest of all, had heard of our quest.

Our eyes narrowed—the Doctor's and mine—as one of us said purringly, "You know we can't offer very much at the beginning."

The other, taking the cue and the tone, added, "In fact, we can't offer anything right now."

And the first chanted, "We don't know when we'll be able to offer anything."

To which Dennis or Denis (we called him Mr. Gurney at the time) replied, "Well, I'd rather do something I like than discuss salary."

The Doctor caught my eye. We'd learned to carry on a fairly complicated conversation with our eyes. The head never moves nor do we make grimaces or obvious signs. I began to plunge into the problems of the present script, but Mr. Gurney stopped me with, "There's one thing you ought to know."

The Doctor's eye met mine again. Then the half-landed director said hesitantly, "You see, I'm not a Catholic."

We breathed more easily and told him that, while it was a most important matter in his own life, it would no more prevent his directing for us than if he had only one shoe. So he told us—volubly for Gurney—that he really had two shoes, but that he had broken a toe and, as it was painful, he thought it wise to leave the other shoe at home. That night, Dennis Gurney (we awarded him two "n's") was signed, sealed and practically delivered at the same salaries that the co-producers were getting.

The next step was actors. They're a great help in show business, although you must handle them carefully. The original Blackfriars had evanesced. I know that's an intransitive verb and so you can mark it down to bad English—but it's the only word I can use. When they realized that one must build a theatre and do a bit of promotion, nothing intransitive happened to them; they just walked out on us—a very transitive action.

The accepted distinction between professional and amateur actor, with the resultant shrug disposing of the latter, is an unhappy one. The acquiring of a union card does no more for one's acting technique than turning pro affects the style of a golfer or tennis player. Naturally, the proportion of good actors is greater among those who have made it a profession than among the millions who dip into it. But it shouldn't be used as a hard-and-fast norm to distinguish the sheep from the goats.

A better distinction, at least for directors in the "tributary theatre," would be the serious actor against the dilettante. The former believes that his craft is important and demands discipline. The latter will skip a rehearsal for a date and phone late with a dubious excuse. Even though talent may be there, nobody wants it at its price. We have been fortunate at Blackfriars, because most of our applicants have been serious about their work and our files which go into thousands are large enough to replace others.

In spite of the obviousness of the above point (which

was made to take the stigma off the word "amateur"), most of the good actors were attached to Actors' Equity Association, at any rate since the time when the members of the illustrious profession organized against the machinations of producers. Furthermore, since in those drear days of '41, the same famed AEA was facetiously called "the union of the unemployed," although later the drums and guns boomed the trade with all the other war neuroses, there was a good chance that some were available. And, since we always go to headquarters, we approached Equity to find out it there were any new or slightly used actors on its shelves who would like to be dusted off and put to work.

What we really sought was Equity's approval to ask the help of actors between jobs without recompense. Equity graciously and promptly agreed, knowing that its members primarily wanted to act. If that statement seems dubious, it may be clarified by saying that as people they wanted primarily to live, but as members of an actors' union they wanted to act. We were chartered as an educational and charitable institution and were so obviously not exploiting peoples' labor for profit that Equity welcomed the new experiment. It was doubtless a relief to the union office to find a new spot to send people for readings.

It was only when a few officials of the Stage Hands Union (which has a large Catholic membership) attempted to bleed us for money which wasn't there that Equity yielded to pressure, and sacrificed—at least in our opinion—the best interests of its members. (Twenty-one people got jobs out of one of our recent plays.)

159

Thus, with permission to use professional actors—and every other permission we could dream up—we set about calling a cast. When one knows the ropes, assembling a cast is a simple process in New York. There is such an amazing grape-vine among actors and students of theatre that, before one gets the last sentence of a call release written, applicants begin to drift in. Even though we didn't know the ropes at this point, about a hundred and fifty candidates appeared for auditions.

There were some good actors among them, but we had taken on an unlooked-for problem in seeking a Dublin accent. I know I'll be disinherited and that many sons of kings will start whirling in their graves if I suggest that English as spoken in Dublin is a foreign language, but, actually, we wanted to get it so right, that it presented more problems than an ordinary dialect play. We could be fooled on stock-comedy Russian or Chinese, but never on Dublinese. I'm sure you know that the Cork man has a singing lilt, reminiscent of Welsh, the man from Donegal the hardness of the Scot, and again, the Dublin of the streets is not exactly the same Dublin accent which has been rightly called the most melodious and beautiful English in the world.—We agree only on articles of faith.

The loose ends got pulled together somehow and we announced a three-performance run beginning October 30, 1941. We had 382 seats, having removed those which would offer difficult sight lines. The price was $1.10 for orchestra seats and $.83 for these in the balcony. This was that historic free enterprise era before the Federal tax rose to twenty per cent. If you're mathematically inclined, you may have figured that we could hope for a thousand-dollar gross. But, since we gave away seats to agents and critics if they were interested and since we had been building for a year, it didn't look like a get-rich-quick proposition. It surely needed a greater incentive than wealth.

The show went on. Four or five of the metropolitan dailies covered us and from the *Daily Mirror* and the *Brooklyn Eagle* came the regular critics—Bob Coleman and Bob Francis. Although Mr. Francis left the *Eagle* for *Billboard* and although on occasion he differs with us volubly and violently, opening night still finds him with us. At this point we salute him and offer to argue any question without anyone dropping a hat.

The gentleman from the South—Mr. Coleman—has seen all thirty-one of our plays at this writing, because he is an unusual critic who has time for non-commercials who can't afford space in his paper. Whether he has been enthusiastic about a given production or not, he believes in our idea and always keeps faith with his public who want to know what is going on theatrically, even though it isn't backed with substantial sums. In this case, he liked our offering and that began a friendship which is a bright spot in our varied press relations.

Grace O'Malley, who got the best press notices, played the role of a housekeeper with much gusto, but she changed her name to Sara Flynn because she was under contract in a commercial which was coming up—and maybe she wasn't sure that the toddling Blackfriar Chapter would come up to her old Abbey standards. Anyhow, after opening night, an agent went to the producer with whom she was signed and begged him to get back Grace O'Malley's contract somehow and to hire Sara Flynn. So, from a few hours after our first curtain, we were getting people jobs, even though in this case it was the actress's own.

As we turned a few patrons away on closing night we decided to run *Up the Rebels* for a fourth performance. With so little time for publicity it wasn't a sell-out, but the holdover was gratifying. However contemporaries and historians rate the production—and we did have much to learn—we look on it with almost paternal pleasure, because after a year of after-hour work we put a play on the fringe of Broadway. It was like planting a flag. And that flag has stayed flying for quite a while.

The next script we decided upon was a biographical story of the poet, Francis Thompson, written by Felix Doherty and done previously by the Boston Blackfriars with Robert Spaeght.

Mr. Gurney was still with us, in spite of the fact that half the directors who had kept us at arm's length returned to say that they had reconsidered. We hadn't. By now, Mr. Gurney had two shoes, not because he was able to buy another from his share of *Rebels*, but because he was able to tuck his mended toe into the one he had been leaving at home. So, conventionally shod, he wandered among his cronies and picked what we still think was a good cast, due in no small measure to Equity's approval.

At this point, two characters stepped through our portals—open only a few hours a day—who became an integral part of Blackfriars in New York for years, until the death of one and the failing vision of the other caused them to leave us.

Bill Schoeller was brought to us as a man willing to design and build our sets. Talking to Bill, you'd never think he was really willing to do anything. But that's where you'd be wrong. An Austrian who was stranded in a Passion Play which toured this country, Bill was primarily an actor, but his accent reserved him for specialized type casting. Like many of his countrymen, Bill was a good craftsman—in this case, a carpenter. His imagination might have been limited and there certainly was a ceiling on his budget. But we all ganged up into an idea department and Bill built the varying results.

Bill had a mannerism which took a little under-standing. As "producer," I thought it in order to ap-prove the sets as they were designed and as they went up. The Doctor, who threw in a good many of the ideas and who handled the budget, sometimes had something to say, too. So, separately or together we would look at Bill's unfinished masterpieces and sug-gest that a door should be larger or smaller. What-ever the proposal, Bill would say, "No!—the most blunt and emphatic "No!" we had ever heard. Then we'd offer reasons to one another quite unemotionally and drop the matter. No matter how small the issue, Bill would walk away muttering, "It's impossible! Im-possible!"—indicating by his tone that we were some-what impossible, too.

Then, without fail, two or three days later, he'd tell one of us he had a new idea. He had come to the con-clusion that that door ought to be changed and he'd give us our reasons right back as though they were his own. Naturally, we thought it a stroke of genius and the game went on for years.

The other impresario who dropped in for a chat and took root was Merritt T. Wyatt. Seeking someone to cover the office for a few hours in the afternoon that we might seem open for business while we were doing our regularly assigned work, we persuaded Mr. Wyatt to fill that opening. Gradually, with his knowledge of theatre and theatre people, he became "the office."

Song out of Sorrow—for that was the labored title of the Thompson script—was scheduled to open December 11, 1941. We weren't to know what a dismal day that was to be in American history. So, rehearsals went on blithely as Japanese ambassadors gave and took the world-old double talk in Washington.

The second act closes with Thompson, filled with gin and laudanum, struggling with a few lines of poetry. One of the actors sitting beside me a few days before opening remarked as the scene was run, "That's pretty good poetry. Did the author write it?"

"Thompson wrote it," I said.

"He did? Did he really exist?"

You get used to actors, too.

The debacle of Pearl Harbor came on Sunday and we opened the following Thursday. The city, the entire country was paralyzed. Perhaps you've forgotten, but there were pictures in the New York papers of empty restaurants except for waiters lined against the walls. Only spots with advanced sales got any business and cancellations were numerous. We had practically no advance, so practically nobody came.

Lacking quantity, we might have been gratified by quality, because more critics came than before. But it was part of their working day and they didn't have to pay. Bob Coleman summed up his review with the words, "The result was one of the season's most rewarding plays." Miss Waldorf of the *Post*, a newcomer to our walk-up theatre, spoke glowingly and Mr. Freedley of the *Telegraph* continues to use this play as a reminder of what we can do whenever he doesn't like a Blackfriar production.

The play, concerning Thompson's rescue from starvation by the woman whose name is now forgotten and who helped him through the major crisis of his life, has moments of grandeur. A well-known producer of bygone days looked at me with accusing eyes after the final curtain and said sadly, "I don't get it. I don't get it . . . You have prostitutes and dope fiends and it's Catholic theatre. I have them and it's cops."

Perhaps we should have taken down the flag at this point. Fifteen months in New York hadn't taken the town by storm. And we might be stressing a luxury when men were being mobilized to die. We did think of that. But another stray thought kept persisting through the hysteria which surrounded us. If the right things could have been said through the media which create public opinion, this war which all sides were to lose as usual might not have been forced upon us.

Since this didn't start out as a political essay, it won't switch at one at this point. I don't think I have much to add to the billion of words which have been ground out on the subject, but I might be allowed a thought about the entertainment field which is regarded by the heresy known as communism as a part of the "transmission belt."

Perhaps that sentence can stand elaboration. I called it the current heresy because the Church has watched "isms" from paganism to communism and is still quietly going along, not merely because it is well organized, but because it has satisfied the human heart, since, for all the human frailties which have been mistaken for it, it is the continuation of Christ on earth.

Chesterton has likened the Church to a horseman who went galloping down a road. While he stayed in the middle all went well, but when he careened to one side or the other he was in or approaching heresy. So, in spite of current opinion to the contrary, most of us who have been subjected to an extensive course in religion know the marks of the various "isms." It is still the balance that interests us.

We're not satisfied to go back to paganism although the human mind, destined for truth, can work out a remarkable civilization along naturalistic lines. But we want much more. We want to take advantage of the fact that God touched the earth in the Incarnation of Christ and made things easy for us. So we are more than a little sorry for those who repudiate Him no matter how humanitarian or sportsmanlike they claim their grounds to be.

The current heresy finds the world overemphasizing the material welfare of man. So completely is this aspect stressed that it becomes man's only goal, at least in theory. But besides being a very secondary goal, the great dream of equality isn't seriously sought in fact. The communist ambassadors do a bit better for themselves than many of the people they eulogize while the latter are in salt mines. And it is not likely that anyone ever really believed that it would work out or that any but starry-eyed children ever wanted it to work out.

The old God-directed communism of the religious orders, which is my rule of life and which has endured century after century, is a lovely and an understandable thing. The counterfeit claptrap of today is a deliberate deception for the aggrandizement of an admittedly unscrupulous few.

This is the crux, however. Indulging in the one selfishness recommended by God—the drive to become united with Him for eternity, I do this sharing or this giving for that eternal compensation. If I were convinced that there were no God and no rewards or punishments I might try to outwit my fellows. I might follow the example of my new leaders and try to become a communist official and get another piece of bread or another palace, hoping the while that those who voted for me had enough to eat. And if I became so important that I wouldn't have to care about votes, I might become indifferent about whether anyone had a piece of bread or no. That is the expected course of the new heresy.

It was a mistake on the part of the communists to get rid of God so completely. They should have taken control of death first. At present all they can do is arrange death; they can't seem to stop it. Of course that's why God had to go. They had to get their rewards before death came. And the thought of God and God's injunctions was a deterrent to hordes murdering the rich and the bourgeoisie and sacking their homes. So God had to be expelled.

But He keeps coming back to individuals. Yes! It was bad strategy. Yet, very simple. Almost every other heresy engaged a few people in proving something about God—His existence or non-existence. This new touch took advantage of the fact that modern man doesn't reason very much. He prefers to listen. So the new proponents of revolution merely seized the media of public opinion and closed the book of the accumulated wisdom of the world. Then they opened a new one—and a host of playwrights, columnists, commentators just assumed that He never existed and civilization plunged back thousands of years.

At least, that was the pattern in Germany, Italy, Russia and the rest of the iron-curtained countries. If I seem to identify communism with totalitarianism it's because I'm talking about the intention, not the bait.

In the entertainment field—theatre, moving pictures, radio and television—Catholics for all practical purposes had done nothing. There had been a parochial theatre here and there, but its materials were cast-off and sometimes slightly expurgated Broadway vehicles. There had been a growing school and college theatre and it is getting healthier by the year. Once, it was entirely satisfied to do edifying pageants or allegorical pieces which gave the participants some recreation. It did little for the audiences emotionally and

168

taught the students nothing they hadn't already learned in classes. More recently, drama has been taken seriously and production standards have generally improved and in a few colleges, especially those with departments of drama, creative work has been of a high calibre.

Yet, my statement stands. Up to now, these have not affected the thinking of the people of the country as have the moving pictures and the network radio productions.

That's what I mean when I say that theatre under Catholic auspices—a much safer expression than "Catholic Theatre"—has not affected thinking in this country. But the theatre of totalitarianism or collectivism—especially that branch dedicated to Russian communism—bit deeply into our thinking, so much so that even actors began to believe it.

The same is obviously true of moving pictures and radio. A few years ago many of my friends were enthusiastic because of the pictures, *Going My Way, The Keys of the Kingdom and The Bells of Saint Mary's.* The McCarey pictures were entertaining stories of good people, not pretending to convey all the dogma and moral of the Church, and served a good purpose. The Cronin picture, in spite of two heresies, was a sentimental study of a heroic priest. I happen to like all three of them.

Yet it seems pathetic that we should be so grateful for three or four pictures out of some seven hundred, when actually we could make the type of pictures we want all the time. I know it couldn't be done overnight. There are obvious problems in the business. But

I still maintain that, if we can erect a parochial school system and dot the country with universities and colleges, we could carry through and make the pictures we want to see.

The radio is even more limited than the moving pictures when it comes to saying anything. This great public servant, paid for by private enterprise and dedicated to offending nobody who might buy a bar of soap, is terrified lest it displease anybody in the world. Occasionally, a picture such as *Monsieur Vincent,* made by public subscription (and a winner of international prizes), can be sneaked into back-alley theatres in our fair land, but such mistakes won't happen on radio.

Conscious of its public-servant role, the radio invites various denominations for fifteen minutes to a half hour weekly over networks and proportionate time on local stations. Those religious groups which have lost interest in dogma and are dedicated to a "common denominator" morality seem satisfied with the arrangement, but the Church, conscious of its teaching role, had the bad taste to talk about communism—and for years the scripts submitted by the best Catholic speakers were blue-pencilled into innocuousness.

Now, with the blunders of the Soviets, many of those things may be said. But we knew them then and thought it an obligation to tell the rest of America. It was less freedom of speech on the radio than the over-reaching of the Russian delegates which has begun to swing American public opinion back to sanity.

That's radio and it will continue to be that way as

long as it is paid for by the merchants of the country, for whom the customer is always right, even though the customers agree in nothing. In the frantic and somewhat terrified effort to offend nobody, it will continue to say nothing.

Nothing else can be expected in a country dedicated to "tolerance." I make no plea that truth or falsehood or the convictions of any group should be aired over the commercial radio. I simply say that if Catholics have spent millions to sustain the conviction that they should teach their children certain things in a school system and that if one hundred thousand teachers have dedicated their lives to teach in that school as a vocation, those same Catholics, in the name of consistency had better build better radio chains, run daily newspapers, produce moving pictures or hold their peace —because the heroic work of the school will be quietly and effectively undone.

Obviously, there is little inclination to organize or finance such vast undertakings. We have to be hit over the head before taking a page from the book of those who are attacking the God we try to serve. Nor had the Doctor and I the means for such effective steps in the interests of what we believed good for all. But we could keep the little 57th Street theatre open. We'd try to keep it open in spite of war, or perhaps on account of war, because we believed and believe what was said a few pages back, before this digression: "If the right things could have been said through the media which create public opinion, this war which all sides were to lose as usual might not have been forced upon us."

With the new year, 1942, the United States Trust Company ordered an inspection made and wrote us a letter telling we'd have to close up. I've forgotten just why they entered the picture, but I imagine they either bought the building or won it in a raffle. At any event, it is of no consequence, because, remember, when you open a theatre in New York, everybody makes inspections. And almost everybody who inspected us told us to close up.

Since the issue had to do with construction, the Doctor took it as his department and wrote a lengthy and devious letter proving our innocence beyond cavil, but in three or four lines the vested interests in question referred us to the Department of Housing and Building. Now, since I had spent so much time softening up that institution that I was regarded as an old Houser and Builder, I essayed to sit on their mourners' bench again.

My good friends welcomed me and answered my question without any trouble. They said, "You are violating the requirement of Section C26-715.0 of the Administrative Code of the City of New York." That dot before the 0 bothered me in the section number. It looked as though we were running afoul of a regulation so insignificant it was placed in subdivision "zero." But I didn't mention that little matter. They

172

have their system and their pride. I merely said, "What should we do?" And they had an answer: "File an application for a variation with the Board of Standards and Appeals."

The camel's back was weakening. I knew that the Board of Standard and Appeals would pat me on the back and say "Go get twelve sets of blueprints." So I asked, "What could I do instead of that?" And after much discussion and a few more investigations or inspections, they said, "Take out eighty-four seats. Then you'll have only 299 and you'll be in a different category and jurisdiction." When the Doctor heard that he glared at me as though I wrote Section C26-715.0, but he shot his cuffs and took out eighty-four seats.

In February we opened with *The Years Between* by Edward Burbage. Burns Mantle said it "is a long way from being the greatest comedy ever written, but it is that rare thing in the theatre these days—an intelligent, timely, clean comedy about decent likeable humans. And that gives it certain restoratives values that are manna for the jaded Broadway spirt." That sounded good. That's what we wanted it to be. Mantle also said it was written by Richard Burbage, but then he was always getting my uncles confused.

It ran for six days, landed a number of jobs for actors, and got a large press, most of which was favorable. Brooks Atkinson panned it wittily and the next day we received a letter from Commissioner Moss:

"I noticed in today's paper an article by Brooks Atkinson, in which he indicates that there is a regular performance going on in your theatre. Please call here on Monday, April 27th, 1942, at 10:30 A.M."

That marked the beginning of my shuttling between the Guild and, White and Centre Streets. Mr. Moss thought that if we got reviewers from practically all the papers, we were a "regular theatre" and should be licensed. I thought that we should do no such thing, because a house seating under three hundred had to pay a hundred dollars for such a luxury, and argued our case through a sheaf of letters and several interviews. Mr. Moss sustained the opinion of the License Commissioner and we bought a nice light brown license with red and black print on it.

It wasn't just handed over on receipt of the money. We had to fill out a questionnaire, checking the word "Theatrical" among "Bocci Ball Alley" and similar ventures. I don't know precisely what Bocci Ball is, but I'll wager it's easier to run than Blackfriars. And I look at all organ grinders with envy.

Lent was the proper time to present a religious play, so I was easily talked into doing *Savonarola,* a play that I had published a few years before. It offered certain challenges, but we were learning the ropes. For one thing it required a large, all-male cast. For another, the leading character was the center of a 450-year-old controversy. Some, following St. Philip Neri and St. Catherine de Ricci, regard him as a saint. Others, weary of defending the Church, in spite of human frailty, prefer to allow him to become a scapegoat. There seemed to me a middle course, which is probably the right one. To doubt Savonarola's personal sanctity and sincerity is rash and prejudiced in the face of the evidence. That his impatience with those less willing to go the whole way at once caused him to flaunt authority is the impression of one who seeks accessible sources. That it is very easy to get caught between divinely inspired zeal and the inertia of any machine is no new or surprising conclusion. But taking a middle course in anything usually offends those espousing both extremes.

Sometimes during this first year the Doctor and I felt like Savonarola, although we never alluded to it. We were convinced that this work had to go on, but we were tripped up from so many unexpected sources that we didn't know just how it would succeed. The increasing demands of our other appointed tasks promised very little stability or organization in the field of theatre. And we might attract unwelcome attention by flaunting this rebel priest of the fifteenth century before those who had more or less forgotten him.

However, we gathered a cast of such doughty Florentines as Brandon Peters, Robert Ober, Morgan Farley and Albert Carroll, built a set that made the little stage look twice as big as it was, clutched our license to our hearts and opened with misgivings. Almost every time we opened with misgivings the play was a success. In the lobby, I watched the faces of a few ecclesiastics and others whom I thought might storm out of the building if their favorite thesis were questioned, but they all said something as unexciting as "Good show. Some fine acting there." It was actually disappointing. Our first bomb-shell in New York went "Pffft." Practically everybody had a pleasant evening and that was all.

The critics offered a display of erudition in varying degrees of accuracy and varying amounts of space.

Billboard's reviewer, for example, had a thesis which he developed for about a column, condemning poor Girolamo and praising the Medici. In a paragraph or two he covered the play, apparently not enjoying it so much as being grateful that we had produced it and given him a chance to show his knowledge of the period. By and large they praised its sincerity and open-mindedness and found flaws in construction and in dramatic tension. But they did write columns about it and obviously had begun to take us seriously. Mr. Atkinson, in the briefest notice of all, alone didn't like it. Mr. Watts, then with the *Herald Tribune*, numbered it among the best ten of the year, and that we thought was a distinction for any experimental theatre to achieve in its first season.

Don't be concerned that my citing of the critics is a sign that, because they were showing approval of our work, I regard or regarded them as infallible or that we sought their good will because it is a means to an end in New York. That end is the securing of audiences to see our efforts. Should we lose that good will, we would have to secure audiences in other ways. We would not change our basic plans.

But I will not use the critics to prove opposite sides of a thesis. That is, I will not approve when they smile and attack them when they frown. They are individuals with individual backgrounds, religious, artistic, political and the rest. I mention them because they are one gauge of our degree of acceptance in a theatre-wise city. Another reason is that we have their opinions in old scrapbooks. What most other people said has been forgotten.

Many of the experts who liked *Savonarola* seemed impressed with the fact we, his brothers, would tell the story so objectively. That slightly piqued us because we have labored under the impression that we have been telling the story objectively for almost 500 years. In fact, a great deal of praise, sincerely meant over the years, has been born of disbelief in either our sincerity or our capabilities. It takes the general form of "I've heard of Blackfriars for a long time, but I had no idea you were doing anything like this. I thought you were a little amateur group." My answering smile to this sort of praise is weak and watery.

Others expressed gratified surprise that we would attempt a big production in such limited space and with no visible means of support, because our box-office for such short runs couldn't possibly pay the bills. We were trying to demonstrate something and the first year's deficit was $3,108, but we owed nobody anything except gratitude.

Another segment of the press discovered us in *Savonarola*. The Catholic papers and magazines were really enthusiastic. Father Gillis devoted two successive syndicated columns to the Florentine reformer. Naturally, he talked more about the man than the play— but that was what we wanted in the theatre of ideas.

The weighing and balancing in the secular press and the sudden enthusiasm of the Catholic press brought us up against a new problem. What sort of audience did we want? The Doctor, who was paying the bills, wanted any audience of people who would pay for tickets, but from a production angle I had to think of so satisfying people that they would come back.

Should we keep on doing Savonarolas (assuming that anybody else wrote such plays) and work toward a more or less exclusively Catholic audience? That was the argument of the near-Blackfriars in Pittsburgh, who regarded it a waste of time to do secular plays. There are many who regard as fit for Catholic theatre only the ecclesiocentric drama—the conflicts of those who are aware of grace and are fortified by the sacramental system. I'm almost falling into the trap of offering a definition of a Catholic play, but I must avoid that pitfall, because, after twenty years of thinking it over, I haven't a pat definition.

We would like to offer that fare to those who want that fare. You have to play to audiences and consider to some degree what they will sit through, especially in the competition of New York. And if we built audiences for the ecclesiocentric play, we would be happy to supply those audiences. If success came our way, we would like to open one or twenty theatres dedicated to this type of drama. It is not goody-goody theatre at all. It merely takes the Catholic background for granted, as do Sigrid Undset's novels of mediaeval Norway. In point of fact, it removes a lot of difficulties. The author doesn't debate as to whether divorce or suicide (as a solution) is acceptable to his characters or his audiences. He knows they're not and everybody accepts that assumption. Likewise, the author can paint his villains as black as he wants (and his heroes as white) without offending any of the millions who shout "discrimination" at anyone who tries to write nowadays. All his characters are in the same boat and hold to the same basic principles.

That would be easy theatre, but from Blackfriars' point of view, it presents a certain weakness. We didn't set up to do a cross between dramatizations of the teaching of the Church and theatre. We set out to do theatre—a theatre embodying ideas.

To limit the appeal to those of one's convictions is to admit inability to bridge the gap and to sharpen sectarian lines. Theatre is no more sectarian than is essential catholicity. Nor could we handle some of the social problems we attempted if we said Catholic theatre is for and about Catholics. A case in point cropped up in one of our interracial plays. The author asked us if he should make his characters Catholic. We told him not to specify any religion. It is not a Catholic problem— as presented in the play. It is an American problem. To make the Negroes Catholics and the whites non-Catholics, or vice-versa, or to put them all in any one sect would have complicated and snarled the problem. It fit everybody as stated and was involved enough.

Then it would be a strain to inject religion into farce comedy and we didn't want to be barred from any dramatic form. If our audiences didn't want to laugh once in a while, we certainly did. And those audiences made known their desires along that line in no uncertain terms. One gentleman who purchased a large portion of the house for a performance of *Savonarola* came out in the lobby while one of the best (I thought) scenes was playing and said, "It's terrific. When are you going to do a good comedy?"

So, on the ecclesiocentric score, we decided to take what of it would be good for a balanced diet and stick to our old principles of doing plays which were artistically and morally right.

There were subsidiary problems in the matter of audiences. Did we want to play to the regular theatre clientele or to build new audiences out of the movie-goers? Did we prefer to teach the young something about theatre or cater to more settled and less noisy audiences? We did talk about those things, but the problem settled itself in a very simple fashion. We tried to produce a variety of scripts and those who liked us came back. Some were young and some were old. Some were veteran theatre-goers and others asked us what time the second show went on. We played to people and asked no questions and made no distinctions—and that is as it should be.

Our file of actors increased both in quantity and quality. But one aspirant was disappointed and made no effort to hide her feelings. A statuesque blonde, who had apparently been in show business for some time, barged into the office one evening when Father Larnen was at the desk. He was rather unfamiliar with our procedure and rather reticent about coping with the high-pressure people who are drawn to production offices. The lady's third or fourth question was, "How much do you pay?"

Father Larnen stumbled through an unrehearsed paragraph (or half paragraph) indicating that we really didn't pay anything.

"Oh, you don't pay anything, don't you?" she stormed. "Why, you're the—you're the sort of people that keep us girls in burlesque."

XV: BLACKLISTED

THE 1942-43 SEASON WAS ONE OF THE WORST WE'VE encountered. We gathered our poorest collection of scripts, annoying the critics and making audiences uncertain of us; one play was pilloried by everybody; at a critical play-doctoring period I got pneumonia; and to make it a beautiful season Equity accepted the mandate of the craft unions and "blacklisted" us.

The trouble lay in the fact that we didn't come on the right material and that we had to go through a trial and error period before we'd know the right material if we saw it. Those who do revivals have the opinion if not the wisdom of those who have done them before to fall back on. There is usually a laudatory notice in publishers' catalogues to reassure them. Those who do originals are on an uncharted sea. (I had to say that. There wasn't a single cliche on this page.) Our scripts come either from established writers, who have a few mavericks gathering dust in agents' offices and which reach us from the bottom of the barrel, or from unknown writers.

We don't pay for scripts and we don't charge for producing scripts either. Twenty or thirty times we have been offered subsidized production costs if we would do a particular producer's pet or actor's vehicle, and as many times we have flatly refused. So if you don't like a Blackfriar script, you can hereby find out

181

whom to blame. In this brash or brave role, I have found out that we can lay eggs, too.

Naturally, I don't subscribe to the harshness of our treatment that year. I merely report. The season's bill consisted of *Inside Story* by Peter Sheehan, *Tinker's Dam* by Andrew Hawke, *A Man's House* by John Drinkwater, and *Moment Musicale* by Charles Angoff.

To begin with, we were broke and extremely busy about other things. The previous season lasted twenty-nine performances, spread over four plays. A few organizations had taken small blocks of tickets, so we asked them what sort of play they'd like to see next. They all said "comedy." Then, comedy they'd get—and we added "a one-set modern dress comedy," remembering the cost of *Savonarola*.

That requisite limited the field. There aren't many good one-set comedies lying around in producers' offices in New York. We settled on Mr. Sheehan's piece with our eyes open, as at least fulfilling the physical demands. He admitted that he wrote it in a hurry and we produced it in the same spirit. Joseph Pihodna of the *Herald Tribune said,* "It may be that the Blackfriars' Guild sought long and arduously for its first script. The organization might have delayed its season until it found a more suitable play." Mr. Pihodna's first sentence is correct. Mr. Pihodna's second sentence was good, but not practical, advice. We had to open when we did to pay the rent for October.

Burton Rascoe said, "With a little tinkering, *Inside Story* might be turned into a first class comedy." That is probably close to the truth. We hadn't the time to tinker.

It was a little farce comedy with an uneven cast. But the audiences who asked for something of this nature found it had the right overtones and expressed their general satisfaction. One of my choicest memories of our work in New York is a scene between J. Augustus Keogh and Patsy O'Shea, who was then about ten. (A few months after we closed, Mr. Keogh, the veteran of the Abbey Theatre, was killed in an automobile accident.)

There was the problem all over again. Should we seek critical acclaim, knowing that these impartial (up to a point) observers were unconsciously pitting us against productions that cost up to one hundred times what we could afford, or should we dig for a while and please our audiences, who were the only ones in sight to pay the rent? Some day we hoped to find the formula. Give them the theatre they wanted by producing so well that they'd want the theatre we gave them.

A few days before opening we had a visit from a representative of Equity, with instructions to withdraw members of his association from our cast. I don't know the background of this visit, but I was sure that Equity wouldn't stop a show practically in production.

The Doctor was elected trouble-shooter and he took off to Theatrical Protective Union, No. 1, because he suspected that there the trouble might best be shot. After several misses, he hit the bull's-eye. Apparently it was only considered a practice shot, however, for grimmer things were soon to come.

Andrew Hawke, incorrectly suspected by John Anderson and the late Burns Mantle of being one of the fathers connected with Blackfriars, wrote a fantasy arguing for a life hereafter. I've forgotten the title it had when it arrived, but the Doctor rechristened it *Tinker's Dam*. The title itself stirred up a little tempest, causing the late Bide Dudley (who gave us midnight radio reviews) to rename it *The Tinker* because, ostensibly, he couldn't use the word "dam" over the air. John Anderson, of the *Journal American*, took an opposite view, saying, "if it does no more than correct the mistaken notion that a tinker's dam is spelled with an 'n' and means an oath, it will have done something." Now, we think it did a lot more than that. Mr. Anderson went on, "As Mr. Ripley, Information Please, the Quiz Kids, or any convenient dictionary will explain (patiently, I hope) a tinker's dam is merely a ring, usually of flour paste, which a tinker uses to keep molten lead within bounds. Since it is cooked by the heat and can be used only once it is not worth much." You'd never get that from the play because the tinker's dam isn't mentioned. So, you see, the critics serve a multiplicity of purposes.

I mentioned previously that we learned to differentiate between the ideological backgrounds of critics. This not too subtle insult to author and producers appeared in *New Masses*:

"Bright note: One of the children in the play was a Negro. Her part was not caricatured in any way and the sentiments she expressed were no sillier than those of any of the others."

While the secular press was in and out, good and bad, praising aspects and panning others (which is its right), the Catholic press was enthusiastic. The secular press in large measure belittled the thesis, throwing in

184

a mixture of praise and blame for the production, but the Catholic press praised the thesis and limited its complaints to the production.

More food for thought. It will take a fool-proof script to bridge the gap between the two schools, so the finding of such scripts is our job. Audiences—again the rent-payers—were pleased and many individuals caught what the author had in mind and were very enthusiastic. Again we served our purpose, and if the author hadn't become ill and perhaps if I hadn't gotten pneumonia just before opening, we might have worked out the flaws which the play had. It wasn't quite finished (we are experimental, you know), but it has the makings of a great morality play.

The bright spot in the season—at least from the viewpoint of pleasing those who steer public opinion—was the combination of Augustin Duncan and John Drinkwater's *A Man's House* which we offered for Lent. It deserved and received a good general reaction and a good press, with the usual contradictions. George Freedly (*Telegraph*) said: "it is not helped by the pontifical direction of Dennis Gurney." Shirley Frohlich (*Billboard*) said: "Under the direction of Dennis Gurney *A Man's House* becomes vivid and real."

Ed Sullivan, in his column, summed up some of the new problems we met in this production: "Augustin Duncan, most famous blind actor in the country, performs today in John Drinkwater's *A Man's House,* at the Blackfriars' Theatre. The blind actor must time his entrance to single cues, find his way around a stage filled with set pieces, climb stairs and greet other actors on their entrances . . . . The remarkable brother of

Isadora Duncan lost his eyesight 14 years ago but refused to be dismayed . . . . "

The play is concerned with the impact of Christ on a Jerusalem family. A blind daughter was played by Cavada Humphrey. Another warm Blackfriar memory is the scene in which Mr. Duncan leads his "blind" daughter across the stage that she may not stumble over furniture.

Some critics called this our best play to date, but, for that matter, one said the same of *Tinker's Dam*. Perhaps when I speak of a poor press I mean that they weren't all as enthusiastic as we were. We never had a completely bad press until the production of *Moment Musicale*.

That was the all-time low. Yet, we did it with our eyes open and to prove a point. We failed. But the point should be explained to indicate that we hadn't forgotten what we set out to do nor did we just go blank for a period.

We had done seven productions by this time and, come to think of it, they included six different types of plays. The Angoff script concerned itself with a temptation against marital fidelity and its thesis fell within our scope. We'd use this as the opportunity to indicate that we were willing to come up against problems— that our idea of theatre was not all sweetness and light. What the play was about was one thing; where the dust got in our eyes was in the fact that it wasn't a very good play about it.

To reassure the most conservative elements of our audience, I wrote a program note, setting forth again our thesis and defending the choice. I will never write a program note again, except to clarify some minor point of geography or history. Most of the reviewers sunk their best barbs into the program note and brushed the play off in a few words. Some had more fun and quoted lines; others quoted lines which members of the audience tossed back.

I was undone. My little explanation looks as good now as it did then. It is still our thesis. But the example we used to prove it limped (as the Scholastics say examples always do) and our stock plunged, taking the box-office with it. It was good, in a way, for our future that not many came, but it was disastrous again from a financial viewpoint. Incidentally, it will reassure me a little to note that the actors and production staff did a pretty good job.

Theatrical Protective Union, No. 1, had not been idle. Gathering strength from allied unions, it finally came out in a massed attack and vented its indignation by "blacklisting" Blackfriars. We've stayed "blacklisted" for the past nine years.

We read it first in the *Times* in an eight-inch stick. I presume it was in the other papers, but, being capitalists, we saved the *Times* notice. A week later *Billboard* elaborated with: "Five major theatrical craft unions with the co-operation of Actors' Equity, are cracking down on what they term 'so-called experimental theatres' which in reality are try-out houses for legit producers who want to see what their untried properties look like upon a stage."

Accused, judged, libeled and condemned without a hearing or a notice, we were to fold up because of that ridiculously false assertion. But *Billboard*'s notice is so interesting I must make a few more selections from it: "Solly Pernick, spokesman for the crafts, said that the acting groups themselves were not opposed, but the owners who lease the theatres. According to Pernick, owners supply their own non-union stage-hands, ticket-sellers, etc., which negates their claim of being 'amateur' theatres."

The last sentence solves one important academic problem for me. If you supply your own stagehands, ticket-takers, etc., because they volunteer to do those unglamorous jobs for devotion to an ideal and without any thought of recompense, you negate the claim of being "amateur." Then what do you have to do to establish an amateur standing? Your answer will be much better than mine.

Billboard continued: "Groups (craft unions) are also mulling a plan to start their own experimental theatre, outside the commercial theatre area, where 'real amateurs' will be allowed to work on plays that could not be suspected of 'tryouts' for commercial producers," and ended: "Dog-housed theatres say they employ union help when presenting pro groups but their budgets don't usually cover the amount required by the unions." This "dog-housed" theatre didn't say any such thing. It didn't say anything. It wasn't asked. It certainly wasn't commercial. It was just blacklisted. Nor was anything done for "real amateurs" in the nine ensuing years.

This notice appeared just as we were moving into our last production. However, Equity said we might go through the production as planned. We didn't go through it precisely as planned, but we went through it.

The question which faced us was one of procedure. We weren't going to close because representatives of a few unions were so short-sighted. Either we'd do without Equity actors or we'd point out the flagrant errors and injustices of the unions' delegates. But how does one go about pointing it out?

So we wrote to Equity. We explained that it seemed strange to lump us with four theatres or halls which were normally rented out to various producers. That they made money, I doubt; that they affected the "craft unions" I doubt more; but they weren't in the same category as Blackfriars which by charter and in fact was a religious and charitable institution which did its own plays. In fact, our charter read much like that of a church—not that we looked much like a church—but when you got through the "whereases" and "parties of the third part" in both documents, it was hard to tell the difference.

Equity arranged a "hearing." As I was out of town, the Doctor attended the meeting, made up preponderantly of union men who couldn't understand what malpractice caused us to be "blacklisted," and he dismissed the matter as a no-decision affair, which paved the way for another hearing.

This I went to and, since it is still vivid in my mind, it may be worth a few words. It was held in a little court-room in Equity's building. Mr. Pernick sat at the main desk or on the main bench (whatever you call the proper place for a judge). The delegates of the other unions and a secretary or two sat around on sort of overflow benches, like the Supreme Court or visiting judges called in for consultation. Earlier in the day I ran into Al Weisenbach and asked him to come along. The two of us sat in the place corresponding to prisoner's dock, press, legal advisors and audience. Not a vast space, I admit, but still a little appalling, since everyone else was raised on podia or elevations.

I did everything wrong (it was pointed out later). I used the word "blacklisting" and the court in a pained tone of voice said "We don't like that word." The unhappy word had been used four times in the *Times* article and that was the sole reason we were there.

I told them how much we had grossed that season and got the hugest ovation of stony silence I've ever encountered. It was chilling. I offered to show them the books. Nobody answered. Then it dawned. It was a hearing for me and I was going to be heard. Nobody else had to talk.

So, with a sense of futility, I ran off the spiel—why we were founded, where we got our operating expenses, what we were doing for authors and actors, where we recruited our audiences, ending up with the chorus that we were not organized labor or unorganized labor. And that we didn't pay anybody because we hadn't that kind of money.

Then a subdivision of the court spoke. A gentleman in an upper box (stage right) : "Where did you get the money to open in the first place?"

I was a little taken back at that, because the list of a few dollars here and a few dollars there would have been something to memorize. I tried to put that idea into words, but he cut in with, "You shoulda got more."

At one point the court said that it didn't want to put us out of business. All they wanted was reasonable

190

co-operation in the way of taking on members of the seven unions.

The court would make some concessions. We wouldn't have to take on a full crew. Just two or three stagehands, and they could be alternated (so they wouldn't know what to do between acts), a ticket-taker, a wardrobe mistress and, of course, a press-agent.

I kept on doing the wrong things. I told them that the books indicated that we grossed six thousand dollars in the current year and had spent just a little more. The entire gross divided by the more than fifty perform-ances indicated an average of a little more than one hundred dollars per performance. If they cared to di-vide that among seven unions including actors, it wouldn't be worth their while. And I added, injudi-ciously, that we wouldn't pay stagehands unless we could pay actors. We liked all unions and played no favorites.

Rather, I was thinking of stagehands who in the best days of the theatre, between overtime and extra-cur-ricular activity in scenic studios, were getting a pay check of about three hundred dollars a week—fifty dollars a day—and I could make up a long list of good actors who were not getting fifty dollars a month.

If we divided that paltry hundred dollars between the innumerable representatives of seven unions, there wouldn't be any money for the rent or the telephone or promotion and we'd be out of business.

The discussion narrowed down to "what could we offer?" I thought we couldn't risk offering more than ten per cent of our gross to something which was head-ing toward a "shakedown" (another word the court

191

ruled out), but that we could offer that to their charities, as that would fall within our charter. The reaction to that offer, I quote from the letter which Mr. Walter Graeza (I'm sure unwillingly) wrote in summary of our proceedings. It reads: "The members of the committee were of the definite opinion that your proposal 'to offer 10% of each production' and your further estimate based on your figures of last year that 'this amount would be about $150.00 per production' could not begin to meet even the most lenient concessions possible."

When we left the hearing chamber, Mr. Weisenbach, who hadn't said a word, pointed out some of my basic errors. He said, first, that they didn't believe we weren't making money. We were putting on shows, weren't we? Then we were making money, because nobody in New York puts on shows if they weren't making money. When they stopped making money, they closed.

I thought rather glumly as I went back to 57th Street that I had written a tremendous outpouring of words editorially in the interests of organized labor, and had preached the encyclicals on collective bargaining for a long time to be branded as a "scab" by my august judges. You learn with age. But we'll keep on preaching and writing on the encyclicals, if for no other end than to save the souls and rectify the minds of the children of unionists who are at the mercy of such shortsighted leaders. The men who gave the Doctor the scenery to open Catholic University's drama school were being taken in by a few, who for money which wasn't there carried on this ridiculous unjust persecution of New York's struggling Catholic theatre.

XVI: AMATEUR STANDING

THE SEASON OF 1943-44, OR THE YEAR 1 A.B. (AFTER blacklisting), was the year of surprises. It was also an experience which jolted the theory that professionals are always better than amateurs. Two of our three authors submitted first plays. They boasted no earlier experience with this difficult form of writing. And we began with non-Equity actors, fearing that union members, however enthusiastic they might be to appear with us, would jeopardize their livelihood. With such unpropitious material, we didn't do badly at all.

Father Gerard Magella Murray, an assistant in the Brooklyn Diocese, was asked to whip up a play for Cathedral College. This meant an all-male cast with accent on youth. Uninhibited by the rules and regulations which weigh down old craftsmen, Father Murray did just that. He took the story of a spy landing at the other end of his diocese, which actually happened but which is still implausible for theatre, wrapped it around eight very average orphans, and found it involving three or four teaching Brothers. It was these who began to grow and, when one of them, who always talked to his guardian angel, saw that heavenly messenger and heard him talking back, the author had a charming fantasy with just the quality that Blackfriars wanted.

But Blackfriars didn't know what it wanted after the confusing reception its offerings got the year before;

Blackfriars had never heard of *Career Angel;* and it never occurred to Father Murray that anybody but Cathedral College might be remotely interested.

The young lady who typed the script for him learned that particular craft from typing for play-agent Mary Prichett. Apparently she read as she typed, because she brought it to Miss Prichett, who took it on and, presumably, tried to interest producers in it. Nothing happened so she brought it to us.

We liked it immensely personally, but that indicated exactly nothing. We had liked plays before which were picked to pieces for the thesis they contained or the production or something. This thesis would be no more acceptable than *Tinker's Dam,* and production standards should fall because we were turning from predominantly Equity companies to acknowledge amateurs. We'd be properly fried for this one with its implausible spy-landing—but the flag was up and the rent was due, and we couldn't quit now. Failure would please too many people.

Obviously, this is a build-up for a success story. Well, that's the way it happened. The Doctor held the fort on opening night because I was making a little speech at the Morgan Fraternity, and if any of my readers remember the episode, I was at the lowest ebb of hope in Blackfriars history. The burden of my story was that if they came to our theatre, they'd probably like the play in spite of what the press would do to it.

Just a quote or two, not to boast, but to prove how wrong we could be. Burton Rascoe of the *World-Telegram* wrote: "Hold everything ! . . . I feel as excited as Johnny Philliber was in Mr. Sycamore when he was

194

trying to tell the earthbound scoffers that he had just seen a postman turn into a tree . . . . Believe it or not, one of the wittiest, most intellectually satisfying, most refreshing comedies that has been produced in New York in years and years is to be seen at the Blackfriars' Theatre . . . . If *The Naked Genius* is worth the $350,000 which Hollywood paid for it, this play is worth more money than the national debt."

Although all didn't share Mr. Rascoe's emotional lift, if was a completely good press—the only slightly chilling breath being blown by the New York *Times*.

Of course, there was the regular allotment of snags. Just before we opened we had an unusual letter from Mr. Moss. I say unusual, because we have a collection of heart-warming notes from his office, all of which read as follows: "Dear Sir or Sirs: Please call at this office on ————, at ————, regarding the operation of your theatre. Please note that this letter is sent you in lieu of a summons, and that failure to respond will be treated in the same way as failure to appear upon personal service of a summons."

I'd take my accustomed place with the inn-keepers, whose customers were a bit noisy, the news-stand operators, whose debris littered the streets, the tin-cup holders, whose blindness was in question, and in the midst of high and hectic activity I'd discover that someone in the endless parade of inspectors took a poor view of our physical equipment and put it in his report.

After a while the Commissioner and I worked out a sort of versicle and response technique. He would point out the window dramatically toward "The Tombs" and say, "If anything happens in your theatre, you and I will spend a few years over there." After I got to know that he was really for us and that our difficulties could be adjusted, I'd reply demurely, "Well you at least will be in good company."

We were always adjusting something to comply with new inspectors' knowledge of laws that older inspectors hadn't bothered about. We made four sets of "Exit" signs for twenty-six doors. I don't mean to imply that twenty-six doors open from our minikin auditorium to the fresh air of outdoors. Obviously, there wouldn't be room for a stage if such were the case. But backstage mazes are a little involved, and if any one chose to leave in a hurry by that route (for what reason I can't imagine), he could total up, if his haste weren't pressing, twenty-six doors.

We began by painting "Exit" over them. Although it is Latin, Shakespeare's use of the word has conventionalized it sufficiently for New York, and we merely adopted it as a precautionary aid to our customers. But the inspectors said it had to be painted on glass with a lighted bulb shining through. So we made twenty-six glass boxes and painted nice bright red letters on the frosted faces. The inspectors said it was an admirable job, but we had to have white letters on a red glass background. I don't remember whether it was another inspection or part of the same, but we were told also that our nice letters were six inches high and they had to be eight inches high. As they stand today, they could be seen from end to end of Madison Square Garden (no doubt the object of the regulation) and we can't get closer to a blackout onstage than Times Square. We thought this would be the end, but the inspectors (who really earn their money) told us we had to number them (this time we asked the size and color of the numerals) and print their numbers on a chart on the programmes.

There are more things to a theatre than Exit lights, but I pick that little detail as a symbol to demonstrate all the unintentional trouble we managed to give Mr. Moss.

The unusual letter from the Commissioner was dated October 22, 1943. The first paragraph had a refreshing directness about it, to which we were becoming accustomed. It read: "It is necessary to suspend the theatrical license of the Blackfriars' Guild for the reason that no approval reports have as yet been received from the Department of Housing and Buildings and the Fire Department."

Back to the old beat at the Municipal Building, I met the new elevator boys, watched the leaves change in City Hall Park and talked to the new crop of pigeons.

We finally got the license restored, and tried to get a reduction for the period in which it was revoked, but it seems to be an annual affair like a church-pew and you pay a flat rate whether you use it or not.

While *Career Angel* was romping through with its non-Equity cast, one of the members was offered a commercial job. His daytime rehearsals—the normal procedure—would not interfere with our production. But since he had to join Equity, he would have to withdraw from our cast.

Father Murray was put on the merry-go-round by a half dozen producers and movie organizations. They sniffed success in the air, and whether they knew or cared what the play was about—the critics had approved—the climax came with a four-column head over a feature article in the New York *World-Telegram*. It actually read: "PLAYWRIGHT-PRIEST WON'T FORSAKE PARISH."

Broadway must have been very happy at that, secure in that knowledge that the vast departments of the far-flung Church could go back to work after weeks of breathless uncertainty. Father Murray would not repudiate the priesthood with its eternally indelible stamp, even to write plays for Broadway and Hollywood which vaguely reminded critics of Noel Coward.

The gap between Broadway thinking and Blackfriar thinking is vaster than meets the eye. Many of our own, knowing nothing else, insist on judging us according to Broadway standards, which will never serve as our guides as long as we retain our basic sanity.

Our next offering was written not by a playwright casting about for a subject, but by a priest who was burning with something to say and who chose the dramatic form through which to say it. The fact that Father Thomas M. McGlynn, O.P., was pastor of a tiny parish in Amite, Louisiana, might indicate a success story, but that would be over-simplification. The son of the late Frank McGlynn, who had attained fame in the title role of Drinkwater's *Abraham Lincoln,* and grand-nephew of the famous Reverend Doctor Mc-Glynn, another priest who created a furore in the days of Henry George, Father McGlynn had attained international acclaim as a sculptor.

Assigned to Chicago, he became interested in what many people like to call the "Negro problem," partially because of devotion to Blessed Martin de Porres, which grew out of a statue he had made of that saintly Peruvian mulatto. He founded and for three years directed a social settlement for Negroes dedicated to Blessed Martin, and during those years became increasingly incensed at the conditions to which his new charges were being subjected. So he wrote a play about it, with perhaps no more right to turn dramatist than comes from a thorough knowledge of the problem and an urge to tell it to the world.

Subsequently, Father McGlynn has made a statue of Our Lady of Fatima, under the direction of Lucy, one of the children who saw the apparition, and has written a book of his experiences and the things he learned in Portugal, called *Vision of Fatima*. I can't quarrel with his choice of subjects, since I have followed his path in writing about both Fatima and Blessed Martin.

In the brief Christmas holidays, I went to Amite, where he was viewing the situation from the Southern side and putting his script into shape. The Doctor and I had thought the script good Blackfriar material, since it tackled a social problem unequivocally, but the pastor-sculptor needed a little prodding to meet our deadline.

The play was a switch on the situation as we know it in Northern cities. The Negroes were rich and powerful with a long tradition of owning the world behind them. The whites were an underprivileged minority, barred from decent homes by restrictive covenants, barred from good schools and good jobs. It was that simple.

199

Before the curtain (both in time and place), a Negro stepped out and made a plea for justice for the down-trodden Caucasians, who were called "Caukeys." Eight or ten of the Negroes in the cast had filtered out into the audience, both up and downstairs (unnoticed in spite of our Exit signs) when the lights went down, and they put up the usual howl. "They let property run down." "They don't wanna work." "But they have the cutest little caukey babies." "Keep 'em in their place." It was a shock to the audience, as people whom they had not noticed materialized beside them and shouted the speaker off the stage.

The trick couldn't hold up for hours. It took the audience three or four minutes to realize that it was a switch, and then the emotional impact of *Caukey* (for that was the name of the play) subsided. Author and producers merely wanted audiences to rid their minds of emotionally toned prejudices and to put themselves in the position of others. It worked and was, from our point of view, a very satisfying production.

The press definitely failed to present a united front. This isn't a complaint. Every man is entitled to his opinion. But it offers a starting point to indicate something of the problem we had to solve. It crystallized some of the things I've hinted at or set forth as generalities before—the ideological backgrounds of individual critics, the policies of certain newspapers, the flexibility of standards, and the general confusion.

We expected some bafflement over *Career Angel*. Many reviewers confused the teaching brothers with priests, and many more, when they dipped into theology, must have confused Father Murray ⎮as they would have likewise confused St. Thomas Aquinas. But this was grist for everybody's mill. This was the great American "Negro problem." And it's fun to sort out some of the reactions.

Coleman (*Mirror*), Rascoe (*World-Telegram*), Francis (*Eagle* and later *Billboard*), the late Burns Mⱡantle (*News*), Wilella Waldorf (*Post*) and a few others understood what we were trying to do and praised or blamed on precisely those terms.

A great middle section, including in this case Barnes (*Herald Tribune*), Pollock (*Eagle*), Field (*Newark News*), Freedley (*Telegraph*), *The Amsterdam News, Cue* and, insofⱡar as I could ascertain, Garland (*Journal-American*), thought the thesis good, but the play—and in some cases, the acting—weak.

Mr. Nichols of the *Times* was not impressed by "the Rev. Mr. McGlynn's play" any more than he had been impressed by "the Rev. Mr. Murray's." I must run through the files and see if the *Times* carried any good stories about "the Rev. Mr. Duffy," chaplain of the Fighting Sixty-Ninth in the first World War.

He sums up his case by saying, "The difficulty is that [the author] settles no problems." I'm afraid that's true. As a result of *Caukey,* the Negroes in Chicago or Harlem or Detroit or Philadelphia haven't suddenly had restrictive covenants lifted. But that's hardly what the author set out to achieve. If legislation, welfare workers, missionaries, and the understandable ambition of a great Negro minority in this country have settled so few problems since the Emancipation Proclamation, it is not surprising that this play hasn't settled them. It did offer a jolt to prejudice and it did set up the only pattern by which they can be solved. But some of our reviewers demand more of us than we promise to give.

The conclusion of the review was reminiscent of the tag line in a Providence review of *The Return of the Vagabond,* the last offering of Providence's favorson—the late George M. Cohan. That critic said in conclusion: "the sound effects deserved better support." Our reviewer in, I presume, a relenting mood and hoping to praise something, said, "As is the custom up on Fifty-seventh Street, the physical production is good, Thomas Fabian's settings being the best part of the evening."

But, if the assigned reviewers from the *Times* continued to care little for what we were doing, we received no such condescension from the drama editorial department. Mr. Sam Zolotov and his associates were always generous with space and always accurate.

Mr. Kronenberger took up some cudgels—and blunt they were—in the columns of *PM*. When I was a student in the house of theology, some of our professors dictated Latin much faster than I could write it down, so along with the others, I developed a code or a crude shorthand system. PM stood for "*peccatum mortale.*" It's hard to shake old associations.

Yet, Mr. K. admitted that the device was "undoubtedly startling. But it is not a wise device. The Negro problem is much too serious to play tricks with, no matter with what good intentions." That sort of jungle prose might deceive people for a brief moment. The "Negro problem" is a set of attitudes and reactions of millions of people. It is like the World War or the battle of the angels. Nobody could play tricks with it. A writer discussing it might say to you: "Suppose the roles were reversed?" That's what this author did.

Another *PM* statement reads: "Furthermore, if white people lack the humanity and decency to be moved by facts, they will hardly be moved by fantasy." If the author of that fantastic statement spent three years in Father McGlynn's settlement house in Chicago, listening to the words which went into the play, being said over and over again in their original settings, he might bow before "facts."

But the best is yet to come. "Beyond that, *Caukey* reveals an attitude that, however, sympathetic, is decidedly unprogressive. The hero is urged to show patience rather than anger, and to remember that it is 'what God thinks of us' that counts. The Negro needs much more militant championing than that." Somehow or other, I prefer our "unprogressive attitude" to the implicit inciting of race riots.

The conservatives, as well as the liberals (whatever those words mean) differed with us, too, and the most satisfying condemnation we came across was in editorial form in the Tampa, Florida, *Sunday Tribune*. A few quotes will be sufficient. Under the title "An offensive play," it said: "The play probably was inspired by a sketch which Westbrook Pegler wrote. . . in which the position of the races was reversed. . . . In

203

the play which, strange to say, was written by a priest, Father McGlynn, the same reversal is portrayed. . . . The reaction to the play by audiences and critics has been one of shocked revulsion. . . . Responsibility for the play rests upon Father McGlynn, the Blackfriars Guild and the American Negro Theater. They could be at better business."

A number of comments come to mind on reading that little item, but to add anything might be insulting to the readers' intelligence.

Westbrook Pegler did take the occasion to tell about his earlier use of the device. He wound up with: "Well, so what? Well, so I know what, but it wouldn't do any good to say what because the solution has been there all the time in a building with a cross on the spire where Father McGlynn works, but neither side is sufficiently civilized to give it a try."

Mr. Pegler's four-line summary of *Caukey* got the plot a little mixed up and Miss Waldorf took him to task on the subject for inaccurate and long-range reporting. In straightening him out, Miss Waldorf got the plot a little balled up herself. Everybody was getting into the act. We didn't mind. She at least used the word Blackfriars'.

Some of the critics of the middle or moderate view—those who were neither enthusiastically for us or against us, but who came to do a reporting job—said that the acting was uneven. That's very true and truth we can never resent. They did not say—perhaps because they did not know or perhaps they felt it had no place in a review—that it was uneven because we were blacklisted and could not use the very actors whom we had developed and who would have been happy to play for us.

But things happened as a result of the play—militant things, I think, although "what God thought of them" was considered important, too. The Catholic Interracial Council of New York met in our theatre on off nights, passing resolutions on legislation for a permanent Fair Employment Practice committee and the like. I'd be curious to know what plays in town since Uncle Tom's Cabin was played straight brought any tangible results.

The Catholic press was enthusiastic—but there's no point in repeating that. Naturally, it knew what we were doing and some of the obstacles we were struggling against. So it helped willingly and effectively.

Lest I do an injustice to author, cast, critics in general and Blackfriars, I must say that most of the reactions were favorable. Just as a sample, I'd like to quote from the *World-Telegram* a few words from Burton Rascoe: "Last night the Blackfriars came forth with a play called *Caukey,* a soul wrenching, hard hitting, searingly sardonic and ironical arraignment of race prejudice, written with great skill and emotional drive. . . . Although at some points, *Caukey* was faultily directed and inexpertly played, it nearly tore my heart out, so poignant is the drama of it, which, in anguish and in sorrow, points a severely accusing finger at me and at you, and you and you!"

It was a gratifying press and it ran an interesting gamut. Many took us to task on the writing or the acting or general production, and to that we can only say, "We'll try to do better next time." The ban on experienced actors scares experienced writers away —but we knew they'd be back because it wasn't an inexperienced press. Those who condemned us on thesis were not likely to be converted by anything we said. If the teachings of Christ as manifested throughout of the world down the ages hadn't gotten through to them, they're not going to succumb to an enforced "amateur" play at Blackfriars.

The enthusiasm engendered by *Caukey* (and by *Career Angel*) gave us a new lease of hope. We were now being talked about from Tampa to Kansas City. Our friends were growing in numbers and becoming increasingly articulate. A large section of the press was openly pulling for us, and most of the dissenters were progressively showing their hands. It looked as though we would weather the attacks.

As a means of garnering a few honest dollars and spreading our theses while the theatre was dark, although the rent was going on, we ventured on a lecture series. That was a mistake, so I'll dismiss it briefly, not because of instinctive escapism from unpleasant memories, but because there isn't much to say about it.

You can pack them in to lectures in any city of 5,000 or better in the country, but New York is something else again. There you have to get the most sensation-causing names of the week. The denizens of the little island have so many things to choose from that they get a little confused and settle the matter by staying home and twirling the radio dial. That's quite all right—but, again, nobody told us. We learned everything the hard way. In the middle of the series, we found we were about six hundrd dollars in the red and called off the remainder with the usual difficulties. They were pretty good talks, too.

Career Angel's late start (due to our troubles) and its long run (due to our surprising success) pushed the season back, so this year we did three instead of the customary four productions. The last, *Earth Journey* by Sheldon Davis, got a cool reception from press and audiences—not hostile, just indifferent—but we enjoyed it immensely.

It was a Chinese fantasy or an American's idea of a Chinese fantasy, in which an idol was brought to life by a princess and, rather than kill her father, allowed himself to be changed back to an idol. Just that—a very colorful fairy story.

Maybe we just like fairy stories once in a while. Maybe we didn't know enough about the Chinese theatre to know what violence we were doing it, because some of the erudite critics said that we tended toward burlesque here and there. But we tried to do what the author told us and I'm sure he knew something about the Chinese theatre. A Chinese director told us we had caught everything but the precise formalism of motion and, of course, the tones, but he could have been practicing his inevitable politeness. All I know is that we thought we had a delightful show and many others did, too—but more perhaps yawned and went on their diverse ways. I'm afraid I'm slowly building myself up as an infallible judge—in reverse. When we're smug, they say "No." When we're scared, they force us to extend the run.

Since we used quotes from the press to indicate acceptance in the two previous offerings, we'll throw in a few here to indicate our non-acceptance. That's fair and we offer no protest in the process.

Variety called it "a little too arch for Broadway"; Rascoe (*World Telegram*) slipped out of the Amen corner, describing it as "mildly interesting as a novelty with a very limited appeal"; Freedley (*Telegraph*) thought it "good for unsophisticated audiences"; Pollock (*Brooklyn Eagle*) said it was "a little too quaint and poetical for these rough and robust days"; Gurnsey (*Herald Tribune*) concluded with the disarming sentence, "It would have been better to let well enough alone." That last sentence out of context sounds much worse than (I think) it was intended. He had been discussing the strangeness of the Chinese theatre to American audiences and suggesting that we play it in a more straight-forward fashion. The admonition was directed to our having so much fun with it. And for all I know they may be right.

Women's Wear called it "well written and capably performed by a worthy cast. . . . A real liking for the Chinese theatre is like eating olives—it is an acquired taste." Coleman (*Mirror*) said "it is very much worth the doing by an experimental theatre such as the Blackfriars, but it is not for Broadway." But, being an understanding person, he correctly added, "And probably wasn't penned with an eye to the Main Stem parade."

Nichols (*Times*), in the briefest review of all, began by saying, "Since the Blackfriars' Guild prefers never to rest, it went on last night to give its third drama

208

of the current season." That's pretty accurate, except for the word "prefer." We'd love to have rested at this point, but something had to pay the rent for the summer. However, a reviewer isn't expected to know that.

"For Broadway purposes," the reviewer said, "it is perhaps a little talky, although the first night audience in the temple on Fifty-seventh Street seemed to like it." And he concluded with the gentle admotion, "But 'Earth Journey' may be just a shade earthbound for the good of the soul."

Garland (*Journal American*) was baffled. He said so. "But 'Earth Journey' baffles me. It baffled me last night as it went on and on and on. It baffles me now, when I'm doing my level best to tell you about it. And I'm certain it'll continue to baffle me, when later on today, I read the piece that I have written. At its opening in the Blackfriars' charming little walk-up playhouse, I stayed on to the very end. What's more I neither drooped nor drowsed as I was doing so. Well, then, maybe only for a second."

I can think of nothing more to say than we who were connected with the production had a marvelous time and Mr. Nichols was right in assuming that the audiences enjoyed it. They did.

Of course that's not a universal statement. Since we weren't equipped to explain our entire story, we took a few by surprise. They came to a "Catholic theatre," expecting a *Career Angel*. They fell consciously or otherwise into the ecclesiocentric school. They thought we were very pagan or very frivolous to do a fairy story at the end of a hard year. A priest

209

who brought such a group still taunts me by quoting the opening words of narrator Ian McLaren's repeated speeches—"I bow."

A gloomy postscript to our season came with the massacre of *Career Angel* when it opened commercially downtown. I'm sure you'd expect merely murder or homicide when applied to an individual and much less than death when applied to an immortal spirit. "Massacre" implies a general slaughter. But, so many things were done to the production—and death came in so many forms—that we'll let the word stand.

The word "downtown" may need some explanation, too, since we're off on a word-study digression. It used to be a geographical term when we were physically outside the unwalled town of Broadway. But with the war, many of the dark houses were reopened and at this point legitimate theatres were operating as far north as Columbus Circle. So the imaginary walls now encompassed us, but we kept using the word "off Broadway" to represent a state of mind and it was directed against commercials who spent fifty times what we did and who on that basis deserved a much better product.

Nonetheless, to be "off Broadway" was equivalent to not existing at all in the minds of some. One of our loyal supporters made a little speech at a tea in Westchester. He outlined to the assembled Catholic ladies the usefulness of a theoretical theatre which could produce the plays we want and operate without subsidy. They were most enthusiastic and promised complete support if such could come to pass. Then he told them it was an actuality and was operating on Fifty-seventh Street. The spokesman for the gathering is reported to have said "Fifty-seventh Street! Why that's like going into the country. Isn't it a pity it's so inaccessible."

Those good ladies were accustomed to driving to the station in their restricted village, then riding some twenty-five miles on the train. From Grand Central Station they took a cab west and up to Fifty-second Street—I'm sure many of them were subscribers to the Theatre Guild. The Guild Theatre is on 52nd Street, just off Eighth. The Blackfriars is on 57th Street, just off Eighth. The distance between them is five short blocks. The extra taxi tariff is ten cents. But we were out in the country. You see, it is a state of mind, and in that state of mind we were definitely out in the country.

Father Murray's script had defects in our production. We agreed with practically all the critics, professional and otherwise, that the spy-plot dated it and injected a melodramatic note in a very spiritual whimsy. But the spy-plot was retained and much of the rest was made slangier and gagged up with even more topical puns. The critics agreed that it had heavy-handed doctoring. I'm sure Father Murray was harassed and high-pressured into a kind of writing which seemed foreign to him.

The downtown cast—which was naturally much more experienced—didn't come over very well. To begin with, the show was paced almost for farce. The gentle chuckles with which it originally abounded—the sort that Barry Fitzgerald called forth in *Going My Way*—weren't enough for the new producers.

You could almost see the windup as a laugh was being built and hear the crack of the bat. It wasn't just funny enough for that type of direction. It was never meant to be.

The eight or nine professional boys who were the orphans downtown were too precise in their actions to be true. They would have outwitted teachers anywhere. So they became, to me at least, unbelievable. Our lads were recruited in large measure from Cardinal Hayes High School and they were human enough to give the teachers a fifty-fifty chance of catching up with them. Director Gurney asked me why they always made the same gestures—hands coming out, palms upward, as though they were asking for a handout. I told him they were studying to be priests or politicians—and to go back to his directing without asking too many questions.

It is quite a fatal mistake to take a play which has been presented with understanding care by experimentalists and throw it on Broadway completely doctored up for gags and laughs. *Career Angel* could have been a minor hit, because enough theatre-goers have good taste and have been waiting a long time for a comedy of its potentialities.

Thus the 1943-44 season came to an end. One episode comes to mind, but I can't date it. The Doctor was acting as host in the lobby one night, beaming at the paid customers and being civil to the dead-heads. But this night he had something on his mind. Some producer was coming with an eye to taking the then current production downtown and the Doctor was waiting for him. In this preoccupation he was introduced to the new Irish Consul for New York. With an eye on the entrance, he missed the newcomer's title and heard only that he was just over from Ireland.

After a pause, the Doctor focused on his problem and realized he should be saying something. So he did. "You're just over from Ireland?"

"Yes, Father," said the Consul. "I arrived three days ago."

Another pause and another glance to the entrance. Then the Doctor's better nature came to the fore and he realized he ought to do something for one of our own, so he said, "Have you got a job?"

I've always enjoyed the Consul's reply in view of the tense situation which followed concerning Irish bases. It was simply, "I think I have a job."

XVII: ACTORS AND PEOPLE

THE 1944-45 SEASON WAS A BIT THIN IN QUALITY. I'll probably manage to modify that statement for the sake of writers and actors who did good jobs—and in the interest of truth. But I'm inclined to agree with the critics. They were on home ground when they dismissed some of our offerings—or certain aspects of these—on merits of theatre. They weren't going after a thesis. So they should be listened to.

I'm not going to offer excuses, either, because my mother warned me as a child never to put on a poor mouth. But lest you have been led to believe that the Doctor and I were able to give much time to this venture, I must in justice correct that notion. Our routine assignments which had nothing to do with the theatre called for seven days a week and our free evenings for Blackfriars were becoming less consecutive.

When we did get together on theatre, we had more departments to handle than any downtown producer. That's a simple matter of union practice. The legitimate producer is permitted by those he employs to choose a script, raise the money, pick a director and hire a theatre. He may share in a few other activities. Under the Minimum Basic Agreement Contract, he may choose a cast, but the author can override any choice in that. The producer may pick a press

214

agent, but from a limited number and usually at a set minimum salary. He may seek a stage designer from among a limited number of union members. He may call in a small number of scenic builders and choose the lowest bidder. He has no choice as to the number of stagehands or musicians and must not dare suggest the name of anyone in particular. His basic privilege is to lose whatever money he himself put into the show.

We were quite free from such restrictions. We were blacklisted. We were out in the country. We could—and had to—do everything with a view to paying the rent at least.

First, we read scripts—a lot of them. The best agents weren't bringing us their best plays, because the best agents were looking for ten per cent, and ten per cent of nothing wouldn't keep the best agents in the manner to which they had been accustomed. We got the scripts that the agents couldn't sell or, more often, that the agents wouldn't take. If sometimes we think our offerings are good, it is by comparison with the other thousands we have waded through.

Then, if we found one with a good idea or a good second act or a good something, we often plunged into the doctoring process. Sometimes we didn't have to touch them. Other times the author was surprised at the evolution—for better or worse, he usually didn't say.

Next, we laid out the sort of set the tiny stage would take. You couldn't open a downstage door off because it would bump into the continuation of the balcony. If

215

you're thinking, "Who ever opened a door off?" let me add you couldn't too safely open it on, because the actors would hit their heads on the continuation of the same balcony and knock themselves out. You couldn't fly in the back of the stage because of the old concert shell, and you couldn't fly in the front because the light pipes were in the way. For those who aren't up in the jargon, "fly" means to lift scenery on lines. (In the strict meaning of the word, I doubt if you could fly either.)

With enough restrictions to scare any scenic designer away, we did a kind of group job of designing a set. In later years, we've put this little task in the hands of more qualified individuals, but in the old days we all took a shot at it. Then two or three of our old standbys built and painted and lit it.

We called in those who had registered recently and held auditions. Agents didn't send us the best in their stables for the same reasons they didn't send us the best scripts. Sometimes this business of casting took a long time, because we tried to give everybody a hearing.

If it was a costume play we had somebody make the costumes. Then we trained a few of those who came in for technical work to run the show.

I know much less about promotion than production, because the Doctor always took care of the former, proud in the fact that he made the money while I spent it. But he built up a list of organizations and individuals over the years, through thousands and thousands of man-hours of typing letters and cards on the part of volunteers. He is not always amused

216

when brash souls ask to borrow his mailing list for a few days.

If you can think of anything else that goes with running a theatre, we do that, too.

We weren't going to risk any more fairy tales for a long time because our own pleasure in doing them was not reflected in box-office reaction. We didn't have any scripts as controversial as *Caukey* nor as bright as *Career Angel* and we were anxious to please. Give them what they seem to like downtown, we said, preserving our principles. Since we were grinding out four shows a year (and I know no other producer who was approaching that schedule year after year), it wouldn't hurt to test reactions on unadulterated comedy with no particular angles.

A script had come in—or rather a bale of paper had come in which might be cut to script length—which met these qualifications. It was a major opus by Katherine Laure, purported to be based on a short story of the author's. If everything in the script was contained in the short story, one would have to take a month to read one of her full-length novels.

Due to my involved appointed tasks, Mr. Gurney cut and pieced until he had something reminiscent of current family radio shows or continuous comic-strip families. Oh, he added nothing. It was all Miss Laure's and when he was finished we still had material for some more plays.

The voice of the departments spoke first as usual and told us that we must secure a Public Assembly License. This was brought about by the tragic Cocoanut Grove fire in Boston. This time our license was held up because the inspection "revealed" that we hadn't hung the required capacity sign in a conspicuous place. That little item, looking like a mural in our tiny theatre, had been hanging in such a conspicuous place for weeks that is was no wonder the the inspector couldn't see it. He probably took it for a wall. But, after an exchange of letters, all was forgiven on both sides and we went into auditions.

But quietly—very quietly—audiences were increasing in numbers and familiar faces were coming back. They were happy about coming back, too. We could tell that. We managed to stick close enough to the work to feel the pulse. The clergy accepted the idea, too, and brought theatre parties. It may seem strange at first glance to note that the biggest response at first came from Brooklyn and northern New Jersey. But Manhattan was coming along very well. That isn't really strange, for Manhattanites—priests and people—feel that they have everything in the world on their island and that anything new has to prove itself. We were meeting that test, too.

Don't George, which is what we called the new package, was all right for the customers and, at the risk of repetition, may I say that customers pay the rent. The press, though hardly knocked on its collective ear, said: "Witty and refreshing," "has possibilities—full of chuckles and not a few guffaws," "good little theatre," "a merry evening."

The Cinderella touch came when the author arrived. It was her first visit to New York. I'm sure that a lot of people in far-flung parts of the world never see New York and suffer little loss as a con-

218

sequence, and perhaps a lot of quiet people in Phila-
dephia don't get there either. But when one writes
hard-hitting dialogue that holds thousands and keeps
them laughing, when one amuses New York critics,
and when that one lives in Philadelphia, people just
assume that he or she is practically a commuter. It's
a wrong assumption—and most of our experience indicates that the American theatre need not be confined to a dozen blocks. It was a real pleasure to watch
this talented young lady listening to her sprightly
lines come bouncing back to her. She went back to
the City of Friends that night or early the next morning and probably doesn't miss New York a bit.

Our next author was the veteran playwright
Courtenay Savage. Of less importance than his Broadway plays to us was the fact that he was an old and
cherished friend. Since the Doctor and I met him,
Courtenay had been trying to find a useful place in
his readjusted world. A convert to Catholicism, he
tried special army assignments and a long trick working for the National Catholic Community Services.
Illness dogged him and with bandaged hands and
dimming eyes he wrote a couple of scripts for us. A
few years later, death came suddenly while he was
helping our servicemen in Rome.

This play, *Home Is the Hero,* dealt with the returning serviceman who found his wife making more
than he could hope to start earning and the consequent
rift in the family. It was a theme that Mr. Savage
knew well from his war work. Most of the reviewers
thought it slow; insisted that *the* play on this important problem was yet to be written. Kelcey Allen of

Women's Wear caught the point in our opinion, when he said, "Mr. Savage doesn't try to solve the problem."

But everybody was happy about the cast and Virginia Dwyer got so many interviews that we realized the play was getting less critical attention than its people.

That we were doing things for actors rather amazed us over the years—not because we weren't happy to, but because at the beginning we simply hadn't thought about it. We set out to produce a certain type of script—or many types of scripts circumscribed by definite principles (which St. Thomas Aquinas might think well of) and we merely hoped to find actors to appear in them. But, because of the lack of experimental houses in New York and the decline in stock, the agents began to drop in. In our auditions we did a lot of seeding, usually with the current play in mind, so we saved the agents tedious work. People got jobs in the process and one thing which actors tell other actors is that they got a job. So the word spread.

Our active registration list is in the thousands and we're not too happy about it. From one point of view we're not too sad about it either, but it has become a responsibility. It really isn't a responsibility in strict justice, but we like people, so it worries us. That's supposed to be a little unique in theatre, too—another indication that we don't know the business very well.

We could always use a few more elderly character actors because they don't have to be seen. They've been seen for so long that the agents have made up their minds as to whether they're good or bad. But three or four hundred ingenues come into the office every year and, with four shows, we can present to the public only eight or ten a year. That's not quite fair, because many of them deserve a chance.

They come from drama schools, they come from Hollywood with movie contracts in their hands, having been told to do East and get experience, they come from parish halls—and many of them, without being dramatic, convey the idea that if they don't get a role they'll go back home and live blighted, frustrated lives. That's too bad, because it isn't always their fault that they weren't even seen. It's the lop-sided system which ignores a vast country and accepts the bottleneck of Broadway. There's no place for them to get started. We've run what has been perhaps the busiest experimental theatre in New York in years and we've been able to present just about five per cent of our applicants.

Instead of jealously guarding the field, we'd like to see more experimental theatres (if the plays weren't dangerous to humanity), but we haven't seen many prosper in spite of constant discussions and some substantial contributions. I'm trying to explain in a few hundred pages some of the difficulties, in case you feel like stepping into the breach.

When in auditions we get down to four or five for the young leads, it's always awkward to make the final decision, because it's going to hurt so many. We can be gay and witty about doing it, but the hurt is still there in their eyes. I'm afraid we'll never get quite tough enough for this business.

I'm reluctant to hazard the number of actors who got their start with Blackfriars' or even that of old-timers who made a come back on our stage, because so many other factors enter into the making of an actor that a single opportunity isn't the whole story. But scores have come back to see us again and again and they keep repeating that they got the break with us and are grateful. Many others who were practically plucked from their dressing rooms by agents have never come back to say anything. Not so many, come to think of it, but a few. We have no facilities for keeping records anyway, but twenty-one actors and technicians got jobs (including summer stock) from one of our recent long-run productions.

How we got off on this digression, I've quite forgotten at this point, but we might as well finish it up. Many of our actors don't believe in the things that we believe in—but, unlike a sizeable section of the commercial theatre in the days when it was popular to be a fellow traveler, they don't have to. We don't ask them what they believe in. Only one actor in the six hundred or so we've presented deliberately twisted lines to water down our thesis and get in a plug for the party. We thought it was a fluff the first time it happened, but when he repeated it with conviction we said flatly what every actor understands, "Stick to the script." It probably tore out his soul, but he went back to the original.

The registration blank which we ask actors to fill out out has space for name, address, phone, whether or not they belong to Equity (so we can warn them against the blacklisting), theatrical background, references, age height, coloring. And that's all.

I have been asked—and rather pointedly—by adherents to the ecclesiocentric school, "What are you doing in Catholic theatre with non-Catholic actors?"

My reply, and it's not a bit facetious, is, "What would we do without them?" I'll tell you now. We'd have been out of business the first year.

Some hundreds of pages ago I told you about dreaming of gathering a troupe of well-known actors, who might be anxious to devote their lives to doing a certain type of theatre. It was my own idea. It was also youthful dreaming—done twenty years ago. The people who propose it again—with zealous fire burning in their eyes—are indulging in youthful dreaming. The few older ones pose it differently. Their attack generally runs: "If I couldn't find an enthusiastic group of Catholic actors who were well qualified theatrically, I wouldn't venture such a project." Apparently, they haven't found such material, for they haven't done it.

The advantage of such an organization is that there would be basic agreement among its members as to the type of plays to be done, and the work could be intensified and aided by group prayer. But it will not happen by itself. It will take money, organization and time to sort out the proper candidates, maintain and train them. It may happen some time, but the sort of support it demands it not in sight.

The fact is that about ninety-nine per cent of the actors of all faiths and subsidiary convictions who come to us are anxious to be seen by good agents with the hope of a few good words thrown by a critic or two. The goal for which they are striving is success in the theatre. Many of them make a point to decry obscenity and profanity on the stage, because they are good and well-bred people. Their basic drive is one thing; their standards another.

The remaining one per cent of completely cause-minded actors would not adequately cast a single production, because they bring to the task varying degrees of acting ability. My critics on this score—I've gone over this many times, so this is not guesswork—insist that, if we set out to build on the cause-minded, we could have found a sufficient number in a city as large as this. Yes! You can do anything with a subsidy sufficiently large and enduring—perhaps. But without any money at all, when you hire a theatre on faith and pay for it through the box-office, you can't wait for a fortuitous series of events—presumably ideal—to fall into line.

Furthermore, we like our companies as they are. That may be experiential rather than theoretical, but it's true. Remember, the object of a theatre of ideas is to put the right sort of plays before audiences. The actor is a means to that end. The more skilled he is in technique, the better he serves that purpose. The object of the Catholic press is to publish sound ideas. It is not too important that the type-setters or newsboys be Catholics or Republicans or veterans. The labor problem—vitally important though it be—is not precisely the same one we're discussing.

By opening our ranks to all, we helped actors generally and helped ourselves immeasurably. It usually made for good performances. That pleased audiences and writers and meant a good reputation among the actors on whom we depended. We hadn't thought it through. We just flailed about to find casts in the early days when we had no organization, asked them if they could act, and did a little checking on that point. We never thought of asking them what they believed in. And that little system of regarding people as people first has paid off magnificently.

We may have performed a slight service also to a few of the young hopefuls who came to town and who listened to the operatives in some of the approved circles. Here they were told that it was smart to think with the fellow travelers, that it would help them get jobs and further their careers. They picked up the jargon of the organizers in an incredibly short time. I recall interviewing an eighteen-year-old girl from the southwest. Apropos of nothing at all, she looked at me intently and said, "What do you think of Franco and Spain?" That one really caught me off guard. I was thinking of the coming production and not about Spain at all. She had been instructed to think very seriously in a certain pattern about Spain if she wanted to get into the theatre. I'm sure her knowledge of that historically interesting country had been rather meagre until she arrived in New York. Since I didn't give Spain as much time as I gave the American theatre that day, I'm sure she went away convinced that I was dialectically incompetent and hardly aware of current theatre trends.

Another actor, who had a sound Catholic training, had listened to the double-talk for so long that one day, when I proposed doing a certain script, he asked: "Are you one of those reactionaries?" I asked him to define the word "reactionary" before demanding an answer. He hasn't as yet—but then it's only about seven years ago.

We had the vanity—the Doctor and I—to think that

we could make out as good a case for God, man and civilization as the subsidized could make out for Marx, Stalin and revolution, so we liked to have actors come to us. (They could at least talk, even if the blacklisting prevented them from acting.) Of course, we had a slight handicap. We couldn't give them paying jobs and our competitors could. That was because Catholics who refused to become aware of the problem thought that God had given us a theatre and that if we were more diligent and ingenious we could raise the money, and we were given to understand frequently, if implicitly, that we'd better get it from non-Catholics.

This is not a complaint. It is a report. It is a report which could be summarized by saying that by taking advantage of the basic drive of non-cause-minded actors—but people with ability, and a careful seeding of scripts, which didn't always please the press, we kept the flag up. We are not enthusiastic about listening to complaints of theorists who insist we should have done it in a very different fashion unless they either show us by accomplished facts that it can be done or provide the means we know it needs.

Simon's Wife was the Lenten offering. It was written by Reverend Francis D. Alwaise, O.P., who has since gone to his eternal reward. Although the press, by and large, called it mediocre writing, it had a good basic idea. When Christ called the Apostles, there is no record that He consulted the wishes of their wives, just as when He calls people to the religious life today He doesn't always get the enthusiastic support of their families.

In this play, Simon's wife was not pleased that her

226

husband dropped his nets and went off with the Galilean. But when she saw the events in Jerusalem at the time of the Crucifixion, her little problem takes on a new aspect. This is the salvation of the world. And when Simon, after his denial of his Master, comes home on the verge of despair, she builds him up to return to the task ahead of him—the task of leading the Apostles and Christ's Church. So well does she do it that when courage returns—courage which she pours into his ear —Simon rises and all but brushes her aside as he walks out to his world mission.

One actor reading for a part walked out on us saying, "It's about time that business was forgotten." It has been—in many places.

On the other hand, the columnist Dave Boone said, "The Blackfriars' Guild is doing in New York what the theatre should do every Lenten season all over the country. That's to produce a play about the greatest drama in the history of mankind, the gripping story leading up to the Crucifixion and Resurrection . . . . Here and there we have such plays, almost entirely amateur, but the theatre of America, should, as a matter of duty, get behind this holy season in a big way."

Much as we appreciate the plug, I don't think that the American theatre is likely to get behind the holy season in a big way, until some of the reasons behind the holy season penetrate the American theatre. Downtown—in the non-blacklisted theatres—the Crucifixion and Resurrection simply make for a period of bad box-office.

An error in judgment closed the season on an entirely harmless note. The piece was called *Slice It Thin* —and we sliced it a bit too thin. It was also called a farce with music. The trouble is that we who made the decisions needed a light inexpensive show to close the season—and by now you know why we needed it. But we listened to the music on one day and an enthusiastic reading (with much terrific laughter) on another, and thought each time that the missing parts might save it. Al Moritz and Lt. Edward N. Heghinian did it and so did we. The critics thought the same thing; the audiences laughed; we were not threatened with setting back civilization nor improperiety; and the rent was paid.

You could have expected more—but, as I implied, this was a year we didn't have much time to spend at Blackfriars.

But there was a bright note and I'd like to end the season on it, although it dragged for months and become an accomplishment in the spring. We had a law passed by the City of New York exempting us from requiring a license. Perhaps for Bocci Ball or a tavern we'd have to contribute something to Mr. Moss's office, but for a theatre according to our original charter we didn't have to pay. That was a wonderful feeling. It meant that our license wouldn't be suspended or revoked any more, because we didn't have one.

Of course, we didn't want one in the first place, and we explained fifty times that we were in the same category with many other organizations which were unlicensed, such as Masonic Temples, YMCA, YWCA, YMHA theatres, etc., but in New York it apparently doesn't make any difference what category you're in.

You have to have a law passed. That gives New York a very thick book of laws and that keeps a lot of experts in various departments busy reading all those laws and all that helps make New York a very big city. Being a big city, it can afford a lot more theatres than a small city, so we should be grateful.

We actually secured an amendment to Section 1, Title B, Article 1 of Chapter 32 of the Administrative Code of the City of New York, by adding to section B32-8.0 (there's that point 0 again) a new subsection to be subsection 11. And subsection 11 tells all and sundry who get that far that we don't need a license. No more mimeographed subpoenas to Mr. Moss's office which bind under pain of a life in The Tombs.

I went to City Hall with Jack Delaney, who was our legal advisor at the time. It seems we always had a different lawyer for each major problem, so diversified were we. Maybe it was because there were so many laws in New York that the lawyers divide them up. Maybe it has something to do with the fat fees we preferred to spread around evenly—a pair on the aisle on a bad night. Anyway, I met Mr. Delaney on a gusty day when even my friends, the pigeons, were keeping cover. We edged into the hearing room after a little reconnoitering and found a lot of people apparently trying to get laws passed. Sitting at the end of a long table, we heard a great deal of discussion which quite confused me, because when I go to a hearing (like the craft unions), I have come to expect to do all the talking.

Finally, my name was called. I arose and cleared my throat. Nobody who was talking before stopped—

in fact, I think a dozen or so more started—and I looked around for the anticipated silence. Jack plucked my sleeve and said, "Don't make a speech. Just answer questions. And don't mind if nobody else listens. You can write a book some day, but let's get this bill passed." So, at my monosyllabic worst I offered a few "Yeas" and "Nays" and we haven't had to buy a license since.

In my farewell to the License Department, where I had become a minor fixture, I did manage to say that since we were license-free, then licensed, then license-revoked, then license-restored with back assessments, all under the same prevailing conditions, they must have been wrong, three out of those four times. But they smiled, too, so nothing came of it.

Our thanks to Mr. Timone, Mr. Sharkey, the Mayor, our legal staff, and all who helped us achieve this long awaited triumph. We'll always cherish subsection 11 under .0.

XVIII: MIRRORS AND MIRACLES

THIS YEAR 1945 BROUGHT INTERESTING MATERIAL, a divided press—mostly on old lines—and, except for one production, enthusiastic audiences. It also brought me a new home with more time for the work, although with a little daily jaunt to get to it.

Our first play had a swarm of authors. So in accordance, with the wishes of the copyright holders, we announced the fact as follows: "*Seven Mirrors* is an experiment in social drama. Some of the scenes are factual; others are rather concretizations of feelings and tendencies gathered from the news and personal observation. These are focused on the brotherhood of man under the fatherhood of God. *Seven Mirrors* came into being as a college production on the stage of Immaculate Heart College in Los Angeles, where the following members of the classes in production under experienced professional guidance collaborated in its writing: Annabelle Crabbe, Fleurette Dillon, Lorraine Johnson, Diane Mellos, Patricia Murphy, Eulalia O'Sullivan, Antoinette Petrasich, Patricia Ronayne, Lorraine Sprafka, Frances Swain."

Although I had resolved never to write a program note again, how could one explain the work of ten authors and give the college credit without saying something? If we merely listed ten names, we'd get reviews on that fact alone. So I wrote the above, and it was a mistake. Most of the reviews dealt heavily with the above paragraph, stressing the "experiment in social drama" and the "professional guidance." Mr. Zolotow of the *Times*—drama editor and not critic—who found out things almost before they happened, announced that Emmet Lavery was the professional guide and that little item had its pros and cons in the reviews.

Perhaps I had better begin at the beginning. Mr. Lavery and Mr. Joe Rice supervised the students named above in the writing and production of an extremely interesting and provocative idea. Seven concepts of Our Lady speak as one in a choric prologue and epilogue and then introduce seven scenes—each in her own territory—indicating the influence of women in the world towards peace. That could be very flat, but some of the scenes were extremely arresting. Of course, we thought that those which came directly out of current events should be brought up to date, but knowing that Mr. Lavery was an exponent of the living newspaper technique, we foresaw no problems.

From a production viewpoint it was a challenge and a joy. Calling for a cast of fifty-seven, the challenge was hurled at our two pigeon-holes of dressing rooms. But we converted storerooms and corridors and met that one. The stage was a ramp built in the form of a huge tilted cross and the backgrounds were done with projected light through slides. That offered problems to what was left of our technical staff, because the war had made heavy demands in manpower. But by the same token, the cast was composed mostly of women and we were anxious to say for once that we had a lot of roles to offer.

Mr. Lavery not only admitted that he had a hand in the play but that he liked it just the way it was. He said he didn't mind rewriting for the movies, but beyond a certain point he didn't care to rewrite for the stage. We gently hinted that we'd be quite willing to take care of that matter if we could secure permission—but that was one instance in which our play-doctoring (no charge) department was put in its place. *Seven Mirrors* went on as written. The critics did as we expected.

As a production, it was big and impressive. Although slide projections were far from new in the theatre, the ones we had seen weren't particularly sharp, so we called on Ed Rutyna from Lowell (death of *Dymphna* and set of *Up the Rebels*) to come down week-ends and work out a sharper picture or eight sharp pictures. Bill Schoeller built the ramp. With black drapes and a few small props, this constituted the settings.

Dropping in the theatre one day, I came on the following internal drama. Bill was sawing and hammering away just in front of the stage. Ed Rutyna was adding a line to one of his pictures. With a single point of light, the perspective of the drawings is much distorted. Rutyna drew the line with a flourish and then doubted his perspective. So, without warning he turned on the lamp, put out all the other lights and sat in the back of the theatre to meditate on the results. It was apparently a last straw. Bill stomped back to me, falling over everything in the process and said, "How can I build anything if that Polack keeps putting out the lights?" I roused Rutyna from his reverie and told him that, since he now was an established artist, he ought to try two lines at a time. He agreed, but asked if I couldn't stop the Dutchman from hammering all day while he was trying to think. That little variation of a ceaseless series of events—is theatre.

The same Mr. Rutyna worked day and night during his limited weekends and bought himself a coffeepot so that, by brewing quarts of the black drug, he might keep awake, especially in the meditative moments when he was criticizing his work. One morning he dashed up to the office and said in a most aggrieved tone, "They used my coffeepot."

"What did they use it for?" said the management, not impressed.

"For coffee," Eddie answered, unsmiling.

"You're lucky. They generally use them for glue."

But—Bill's ramp held twenty people at once, and Ed Rutyna's backgrounds won praise from all.

Dennis Gurney went all out as director and built himself a booth in the balcony—a prototype of television directors' booths—and called light and sound cues by phone.

Our audiences were pleased, and quite sincerely. Some balked at certain spots, but we had gone over that before and failed to get concessions. Documentary material—even though it be couched in imperishable prose—doesn't seem as sharp a year later.

To indicate the usual cleavage of the press, I'll quote two of our friends—Mr. Rascoe and Miss Waldorf. The former said in part: " 'Seven Mirrors' as presented by the Blackfriars Guild makes a thing like 'The Miracle' (which was presented by Max Reinhardt) a cheap and tawdry spectacle." The latter said in conclusion: "Certainly it is something upon which professional critics should never have been asked to comment." Take your choice!

About this time my numerous assignments, plus a few germs, made for a complicated picture, so I asked to be relieved of the editorship of *The Holy Name Journal*. The request was granted, but in the process I was transferred to Sacred Heart Priory in the Greenville section of Jersey City.

The first night I made my way from the theatre to my new home had something of the triumph of most first nights, but since then I've settled down to a rather routine run. First, I was directed to a particular bus, which I found without too much trouble—but as I knew no landmarks and as it was raining enough to blur landmarks anyhow, I asked the driver to let me off at Bayview Avenue. We rode and rode until the driver and I were the sole occupants when we went into a terminal. He looked at me in some annoyance and said, "Stay there. I forgot ya." And he drove me through back streets, depositing me at my door. But it was a quiet triumph, as nobody was up to witness it— but for that matter, because of my late hours, nobody has waited up since.

The next play was our second venture in the interracial problem and a good job it was, if I do say so. Edwin M. Bronner wrote it and called it *A Young American*. It was the story of an orchestra conductor who received a very good score through the mail and invited its composer to spend the rehearsal weeks with him to smooth it out. The composer arrived and threw a bombshell into the family because he was a Negro.

The conductor stuck to his bargain, but his servants—black and white—became very superior. The daughter of the house was understanding and sympathetic, but her fiance brought a vigilante mind with him and got generally difficult.

An old colored teacher came in at the major crisis and offered some very sound advice about the solution of the "problem." The boy finally went home determined to devote some time and thought to eradicating the hatred and bigotry on both sides.

Our play-doctoring department—which had been dormant during the preceding months—had a hand in the fundamental thesis about a solution and Mr. Bronner thought we had a good idea. As a result, he came out with something different from most racial plays, because he put the blame and the hope on people—all people, regardless of their color. We got a good cast, including a composer who could play the piano, and offered the public a sensitive and solid show.

Instead of breaking down the first-night press and perhaps being accused of prejudice, I'd like to reprint *Billboard's* article which has done that for me in its succinct and breezy style.

After headlines and a list of cast and credits *Billboard* for January 26, 1946, reads:

"Well, let's be honest about it. Half a dozen of the daily drama defenders caught *Young American* and came back to their machines to pound out everything from A (for applause) to Z (for zero). Since this Edwin M. Bronner problem piece under its aegis is not important in the commercial theatre, tho it would figure to arouse attention and special audiences if thrown into a Broadway house where values rise in direct ratio to (1) theater and location; (2) producer; (3) director; (4) cast, and (5) build-up, this is as good a time as any to review the show on the basis of its reception by the two-on-the-aisle gentlemen whose lines are said to influence public opinion slightly more than a nonconsumer sheet.

"That was a helluva long sentence to struggle thru, but what happened to the Blackfriars-Bronner duo is much worse.

"Robert Garland (*Journal American*), in a trick notice on the comedy side, said *Deep Are The Roots* and *Strange Fruit,* which also tackled the Negro question, 'are equally controversial but more fundamentally honest dramas.'

"His afternoon colleague, Burton Rascoe (*World-Telegram*), said the play is 'a better drama of racial discrimination against the Negro than *Roots* or *Fruit.*'

"Vernon Rice (*The Post*): 'What it has to say it says rather badly and most tiresomely.'

"Otis L. Guernsey (*Herald Tribune*): 'A creditable new drama (with) moments of intelligence worthy of a more prominent production ... presentation of which Blackfriars' Guild may well be proud.'

"Lewis Nichols (*The Times*): A work of fine dramatic unity (discounting a few minor faults).'

"Robert Coleman (*The Mirror*): 'Written with evident sincerity.'

"Garland: 'I see no urgent reason (for it). Except that the Blackfriars just had to put on a play.'

"Coleman: 'It is a fine thing, indeed, to have an organization like the Blackfriars to give young, idealistic dramatists, like Bronner, the hearing that is so often denied them by the professional managers further downtown.'

"Rice: 'A number of promising problems present themselves, but nothing much happens except a lot of talk.'

"Guernsey: 'On the occasions when this play strikes the right key, its note is eloquent indeed.'

"Rascoe: 'Faces the issue of discrimination against Negroes with utter honesty and truth.'

"Guernsey: 'Gurney's direction is adequate.' (50 per cent.)

"Nichols: 'Gurney's direction is sound.' (65 per cent.)

"Coleman: 'Gurney has capably directed.' (80 per cent.)

"Rice: 'Dennis Gurney again directed and showed once more that he is a very capable man.' (90 per cent.)

"Rascoe: 'I . . . consider Mr. Gurney one of the five most expert directors in the business.' (Other four not disclosed.) (100 per cent.)

"On the statistical side, four of the crix turned the play down but had enough pleasant things to say to add up to customers. The two yeah-men also reversed themselves in tackling other phases of the work.

"So if you add it all up, there were a lot of words kicked around, but with the lone exception of Rascoe, no one was definitely all out in his beef or bravo. Rascoe happens to operate on the strong opinion shelf."

This is not a collection of quotes carefully selected to prove a point. It is the cold recording of the not

238

exactly philosophical *Billboard,* attempting to estimate
whether the play was approved or not. It can stand as
written to justify us in going back to Aristotle and St.
Thomas Aquinas in seeking norms and standards. We
could balance the American critics until the end of
time and be little wiser in making our selections.

Let me juxtapose two items not included in the fore-
going:

George Freedley (*Telegraph*): " 'A Young American' obviously has no importance as far as the Broadway scene is concerned."

Times: "Bidding against some keen competition, the
Messrs. Shubert and Albert de Courville have succeeded in obtaining the rights to the Edward M. Bronner play, 'A Young American.' "

Suppose we continue the tragic story of this play in
quotes from the newspapers. It spares a perhaps faulty
memory the accusation of bias.

Jack O'Brian, in a nationally syndicated article,
wrote: "Its Broadway engagement will follow almost
immediately its current Blackfriars presentation . . . de
Courville will direct . . . the Shuberts won out in competition with several producers and at least two Hollywood film firms . . . the Shuberts, you see, have Broadway theatres of their own and none of the other producers could guarantee one would be available."

The *Times,* answering its own question "Why the
rush?" said: "By the way the national company of
Deep Are the Roots has been trying to get into Chicago
as quickly as possible."

Blackfriars closed *A Young American* on February
11. The Shubert-DeCourville version opened fifteen

days later in Chicago with a partially new cast and some hasty script changes.

Concerning the latter, the Chicago *Journal of Commerce* reported: "A prosperous conductor has announced him (the composer) as the winner of a music competition." There goes the plausibility of the situation and the impact of the first act. National contest winners have a way of getting discovered.

Robert Pollack of the Chicago *Times* said: "Constructive suggestion department . . . . Get a new offstage piano or have the old one tuned. If the management must give us a sample of the composer's talents let his music sound more like Sibelius than Ethelbert Nevin." Blackfriars, incidentally, cast a concert pianist in the role and used a tuned piano.

Claudia Cassidy of the Chicago *Tribune* said, "It is cheaply staged and badly directed in the ugly setting abandoned here by 'The Ryan Girl.' "

The New York *Times* chronicled that the play lasted only twelve days in Chicago. Thus the saga of *A Young American* through the eyes of others.

That season we made a direct appeal to the priests and Sisters who had seen our productions. They came through. Rather preposterous to write religious Brothers and Sisters who have no money of their own. Of course it's preposterous, but we thought they might have the vision to keep us going. They had. It didn't take much. But, then, it didn't take much to start us off.

The Sisters were particularly staunch friends of ours. Every play we've ever done has had least two matinee previews or dress rehearsals on the Saturday and Sunday before opening. Some, because of community regulations, are not allowed out on Saturdays and some are not allowed out on Sundays. Some are not allowed out at all, but they seem to have a way of finding out about us.

Our only curtain speeches have been made to them at these exlusive performances. Since the rules of some forbid them from attending a public theatre, we make this an exclusive, and one sees all sorts and colors of habits. We sort of make an accounting to them, too. We tell them our troubles and joys. We don't break it down to dollars and cents. That would be boring. But we do tell them how much praying it will take to keep us open for the next production. And they keep us open. If we hadn't faith in their prayers—and it's one of the most genuine objects of faith we possess—we'd still have assurance that they keep us going from the indisputable fact that not much else does.

They come early and make it quite a holiday because they're almost sure of meeting old friends. Some who travel a distance to attend morning classes in New York arrive about noon and eat their lunches. Some prepare classes, others read their Office Books, but they come early to get good seats. We've often been caught in the act of cleaning up the theatre, and I used to thank them for dusting the seats with their voluminous habits. I've stopped saying that, because they all believe it and no amount of polishing up the theatre prevents them from drawing a fastidious finger across the seats before sitting down.

As audiences, they're a little disconcerting to the casts who are priming for a cold opening audience, because the Sisters like everything so much. But by the same token, they're doubly deceptive, because among them there are some of the best critics in town. I'm sure they enjoy Blackfriars, shining or dusty, because while the sweepers have no trouble with cigarettes, they present an amazing collection after each performance of twisted programmes, black gloves, an occasional book and a wonderful display of candy boxes and wrappers. It's a Roman holiday in the narrow sense of the term. Incidentally, they're going to get us a bigger theatre with plush seats.

Up to this point we had no formula for a Lenten play. The simplest and most proper presentation for this season would be a story of the Passion and Death of Christ based on the Gospels. Simplest, that is, in concept, but far from simple in execution. It demands a vastly superior script with a multitude of settings or acceptable substitutes. In the prevalent tradition that the figure of Christ should not be presented on the stage, because no actor could satisfy the idealism of people, the factual play in which He is the central figure and reason for being would have to be doctored up beyond the skill of any playwright known to us.

The next best thing seems to be a play about actable, approachable, entirely human characters, real or fictitious (in the sense of representatives for the rest of us), showing the influence of Christ's coming among them.

We found such a script in Ernest Milton's *Mary of Magdala*. Without going into exegetical studies on whether the Marys of the Bible are one, two or three women, Mr. Milton (an American actor who has spent much of his life in England) followed the prevalent Catholic tradition that they are all the same person referred to and he made her a prototype of modern cafe society. Her parasitic, man-enslaving life is clouded by having met Christ and the play is about her struggles against and finally enthusiastic acceptance of Him.

It is a thought-provoking piece, because three of her competing devotees—a Roman, a Jew and a Briton—watch the process and adjust their lives to it, each in his own way. This sounds talky, but it held up with a good cast and an impressive single set.

The press thought it a good job—at least for Blackfriars and in Lent. Eight out of twelve reviewers listed it from "Good" to "Excellent"—although some noted it was not for Broadway and Mr. Rice of the *Post* said, "It could be completely lost in the Broadway mill, and it is devoutly hoped, in this instance, Broadway stays away from its door." Three of the remaining four critics said "Pretty good" or "Fair," while Mr. Rascoe, perhaps to prove he wasn't on our pay roll, switched from the pack again and said, "To put it bluntly, it is a very bad play, lifelessly projected."

We thought it said some important things and had some very good acting, and our audiences agreed with us.

Actor-agents had been taking Blackfriars seriously for some time and were summoning more and more from our ranks. It wasn't a regular progression, because some seasons of the year saw more casting than others. But each year more of those who were seen on our little stage got commercial jobs.

Agents are very much like people. This bit of en-

lightenment is for those actors who meet their recep-
tionists daily, but who've never seen a real live agent.
The big ones—and this includes most of the successful
ones, but not all, because big people are not always
thinking of sucess—ask for seats well in advance or, if
they drop in unannounced, they take any seat in the
house. In fact, they frequently offer to stand, but we've
always managed to dig up some sort of seat, so that they
can concentrate on our actors without too much resentment.

But we've met others—listed in nothing closer to
the theatre than the phone book—who are very demanding in the matter of locations. (They often try
to get their families in, too.) One aggressive woman
who claimed she was an agent put up quite a protest
to Mr. Wyatt because on a sold-out night he put her
on the side in the only empty seat in the house. He
remonstrated quietly that he would like to have done
better, but we had no notice of her coming and the
house was simply sold out. But she was an agent, she
went on, an important agent (which thoroughly dis-
proved that point) and she had to have a better seat.
At which Mr. Wyatt rose to his full height, looked
down his nose and replied: "Madam, I am not a
cabinet maker."

On another occasion, a woman rushed back to the
box-office just before curtain time and said, "I'm
sitting in the last row. I can't see a thing."

Mr. Wyatt met that with, "You're in the tenth
row, Madam. It shouldn't matter how many people
are not in back of you."

But she was persistent, and repeated, "I can't see
a thing."

Wyatt looked at his watch deliberately and said soothingly, "I dare say you're right. But in three minutes the curtain will go up and then you'll see something."

Come Marching Home by Robert Anderson was our windup for the season. I always get its title confused with Courtenay Savage's *Home Is the Hero*. It was the story of a veteran who returned to a pleasant home where he decided to putter around with his writing and his garden, until some of the local politicians thought his war record might help him (and them) in their political aspirations. He ran into the not-infrequent smear campaigns from his enemies and finally wasn't satisfied with the intentions of his friends who deserted him, too. Becoming conscious of the obligation to keep on fighting in peace as well as in war, he ran as an independent candidate, sure of defeat, but ready to keep on trying.

The play won top place in the National Theatre Conference contest of 1944 for plays written by servicemen overseas. The entire press—except Mr. Garland—called it good—but not quite good enough to startle Broadway. The critics found it "sincere," "honest," "credible," "sometimes a little preachy," and the *Times,* which sent a new reviewer, said, "Nowhere in Times Square will one find more honesty of purpose than was revealed last Saturday evening at the Blackfriars' Guild's intimate theatre by all engaged in the presentation of Robert Anderson's 'Come Marching Home.' "

So, we'll march home to the finish of a season. Ninety-four public performances, added to eight for the Sisters, took us just over the one-hundred mark in our four plays.

H E SEEMED TO BE ON A SEE-SAW, SUPERIMPOSED, of course, on the customary merry-go-round. The 1946-47 season was a year of many critical frowns— perhaps some of the critics thought we were a waste of time—and it was a year of specialized audience reactions. If we were looking for universal approval, it might be regarded as the usual off year (we had operated on a Yes-No cycle, you've noticed), but if I may tell it from our point of view, it wasn't bad at all. We did the usual four plays, audiences came and liked three of them, and we paid our bills. What's more, we got a number of experimental ideas out of our system and from this season settled down to a more definite pattern. Six years of operation showed us the futility of trying to please a number of diversified interests. We'd please ourselves from this point on, and the results of that decision have been eminently satisfactory.

Indicating that time was passing and that old posts would have to be replaced with new faces, the news of Courtenay Savage's death reached us at the beginning of this season, and just before we went into rehearsal Bill Schoeller died suddenly at New Hope, Pennsylvania, where he was doing sets for the Bucks County Playhouse. I said the funeral Mass for Mr. Schoeller in the presence of a few Blackfriars and

those who stayed over at New Hope for the final
week. It was a small group and a mixed one, repre-
senting almost as many religious beliefs as there were
people, but we had a strong bond in our respect for
Bill as we laid him away on a hillside in that peace-
ful part of the world.

On the unexpected side, our clipping bureau sent
us a notice from a Boston paper announcing that a
man in that city was suing his wife for divorce because five years before she played a show with the
Blackfriars' Guild which took several evenings a week
of her time. Even Boston was learning about us.

We had a lot of scripts, most of which we read
with lowering spirits because they didn't represent
what we stood for. Most were based upon absolutely
wrong premises, sympathizing with or justifying
wrong living. Others were sound enough in thesis, but
just weren't theatre. And then Father Larnen brought
us a script by Michael O'Hara, who was, interestingly
enough, also from Sligo. The script was thin, and if
we hadn't known it the critics would have told us,
but there was one charming feature about it which
sold us almost immediately. The Irish in it were
laughing at themselves.

They'll do that eloquently among friends, but years
of persecution have made them a little thin-skinned,
and if the English have a conspicuously disarming
quality it is that they will laugh at themselves even
among enemies. I'm not going over all the background
for those different states of mind, but knowing quite
a bit about the Irish and their hardships and struggles,
I would still point out that there were times when the

247

chips were down for the English and they still laughed a little.

So, to find the Irish laughing a little, too, because in adherence to a principle they were better off than most of the world, was a refreshing thing. That was what we saw in the O'Hara play.

The American press—and I suppose the press of the free world—printed an accusation that there were very many Axis spies in Eire, including some 3,000 Japanese. Now, the average Irishman is willing to admit a mixed heritage, from the Milesians through the Danes to the Spanish, but he still thinks he could recognize an Oriental if he saw one in the hills of Kerry. And the Irish were quite surprised that the infallible American press (even though it was only reporting an accusation) would do it with a straight face. Dublin officialdom had a record of six Japanese in the country, and these six were at the Legation and had never been mistaken for the sons of Kathleen. It was obvious that, if what the papers said was true, the invisible 3,000 were as interesting a problem as the vanishing race of leprechauns.

It might have been reasonable for American and British interests to be unhappy that a number of Germans and a half dozen Japanese were at large in Eire, but it could hardly be a threat to that country's neutrality. Every Irishman will tell you that the thousands of Englishmen who came and went at will were for all practical purposes British agents, and nobody ever suggested seriously that they be removed. Ireland was conscious enough of world issues to forgive centuries of persecution, but she wasn't quite

248

ready to make that forgiveness official and become a holocaust in vain into the bargain, unless England finished the job of granting the freedom she said she was fighting for and reuniting the divided country. It's the first time that the Irish had the upper hand in centuries. The cost of securing it was a bitter one and still rankled. But they had it and they couldn't help smiling.

Derryowen, for that was the name of O'Hara's play, was in just that spirit and I'm afraid we liked it. My apology for doing so thin a script is made with head lowered in mock chagrin and with tongue in cheek. The critics told us it was thin.

The Bronx *Home News* began its review this way: "Blithely unconcerned about the mighty Theatre Incorporated's exciting new revival of *The Playboy of the Western World.* . . " There you have it, and very true. With proper blushes let me commend that reviewer in his use of the world "blithely." We are blithely unconcerned about all the might of Broadway; we are blithely unconcerned about the mighty Synge; and we are blithely unconcerned about the "mighty" *Playboy.* They happen to be saying something other than what we want to say. We'd like to have the pen of Synge saying them for us; since he hasn't done it, we'll not complain, but go right along with our story.

From the time that Synge discovered the realities of people like the Aran Islanders and outmoded the type of Irish play in which the heroic son of a poor farmer outwitted the English landlord and won the hand of the most beautiful girl in the town land, the

Playboy, although booed and hissed and in its early days generally broken up by Dublin audiences, has been regarded by many as his best writing. When it opened in New York, the night that the *Titanic* went down, it got a violent adverse reception from many Irish-Americans. Their missiles indicated that they took a poor view of what it said.

Fortified with this knowledge that the controversial classic was rearing its head again in New York with a good company, the critics whetted their knives to dissect learnedly the changing position of Ireland and the changing standards of Irishmen in a changed world.

We had the misfortune to come up two days later with a light farcial script that laughed its way through. Mr. Hawkins of the *World-Telegram* said: "It deals lightly with serious subjects such as Irish neutrality." True—too true.

Just to strike the balance in an evenly divided press, may I quote what one of the few with Irish names had to say about it. John C. Wynn of the *Enquirer* said: " 'The Playboy' is being acted with verve and spirit by a cast of capables and directed with evident zest by Guthrie McClintic—but it still isn't a true picture of life on the west coast of Ireland —as any Mayo man will tell you. On the other hand, the ever-striving workers at the Blackfriars' Guild have turned out an amiable and refreshing little comedy about today's Ireland in *Derryowen.* . . . Should there be those who might feel that Eire's neutrality during the recent war still needs explaining—*Derryowen* does just that."

Two notes of gratitude may be mentioned here, although there hasn't been much time or space to single out individual performances. But we had some casting problems in this play and James Maloney popped up and learned sixty-four sides in three days. That's a feat in any theatre. And Jerry Buckley gave me and a good many others some of the longest, loudest and best laughs we can remember at Blackfriars. That's cause for gratitude in this sombre world.

We stopped laughing (having pleased the Irish) when we tried to please the classicists. The next play was *If in the Greenwood* by Victoria Kuhn, and it didn't go down very well. The reasons, apparent in hindsight, were simple enough. It was a new version of the ageless Tristan and Iseult story, set against present problems in the United Nations and done in blank verse.

Dennis Gurney was really the champion of the script. I had no knowledge or assurance that it would be a hit—just a vague, questioning feeling. We were dealing with something new to us. But the audiences, geared to *Derryowen* and *Seven Mirrors,* were uneasy in the story of infidelity with suicide as the solution for the wrong-doers. We had checked the matter carefully with outstanding theologians, but the intrinsic justification of the solution probably can be confused with many things not so justifiable in modern theatre. Whatever the strict merits of the case, our audiences weren't happy with the scholarly approach, and their uneasiness was further stirred by the purring innuendoes of a few critics.

Most of the gentlemen of the press who didn't like

the play gave as their reasons that it was vague, unspecific, and that the verse form blurred it the more. A point I think they missed—and a matter which drove Gurney nearly mad—was that the play called for broad acting, and we had great trouble shaking our troupe loose from the drawing-room conventions of modern technique. Had Judith Anderson's *Medea* come along, we might have had something to point at, but with a subconscious dread of the melodramatic posturings of the last century, most of them inwardly fought against letting go. And it was a good cast, too.

That brings up a point I've often thought about, although it isn't particularly important. It's that a critic or anyone in the audience for that matter, seeing a play for the first time, doesn't always distinguish acting from directing and sometimes from writing. If that sounds like a superior generalization, let me explain it. I grant that, since the play is prepared for the audience, a fresh mind is its best critic. I more than grant that each witness should know absolutely whether he likes it or not. I merely question whether or not he has the time—as the story unfolds—to thoroughly analyze why.

Director and producer working with a script set up certain norms they want to attain. But, sometimes, an actor, just doesn't deliver. Again, a better actor takes poorer lines and makes them come across. The theatre-goer, therefore the critic, be he professional or not, may be entirely justified in his over-all opinion of the piece or a part of it without always knowing why. I don't think the director or producer makes a good critic, because he is too close to his ever-growing or changing organism to have any perspective left. But more than once I've been quietly amazed at the assurance with which critics become very specific in condemnation, when from weeks of watching it grow we were quite sure the fault lay in another department.

However, the thing that brought us up most sharply with a sense of the slowness of our progress was the reaction of part of our audiences. They were afraid it was a dangerous play. Sex had been treated so shabbily and so cheaply in a large portion of the theatre that they weren't quick to discover in its treatment either a good thing or the simple labeling of its misuse as a sin. It was going to take some time to reconcile the theological or academic matter of standards with the popular feeling tone. That meant we were going to be condemned by our own for doing what we were sure was a good thing—the building of an adult theatre which distinguished elementals from accidentals. In this instance, Mr. Lewis of *America* headed a good Catholic press and that promised to make the task somewhat easier.

Then I committed the unpardonable sin. I mentioned the press in a play. Yes! I'll take full blame because I wrote this one—*On the Seventh Day*—it was our usual Lenten problem. We hadn't a good new script suitable for the penitential season, so I stepped into the breach and offered to finish up a modern morality play that the customers might have something to "offer up." It was about the education of John Smith—or modern America. I thought it was rather mild, because I'm of an outmoded school of thought which doesn't believe we have here a completely perfect world. It seemed safe to mention divorce or separation, because divorce has increased sixty-fold or six thousand per cent in the last century here. So it isn't exactly a new idea. It seemed safe to hint at neuroses and psychoses, since every psychiatrist—genuine or quack—is booked up months in advance. It seemed more than safe—it seemed useful —to mention the causes of some of these changes. That part was rather cold reporting, if one believes stacks of monographs on the education of children— the influence of movies, of comics, of radio, etc.

That was the heart of the play, but it had a little frame around it to indicate that God still has a hand in things and we don't just get along by "the skin of our teeth."

The frame indicated that Lieutenant Oriel (a mere archangel and consequently way down the scale of the nine choirs) had been in charge of the department of human relations, but he was tired of humans and had come as close as an archangel could to having a nervous breakdown. Colonel Advocatus (a principality), top brass in all dealings with creation, was hard pressed to find an archangel who would take the job. But he thought of Lieutenant Raphael who had been working with the engineers, keeping the celestial spheres in their orbits, ever since he had been a little smug because of his handling of the Tobias case. Realizing it wasn't fair to let the unsuspecting Raphael face humanity in the belief that it was as simple as in Old Testament days, Colonel Advocatus sends him down with Oriel for a conducted tour and

254

suggests that they look into the education of John Smith.

The two heavenly lieutenants in their snappy white uniforms and little efficient white wings look over the American home and talk about it from time to time.

On a still lower level (than angels and men) we had a few symbolic figures who threw in a few thousand words and generally defended themselves, or rather their lack of responsibility, being quite inanimate and at the mercy of men. The schools, books, magazines, newspapers—writing in general—were embodied in an animated typewriter. The camera, a second gadget, took care of movies, picture magazines, all our visual aids; while a microphone, rather brash and youthful, took care of the endless talk which beats in our ears through radio and its variations.

All that sounds pretty harmless, reading it over, just as it did in the writing and the production. But one of the many arrows, dissipated by their very numbers, grazed the sacred cow—the newspaper—and nearly all its employees, who didn't seem to mind what happened to the other forms of propaganda, let the world know how grievous a sin it was to disapprove, or better still, to say simply what the whole world knows.

One reviewer said: "Father Nagle's indictment of Mike, Cam and Mr. Press is as sophomoric as it is one-sided. He sees them solely as means of propaganda, wholly ignoring their other functions as enlightenment and education."

This in face of the fact that Mr. Press makes quite

a speech explaining his responsibility for the printing of the Bible, and the others get a fair shot at defending themselves—if a defense is necessary.

Mr. Hawkins in the *World-Telegram* wrote: "The author attributes to them [forces that influence man] nothing but the most destructive influences. He goes so far as to suggest that the funny papers are an evil force because such strips as Superman teach the creation of enemies to destroy with force. Men like Otis Swift are ignored."

So are Dick Tracy and Li'l Abner. Broad as the canvas was, it didn't attempt to give a list of names. And what he went so far as to suggest, and very definitely, was that the magnificent powers of the spiritual world as manifested by angels are removed from the child mind by the fantastic creations of interplanetary wars—with material power as the sole motivation.

Mr. Watts of the *Post* said: "in the case of the press he seemed slightly ungrateful, since at least part of it has supported him in his contention that America was lured into the recent war by hypocritical propaganda." Then we're in accord. I'm with that part of it, unless it shared in some hypocritical propaganda. Mr. Press did make a defense. All I tried to say was that John Smith has come upon his confusion because of the forces which set out to direct his thinking. Anything less doesn't add up to a declarative sentence. We are the result of our teachings and today the modes of teaching are multiple. Can't it be said without one being ungrateful? I'm grateful for the right things in the press and not for the wrong ones.

An old friend, Kelcey Allen of *Women's Wear,* obviously looking for something nice to say, phrased it this way: "The cast does very well with the enormous amount of words entrusted to them." Another old friend, Bob Francis, said in *Billboard*: "Why, when he [the author] sets himself to write a play, he tosses wit in the discard in favor of unadulterated dogma, is a question. Maybe it's the Lenten approach." Maybe that's it. If it was thought bad taste to wring out a smile at Irish neutrality, it would be worse to laugh at the state of the world. Yet, our audiences slipped in a few chuckles.

Now, in all justice, the critics might have thought this broad canvas Lenten morality dull and talky for the good reason that it was dull and talky. But whether it was or not, let me warn young playwrights not to include the press—even in a minor capacity—in analyzing the evils of the world, because the press doesn't like it. And there are enough trees left in the world for the press to get in the last word.

Over the years, the *Brooklyn Tablet* had been making our cause its own. This time, in almost three columns, between reviews and editorials, Mr. Bennett wrote hard to forestall the expected cold water. In one article he said, "The play is unusual—so unusual that the newspaper critics will probably pan it in print and confidentially advise their friends it should not be missed." And he concluded another militant blast with the significant remark: "Catholics may now safely climb on the Blackfriars' Guild bandwagon."

For all our defenders, however, we're slow to recommend this piece to any but the best-equipped theatre, because, although not a single prop is moved, the sound cue sheet takes up three single-spaced typewritten pages.

We closed the season with *Respectfully Yours* by Peggy Lamson, a nostalgic (for most of us, since its setting was 1912) comedy about the wife of a college faculty member, who wrote a book, upset campus life generally, and finally won respect and understanding from her stuffy professor husband. Under other titles, it won a prize at the Dock Street Theatre in Charleston (where Dorothy Gish played the lead) and it was held for a while by the Theatre Guild.

It played well for our audiences and broke in some new people under the Blackfriar flag. Although Anne Follmann deservedly picked up the best notices for the leading role, Marjorie Hildreth gave Gurney a breathing spell by staging it, and Hugh Rogers, fresh from *Time,* supervised the production. This last-named gentleman asked me what a producer had to do at Blackfriars. I told him, "Everything that you can't get someone else to do."

He managed to get the right rolls for the player-piano, but ran into difficulty with an old flash pan for a photographer. To begin with, he couldn't find one, and, if he had succeeded, it couldn't be sold because of some law or other. So he made one which had all the requisites of theatre except for the slight difficulty that it wouldn't work. Then he dug one up in a prop shop which went off once out of four times. Finally, one came to light in a firework shop out in the country where firework shops are supposed to be. We tested it at night and in the rain, dozens of times,

258

illuminating, I'm sure, the skies of Long Island to the surprise of the natives. Rogers left us for the more lucrative field of television and advertising, but in passing, he found out what a producer does at Blackfriars.

The press liked this too. We got nine good reviews, three so-so. The *Times* wasn't impressed (with its customary brevity) and Variety has the same feeling in the same amount of space. Mr. Francis of *Billboard* said "No" because his old friend Mr. Gurney didn't direct and Mr. Garland of the *Journal American* said the only good thing about it was that his old friend Maggie Hildreth did direct.

I suppose Aristophanes and Euripides got caught between critics who had friends among directors. But we'll continue to invite new directors if we think the pace is too much for Mr. Gurney or if he chooses to go downtown to make a few dollars, and we'll be happy to invite Miss Hildreth back because she's a good director, too.

Respectfully Yours ended the season on a pleasant note and some reviewers thought it would fare well with the commercials. But nobody bought it, so with its title we'll sign off this season.

XX: LADY OF FATIMA

T HINGS WERE LOOKING BETTER BY THE END OF THE summer because we had two exciting scripts. Taking them in order of accession (as the libraries say), the first really concerns itself with the drama *Les Gueux aux Paradis*. Two or three of my GI friends—or should I say "friends among the military"?—told me of catching a terrific play in Paris, written by G. M. Martens and Andre Obey (whose *Noah* we had done in Providence and Nabnassett). It made such an impression that each of my informants outlined the plot, but—as it was always with much clatter in the lobby—it was always filed away for a future memory jog.

Somehow or other we secured a copy of the script and memory was jogged. This would be our opener. Of course, there was the matter of permissions, but we had done British plays before. It shouldn't be too difficult to reach across the Channel and clear this matter up. So, when we reopened the office in the fall, we started all departments working at once. A little translation went on, a little casting and set designing and costume designing, while we allowed ourselves ample time to get all the necessary approbations and permissions. Robert Healey, who, when a student at Providence College, helped me in my struggles with undergraduate musicals, did a rough translation, but we couldn't announce it until proper permissions were secured.

The printed book carried the name of a publisher to whom one was supposed to write and we sent a cable to this firm, guaranteeing enough money for a reply collect up to ten words. Thus, they could say "oui" ten times or compose a whole sentence. A few weeks went by and we became uneasy. This time we sent the publisher another cable and one to "Auteurs" —the equivalent of our Dramatists' Guild—carefully establishing funds that they might spare ten words for us in any language. The translation was ready, the cast was almost complete, the sets were started. No reply from anybody.

These cables weren't all, by any means. We appealed to the American agents who had handled *Noah* for M. Obey, but they had no recent address. We phoned known or suspected friends of both authors, with no success.

As time was running out everywhere, I went to the cultural attache of the French Embassy, who allayed my fears and made my excitement look like a reversal of national traits. With the authority of his office, he smiled and said, "I will cable the proper people. Your permission you will have. Phone me tomorrow."

To my phone call of the fifth consecutive day he said with all my former perturbation, "It's impossible. It's incredible. They don't answer their government." Well—I felt better. Maybe France doesn't hop to answer a cable signed "Blackfriars," but the insult was effaced. It doesn't answer anybody—not even itself.

Personal announcements had to go out that we might get an audience. We were afraid to break in the newspapers because of legal complications. We had cabled every name in Belgium and France (except Napoleon's) that anybody gave us and mortgaged our future posting money for their hoped-for replies. Europe remained silent. I walked out of the office one day absolutely stumped and remembered a phone call I should have made, so I dropped into a drug-store. I fumbled through my pockets and found nothing smaller than a quarter. Walking up to the tobacco counter for change, I held out the quarter. "Will you give me a nickel for a cup of coffee?" Three people said, "What?" knowing they couldn't have heard aright. Shaking my head, I corrected the remark with, "Will you give me a nickel for a phone call?" Everyone was relieved and I got the change. I'm not going to explain the psychological process, but if a bit of advice is in order here, let me say, "Keep out of show business."

The French consulate, still miffed at its slight, came through after examining our documents and told us to produce the play and that we would be defended in the event of legal action, because we certainly tried to get permission. So we announced in the newspapers (which have really been good to us and which we do like in spite of regular tiffs) that we were presenting *Hoboes in Heaven*—a most inadequate translation of the title, *Les Gueux aux Paradis*. I've come to the conclusion that after twenty years of experience I keep coming up with the worst titles in the business.

The plot itself—which had been recounted to me

many times by its avid salesmen—had to do with two local characters in a Flemish village who had long maintained the custom of masquerading as St. Nicodemus and St. Nicholas on the latter's feast day and distributing toys and sweets to the children. But the joy in doing brought them an excuse for their favorite sins, for one was a glutton and the other a wine-bibber and their pious custom had been deteriorating over the years.

The pair dug out their costumes which faintly imitated Church saints and "St. Nicodemus" roughly smeared his face because his prototype (one of the patrons of the village) was a Negro. I failed to find sources on this matter, but, after all, we were producing a play and not writing one.

Having consumed a foundation for the night's work, they stepped outside the door, to be struck by a whizzing automobile and brought in for dead at the curtain of the first act.

Whether in a dream or in some unexplained transition period, they wake up in an anteroom of Hell. Perhaps if we, as producers, aren't sure how they got there, you might think us rather vague about our business. But, so many of the French plays I've read have so little rational progression and so much impulsive jumping about that I accept it as a characteristic of a French play. They don't painfully jockey a character into a situation. Rather, the situation jumps at him—and there he is. We dull spectators take it or leave it. Parenthetically, we took it; the press left it.

Well, Hell unfolds the Duke of Alba, whom the Flemish don't like, the devil, whom the Flemish don't like, and a hot-spot Negro bartender based on imaginary American types which was probably twice as funny in Belgium as in the region round Columbus Circle. By begging for a trial, the two pseudo-saints are whisked to an anteroom of Heaven. Here they are getting by the guard of Michael with his sword, because the real Sts. Nicholas and Nicodemus were out dispensing gifts to their children and are about due back. But—and this became serious trouble—the real ones got back at the precise moment and puzzled St. Peter a little, until he asked for the password. The earthbound saints failed to meet the test and St. Peter discovered their identity and turned to their record. It was a sorry one, indeed, and Peter's anger mounted until the Blessed Virgin entered. She quickly sized up the situation and asked God to give them another chance—because they were weak rather than malicious.

The third act is rollicking comedy—although not always painfully logical. Coming back to consciousness, the wayward pair discuss their experiences or dreams and can't believe they are alive, so they play dead as the carpenter measures them for a coffin and the sacristan arranges for their burial and incidentally proposes to the wife of one, who indignantly refuses him—or at least indicates that it is rather soon for such a proposal. The barber who tries to shave them finally convinces them that they are alive and in a happy ending they go forth to dispense their gifts, fortified with good resolutions to amend their lives.

That's the story inadequately summarized, and if we believed in signs and omens we probably would have taken the difficulty of securing permission as an indication it wasn't to be a critical success. M. Martens finally approved our production plans and we went rather merrily ahead.

The press—rather a light one, perhaps expressing disapproval of our preceding year's selections—brushed it aside for the most part. The *Times* headlined two inches with: "A Heavy Foot on 57th Street." The little gem under that title remarked that it went from Flemish to French to us, adding that "the current adapters have carried Hoboes in Heaven one translation too far."

Of course, there was the usual other side, too. Coleman (*Mirror*) said: "Hoboes in Heaven is one of the most enjoyable shows yet offered by Blackfriars'."

The most revealing and pathetic review came from the typwriter of Mr. Garland, who concluded a column of his incomparably witty ridicule with this explanation of what went before. "Which is to say that it is dull, uncalled for and almost unflaggingly impious." Whether the critic writes his headlines or not, it was called "impious" in a two-column spread, and I was called on by my superiors immediately to explain just what we were doing.

It would have been ironic had Blackfriars been closed by ecclesiastical authority because of an irresponsible headline. It would be doubly ironic if the New York newspaper which has consistently and blatantly fought communism were to be instrumental in closing the theatre in New York which was known by all to be carrying on the same fight.

How would a Flemish peasant dream of heaven except through the statues he had seen in his churches?

265

How would he dream of salvation except through the intercession of Our Blessed Lady? Is the juxtaposition of comedy and solemnity reserved for mediaeval mystery plays? Has Puritanism so eaten into our lives that we can't feel at home with the saints? And is laughter in the presence of a Father and a Mother a lack of piety or filial devotion?

This play was done under Catholic auspices in Montreal. Dozens of priests saw it here and have written for copies. Many of them said it was the most refreshing thing we had ever done. And I was criticized just a few months before for my abysmal lack of wit in a morality play. *Hoboes* is still discussed with affection by many of our customers.

The second production of the season—and our twenty-fifth in New York—was a biting "documentary" about race prejudice. Father George H. Dunne, S. J., champion of democratic civil rights and an enemy of "the sin of segregation," was justifiably incensed at the murder of a Negro family who had dared build a home in a part of rural California where the best people still worship the whiteness of their skins. He protested in magazine articles and lectures—not that the dead would be brought back to life—but that the land of freedom would not insist that this murder was an accident, because he hoped that others with illusions might have grounds for hope. The articles did little more than most articles do, so he wrote a kind of play—more like the living newspaper—with emotional overtones and called it *Trial by Fire*.

There was gentle irony in the title. The ordeal of

which trial by fire was a species was an exceptional juridical procedure of Germanic origin, which the Church slowly fought against (along with the duel) until it was finally outlawed. In the absence of conclusive testimony, the survivor or winner of an ordeal was regarded as innocent of the crime charged, because of the testimony of an omniscient God. Father Dunne's reporting indicates that this family failed to pass the test and was thus proved guilty, but the crime had long been acknowledged—the crime of not being the accepted color. This time it was expiated.

In production, the theatre became the hearing chambers of the coroner's jury. In Fontana, California, the Short family was killed when their home burned down after an explosion, and the jury was to decide whether it was an accident or caused with malicious intent. Most of the lines in this before-the-curtain section were actual transcripts from that session. But the author flashed back from time to time, so that onstage, behind a scrim, the actual story was told, and this information came from witnesses or people acquainted with the affair. The decision was "deaths caused by accident."

The play had been done first in Los Angeles and, although it received an enthusiastic press, we weren't so sure that it would fare so well in New York where the original story received little notice. But we were gratified by a large and warmly applauding group of reviewers. It was a novel presentation and had a good cast and the newspapers unanimously acknowledged the fact. Albert McCleery, Fordham's director, came down to do the staging and got acclamation from all.

Perhaps that unanimity demands qualification. Those who came approved. Some reviewers had crossed us from their lists. Perhaps their readers wouldn't be interested. Among those who came and wrote favorably were Mr. Rice (*Post*), Mr. Coleman (*Mirror*), Mr. Freedley (*Telegraph*), Mr. Francis (*Billboard*) Mr. Wise (*Wall Street Journal*), Mr. Dash (*Women's Wear*), Mr. Shipley (*New Leader*), Mr. Currie (*Brooklyn Eagle*), *Variety, Amsterdam News, Peoples' Voice, New York Age, Brooklyn Tablet, America, Commonweal, Catholic World, Catholic News* and a number of sectional and occupational papers.

The *Sun* covered us by an interview as did the *World-Telegram*. The only old reliable which missed us, if my records are accurate, was the *Herald Tribune*, but this was apparently an oversight, as some of the soundest reviews we have ever received came from that paper.

The *Times* gave its usual two-inch announcement, hardly for or against, but it did mention our name. The *Journal American* was not represented. The *News* has not deigned to cover us since Mr. Chapman has taken over the department for that paper. His predecessor, the late Burns Mantle, never missed us, saying that we were his favorite little theatre. *PM* was missing, presumably holding to the theory that only the leftists should deal with the "Negro problem." Perhaps the reviewer who was disappointed in *Caukey* feared that we were so reactionary we still believed that what God thought was of some importance.

In spite of this extremely gratifying press, audiences weren't as large as for many plays which fared badly with the reviewers. Perhaps some of this falling off was

268

due to the fact that our opening followed closely upon the Christmas season, but nearly every year we had a January production and some did very well. I think the answer to the question which suggests itself is that it wasn't particularly good entertainment. It was rather the cause of an examination of conscience—a soul-searing experience. People want to be entertained and not jolted to the core of their being. They don't want to stir up sleeping fears and, in this case, the fear in the heart of almost everyone is that he has been at fault.

There were incidents—big and little—surrounding the production. William Riva, justly famed for his sets at Fordham, volunteered to design our sets, since Mc-Cleery was directing. One of his requirements was a huge drum, or, rather, a frame covered with the stretched skin of a mastodon. No extant animal would be big enough, I'm sure. The monster arrived and Mr. Riva demonstrated its proper usage by belting it with a sort of baseball bat which went through the skin on the first swing. Home run! We paid eighty dollars for a few feet of four-by-one and two used electric light bulbs.

One night during the run, word came up our marble stairs to the lobby that we were being picketed or something. So we sent the picket-caring squad down to see what we had done. The new attraction outside our door consisted of a few people selling booklets. Not knowing the next step, as our legal department was not at hand, we bought a booklet. It was entitled *Vigilante Terror in in Fontana* and was put out by the Socialist Workers Party of Los Angeles. We read it quickly. It was our story, with pictures of the original cast. So we dashed down to buy out the entire supply, intending to give them out where they'd do the most good, but by that time—a matter of ten minutes—the supply was exhausted.

Another incident which touched us was the story of Nappy Whiting. Nappy is a colored gentleman who has done bit parts—and better than bit parts—in the movies for a long time and he knows the inside of a lot of night clubs from the performer's viewpoint. By some process unknown to me, he got into the Los Angeles production and the small role he played became an important thing in his life. So, when he heard it was opening at Blackfriars, he got the urge to come East and "look things over." We exchanged letters, but my invitation wasn't too important because his addresses were always moving eastward. He was coming towards us by easy stages, anyhow.

On arrival, Nappy came to Blackfriars and was so right for the President of the Negro Chamber of Commerce that he picked up the part without competition —something which, I'm sure, he had always taken for granted. Naturally, he played it to the applause of critics and audiences.

At the cast party he made a little speech, and it was only then that I realized the extent of his sacrifice and degree of devotion to the cause. It wasn't a speech which will get into anthologies as a masterpiece of prose. In fact, he laughed all through it. But it got hold of me and a good many others. Beginning by telling us that he just wandered into the Los Angeles production and sort of got caught in it, he went on to say that it began to mean something to him. Then he heard of Blackfriars production and thought he ought to get re-established in the cast. Not being proud of his compositions, he said he got a "secretary" to write to me and put in a lot of big words. My letters which caught him all over the country were full of big words, too, he said, and, as he hadn't any secretary, it was only later that he realized we didn't pay any salaries. Nappy didn't mind that too much, but he wasn't sure how he was going to manage in New York—having been away for a good many years. But he kept that fact to himself and played the show.

That night at the cast party, instead of blaming us, he paid tribute to Blackfriars for taking up his cause —Blackfriars and the Church. It might have seemed insincere—even out of place—coming from many of the more sophisticated members of the cast. But Nappy made it real. And then he topped it all—like the Jongleur of Our Lady—by singing a blue song, his night club hit, which was definitely "not Blackfriar material."

So, in the fall of 1947, all I had to do was find a Lenten play—and I hadn't found one. The rebukes were gentle but constant.

We had a couple of psychological plays exploring the mind of Pilate during and after the Crucifixion and they were quite well written. But I couldn't feel that our audiences, especially the Lenten ones, really cared about what Pilate thought—or what an author said he thought. What people themselves thought was the stuff out of which Lenten drama should be made. We're prone in these days to wander up little alleys of the mind, shifting blame by way of unconscious escapism, and forgetting universals. There was something ingenuous about mediaeval drama, because Everyman in audience and cast thought less that he was being talked to than that he was walking on the stage.

The old look in the Doctor's eye more than implied that everybody was coming through with a good job and that I couldn't expect things to be handed to me on a silver platter. He didn't put it into words, but his forbearance was all the more eloquent. The questioning eyes and the strained silences indicated definitely that I had better come up with a script.

On the eighth of December, Father Reilly of Nabnassett and Cliff Haven memory dropped in and, after discussing everything under the sun, said simply, "Did you ever think of a play about Our Lady of Fatima?"

I had thought of it, but in a very indefinite way. Once, when Archbishop Finbar Ryan, O.P., of Trinidad, the first to write extensively in English about the apparitions in Portugal, was guest of the Catholic Writers' Guild, I was asked to introduce His Excellency. When he had finished speaking, the sponsors looked to me to announce that it was over. I think that chairmen should simply gavel such endings with a stock phrase like "Exeamus" or "That's all there is; there isn't any more" or even "Forever hold your peace." They rarely add much to what the speaker said and nobody listens to them anyway. But, following the pattern we use, I tried to wax, and being caught with the spirit of the gentle yet forceful Archbishop, I said that someday I must try my hand at a play on the subject. It sounds awfully stuffy now, but there was a spell cast that night and I think I half meant it.

You know—and I should know—that you can't make

promises to the Blessed Virgin and blithely forget them. She doesn't exactly nag, but like a mother, she reminds you, and until you come through you don't feel quite right with the world.

Of course, I knew about Fatima in the vague way I knew about Guadaloupe and LaSallette. I knew more about Lourdes—which was really her nineteenth-century message and she used the miraculous cure of bodies to temper our adoration of science. Fatima was her twentieth-century message, warning us that all-out wars and treaties were not going to stamp out the ideological assaults on her divine Son.

I was being prodded by these thoughts and a few accidental circumstances. Not protest, either. Why didn't somebody else do it? I wasn't equipped. I had never been to Fatima. Some Americans had been talking Fatima for years. But I hadn't paid much attention to them. The next day I was going to Pittsfield for a lecture and I got to New York early to pick up a few books on the subject of the apparitions. It was a far cry from a decision to try a play. I wanted to see if a simple story line could be found. I told her all that on the way to Pittsfield—that little citadel in New England's mountains—but no excuses were accepted. Of course, there were mundane reasons, too. We had to have a play. She didn't appear to me. Such favors are reserved for the Bernadettes, the Lucias, the Franciscos and the Jacintas of the world. But the gentle pushing was perceptible.

When I got home from that trip and assembled the envelopes, the backs of which bore nearly unintelligible scribblings due to the smoothness of the New Haven

273

Railroad, I knew that one could write a tightly knit and critically acceptable script about some fictitious happening foregrounding Fatima, or simply tell the story. The latter would be much too rambling for a play; it would require more sets than anyone would want to touch; it would be a huge, unwieldy production. But I also knew that was the script I was going to write. Playwriting form and critical acclaim seemed unimportant. The things that happened in Portugal thirty years ago should be made known to America—and, though it was late in the day, a dramatic representation might serve something of that purpose.

The staff agreed to plunge into it from an outline submitted in the middle of December. Mr. Wyatt moaned that I wouldn't consider a script with more than three sets ιand here I proposed to write one with twelve. *Lady of Fatima,* for that was the name of the proposed script, got written—or had one page set down after another—under pressing circumstances. I used to get back to Jersey City between twelve and one after performances of *Trial by Fire,* look briefly at the outline, spread out the half dozen or so of secondary source books and pound the typewriter for an hour or two.

Because of the shortness of time, we had to get at casting directly. Since the play was basically built around three children, they should be cast first. We opened readings to selected children from New York City's parochial schools and the professional schools. That took days and days, because we ιactually read 230 young aspirants and, since the very littlest couldn't read scripts, we had to invent new techniques.

David Reppa pondered the problem of twelve scenes

and came up with a unit set which solved the problem. Gurney and I pondered the problem of thirty some actors—many with bit parts—who looked sufficiently Portuguese to satisfy American audiences. One lady who was rejected because of her flaxen hair said on the way out, "Well! This is the foist time in the hist'ry of the American theayter it's been a handicap to be a blonde."

By hurrying home every night and pounding out a few more pages, I kept ahead of rehearsals and had a first draft ready by New Year's Day. On the twelfth of February we opened one of the biggest productions we had ever attempted. And we went into it with fear and trembling. My own trembling was more than a figure of speech. I had what my grandmother would have called "a case of nerves." I even went to a doctor and canceled speeches. The doctor said that it was good to sleep once in a while.

No one seemed to understand what was at stake. We had announced and cast a show from an idea. It was much too big and difficult for our stage. It didn't conform to any of the rules of the trade. It made impossible demands, such as a dancing sun. Yet we did it under a compulsion which we couldn't seem to divert. Although in the beginning it was just another play to pay the rent, it became an absorbing thing and we were living in the Fatima we had never seen. If it failed to come off—and nothing is as dangerous as tampering with sublimity—if we tackled something out of our depth and missed, she wouldn't be too pleased with us again. And the onus was on me. I said I'd come through, because every other department had come through magnificently. So we were tense and afraid on opening night.

The Doctor was reasonably afraid, too, although he didn't show it. He wrote the critics it was our Lenten play and perhaps they wouldn't be interested. He didn't want the anticipated beating which we could foresee from similar offerings before. This was too important for us to be taken to task on dramatic structure. The only important thing was to tell her story to our audiences. We didn't want the papers to confuse them. Those papers had practically ignored the apparition when it happened, although correspondents in Portugal had cabled the entire story. So only a few came.

The curtain went up as it had done so often before. The director had to step into a last-minute replacement. The Doctor and I huddled together for what seemed like interminable hours until the last curtain came down. There was no applause for minutes. Then it was weak and trance-like. There was no curtain call. The people left quietly. We still didn't know.

Then it broke. The people had been hungry for the simple story of Fatima. Within a few days, every seat was gone for our projected six-weeks run.

The slender press was divided. The trade papers paired this time, *Variety* saying, "Pretty good," and *Billboard*, "Not so good." Bob Coleman of the *Mirror* called it "inspiring" and told those who had materialistic jitters to visit us. The *Times* (in its two-inch habit) said: "Its sectarian appeal should be strong." Of course, the Catholic papers knew what we were about and were unstinting in their praise.

After Easter, we reopened for three more weeks and

perhaps could have gone on if we could have held our casts. But holding casts isn't our idea in the first place. We ask actors to stay with us long enough to get our investment back as compensation for being seen by the agents. It is not Blackfriar policy to run on and on. On this occasion we were torn between the wishes of our audiences and our regular policy. The fair solution was to release the play for the amateur market and close for the season.

The decision caused a few complications. Allen Kramer, our stage manager, was meandering through the haunts of actors around Times Square toward the end of the second run, looking for a few walk-on replacements. People were getting jobs or getting tired and the bit parts were hard to keep filled. An old friend, knowing his connection with the Guild, said to him in the confidential manner known to the trade, "Can you get me a pair for *Fatima?*" Kramer replied very honestly, "I can't get you a ticket, but I can get you a part in the show."

Early in the run, when seats were available, a lady with a delightful Irish accent called for reservations. "How much are they?" she asked.

"Two forty, one eighty and one twenty."

There was a pause, then the customer said, "They tell me Herself appears."

Now, that was a poser. We were having trouble enough stimulating a miracle without promising a real one, so our office said haltingly, "Well—yes. There is an apparition."

Another pause—and the voice said proudly, "I'll take the two-forty. It would be scant courtesy to view

Herself from a cheaper seat if I could afford the best."

And that is the most beautiful reason that Blackfriars' Guild ever heard for selling a good seat.

Just before curtain time on the last Saturday night of the second run, a woman appeared at the box-office with five little ones all scrubbed and shining like new pennies. She had a ticket, but since watching over the five and entertaining them was part of her Legion of Mary task, naturally she brought them. The particular night had been sold for weeks. There wasn't a place in our tiny theatre where they could stand. We had established a good relationship with the Fire Department and had no intention of jeopardizing it. Reluctantly— very reluctantly—we said "No." The issue was momentarily forgotten, but in the tension of "Curtain Going Up," we noticed the five huddled in a corner of the lobby, weeping copiously and reciting the Rosary. The Fire Department lost that one. When people ignore our authority and go to Headquarters, we accept new orders. The five saw *Lady of Fatima,* although some of them sat on windowsills.

The quiet compulsion of *Lady of Fatima* was felt in other ways. Long before we closed, requests came in for copies of the script for productions in schools and community groups throughout the country. Publication of the play came in May. Our audiences—even our critics—were serving a purpose they hadn't dreamed of. They were helping to get the "bugs" out of scripts that people seemed to want. Some day we'd get a script which would please everybody, but our first obligation was to our audiences and the great potential Catholic theatre of the country. That story could be told in such

278

a way that it would compel Broadway to listen. But Broadway's listening isn't as important as telling our story.

We had endured for seven years on 57th Street and many people had come and gone. But at this point Mr. Wyatt, one of the fixtures of Blackfriars'—a name synonomous with our work for seven years—relinquished his desk because of failing sight and general ill health. His place with us would be hard to fill. He was with us through seven lean years. Could we hope for a share in the analogy of Pharaoh's dream and go forth into seven fat years?

Mrs. Gerald Tyne stepped into the general management of our illusive fortunes and manifested a faith in our abilities which was sometimes disconcerting. If, as happened, there were no blocks of seats available for the last days of *Fatima,* she thought nothing of selling a house for sometime "next year," ignoring the fact that we, as friars, might be transferred, or dispossessed of our theatre which was becoming more desirable in the minds of organizations which could stand a higher rent. Fat or thin, next year wasn't going to be monotonous.

Engineer, writer, inventor, Mrs. Tyne brought us a New England housewife's appreciation for the value of a dollar and a determination that nobody would get off the telephone without buying something. She also brought two daughters who quickly became technical experts backstage, and a husband who found that his scientifically minded family had suddenly been convinced that theatre was fun and this one was important, so in his spare time he straightened out seating problems when his enthusiastic wife sold more tickets than we had seats for.

During the run of *Fatima* I was coming home on the Hudson and Manhattan Tubes (underneath the majestic Hudson, which I "cross" every day and almost never see), when across from me sat two women and four children, ranging in age from five to twelve. They looked Polish and were probably Catholic from their smiles and bows. In fact, the littlest one said, "Good evening, Father" (although it was well after midnight), and not to disconcert her I said, "Good evening," too. The women nodded and looked at the other children, indicating that they were remiss in manners if they didn't speak, too. So, the two older children muttered politely, but the remaining one—about six years old—stared at me uncertainly. Finally, her mother (I presume) said encouragingly, "Say something to the priest." And the little one said solemnly so the whole car could hear, "Bless me, Father, for I have sinned."

Commuting had its compensations, although there is a certain monotony about the pattern. In four years I have traveled just short of 30,000 miles to and from Blackfriars to my home at the Sacred Heart Priory in Jersey City. That is more than the equivalent of a trip around the world at the Equator. Even though the latter alternative seems more romantic, I'm sure I've seen as much and kept cooler in my more circumscribed journeyings.

XXI: MINSTRELS AND KINGS

THE FALL OF 1948 FOUND US SOMEWHAT RE-freshed and ready (after a fashion) to step up to our eighth season. We had a script centered around the songs of Thomas Moore, the Irish poet. It had known several names in its day but was finally called *The Minstrel Boy*. W. A. S. Douglas, formerly of the Chicago *Sun,* wrote it a long time ago. I had done a little rewriting on it when it was held by Frank Fay, the pooka's friend, but Blackfriars didn't get it until the summer of 1948.

Even though it wouldn't pass for precise history, it would give its audience a chance to hear *Believe Me If All Those Endearing Young Charms, The Meeting of the Waters, The Harp That Once Through Tara's Hall, Oh Breathe Not His Name,* and *The Minstrel Boy.* We wanted to try it just to hear them if we could get a singer and the rest of a large cast. Mr. Gurney didn't even offer his tin ear to the musical auditions, so I had the pleasure of hearing and wire-recording some thirty-eight aspiring Irish thrushes. Each in turn sang *The Minstrel Boy* and *Believe Me.* You can believe me that, long before the curtain went up, I'd cringe at even a few bars of those beautiful numbers. You can get too much of a good thing. Besides hearing the singers in preliminaries and the more successful ones in finals, I had to play most of their songs back to myself, because it is difficult to remember voices and we were trying to be fair. Then, again, there was more than voices to consider. They had to be able to act; they had to be young; and they had to look remotely like Irishmen. So many superb voices seem to be developed in middle-aged Italians that the task was fairly complicated.

We picked Tom Donahue—a good choice—and our departments rolled into action. If much of this was routine by now, the casting wasn't. In the past, on three occasions, we had sought—and found with great difficulty—three or four actors who sounded like genuine Irishmen. But this time we had to gather together about twenty. In time, we managed it with the help of people with names like Vraz, Perrault, Press, and Barrs.

Mr. Douglas had complicated the job by having Tom Moore, at the time of his death, hear himself sing his famous songs as a young man. That put two Toms onstage at once. And since he wanted to demonstrate that the poet was a child prodigy, we had Tom as a child to feature, too. Although the resemblance between the three chosen was only in the name on the left hand side of the programme, one must admit that time brings great changes.

The selection of "Old Tom" marked one of my rare excursions into talent scouting. Visiting a Dominican who was leaving for Australia to teach, I heard Charles Dolan of Jersey City sing a few songs. He was seventy-one. Moore died at seventy-two. I signed him up. The only trouble with him was that he was so vital we could never quite soften him up for the death scene. From a box-office point of view he was terrific, because his nine children and his relatives and friends came from all over the country and promised to keep us running indefinitely.

We were doing things in the grand manner that fall because Mrs. Tyne was selling tickets to everybody —even those brash souls who were accustomed to call us up as an information bureau. For example, author Douglas called for a harp. We got three harps: one for the actor, one for backstage to cover the actor, and another for our pit ensemble. That seemed reasonable enough, but in our enthusiasm at one time we had four harps. The Doctor counted them, looked at me, counted them again, and promptly sent one back. I guess I was overstepping. But I wasn't taking up the harp on company time and funds as he seemed to imply.

The author wanted a piano—circa 1800. I got a piano—circa eighteen something early. It was just right except that we couldn't tune it to the harp or it would have burst asunder. If we brought the harp— or all the harps—down to a pitch where the old piano could contain itself, Mr. Moore—or rather Master and the two Mister Moores—couldn't sing. So I sent the piano back and got another one.

Gurney and I always doubted that anyone in the promotion department ever read a script, and our misgivings were strengthened by a casting episode. We were comparing notes one day and he told me that the cast was complete except for a harp-carrier. That strange designation was given one of the characters who brought a harp to Jack Moore's Grocery and Spirits Store and left it to cover his growing bill. It was this harp which started Tom off on that phase of his career. Mrs. Tyne, lending only one ear from her telephone high pressure and not quite getting Gurney's Londonese, made a mental note to right that little problem.

For days after that she kept sending giants down to the theatre to read. The harp-carrier was supposed to be a little mousey man and we wondered why no one showed up except these better than six footers. Finally we asked her what was happening and she replied, "Well, you want a hod-carrier, don't you?"

There was a small but good bit in the play for Robert Emmet. One day a young man walked in and said, "I'm Robert Emmett." Since all the variations of Napoleon and George Washington come into casting offices, we smiled and said, "Yes—but we'll determine that. What is your name?"

To which he replied, "Robert Emmett—but I spell it with two 't's.' " Well, strange as it seems, he was Robert Emmett, and he became Robert Emmet in the play, doing a good job and getting good notices. That's carrying type-casting to an extreme.

Mr. Douglas came to town for dress rehearsals and proved himself an understanding author by agreeing that we were worthy of a substantial percentage in the event of a commercial production, and—having sat to leeward of my pipe—buying us a box of good cigars even before we opened.

On the fourteenth of October, we sang our songs and played our harps and spoke our lines for the public. The Irish laughed a bit and wept a bit and the non-Irish said they felt like it at times. The press was eminently reasonable, with the Catholic papers being pleased most. The *Mirror, Variety* and *The Enquirer* came up a close second. *Billboard,* the *World-Telegram,* and the *Wall Street Journal* approved with understanding reservations. A new era had come, because the *Times,* displaying a new set of initials under its review, at last gave us more than two inches and thought the play better than fair. Mr. Freedley of the *Telegraph* was the least pleased of all, saying it was "strictly for the minor leagues."

Whatever league we were in, we played forty-six times, had some nibbles from commercial producers and sent audiences away with a warm and friendly feeling.

Mrs. Tyne blandly announced one day that, instead of selling single houses, she was giving customers a new kind of two-for-one. For the same telephone call they were permitted to reserve a house for the following show, too. The advance sale for Lent had thus become so impressive that we decided to open the Lenten play earlier than usual and skip the customary mid-winter offering. She had been telling them of an unusual script about Blessed Martin de Porres which I was working on, but the most unusual thing about it was that it wasn't nearly finished and I wanted to throw it up on more than one occasion.

The full story of this biographical endeavor is perhaps worthy of telling, because, while it breaks all the rules of technique, commercial procedure and common sense in promoting, it won us a large and glowing press, the longest run in our history and results—tangible and intangible—which seem to be endless.

About twenty-five years ago I discovered Blessed Martin and read the little literature in English which had been written on him up to that time. It has been augmented greatly since. Thinking there was a story in the life of the gentle mulatto, I wrote to Peru and asked the Dominicans there to send me what books they might have. Months later, two slim volumes arrived and I began to apply my Spanish—which boasts a thousand nouns and no verbs—to the task. There was almost no chronology in the Spanish books. They offered episodes taken apparently at random to demonstrate his faith or his charity, but, since nothing was dated except his birth and death, there was no indication of growth or development.

This was during my novitiate days and I even induced a Spanish novice to give me an insight into some knotty passages replete with unusual verb forms. As he read in a curious English, I made notes, but when he got onto a particularly syrupy passage filled with Latin "Ahs" and "Ohs," I put my pencil down. He continued awhile and then asked, "Hwat ees thee mahter?"

I replied, "I think that is the bunk."

He shrugged: "Bot—eet ees preety good bonk."

With a mess of notes, I debated whether or not to attempt a life of Martin on the lines of Willa Cather's *Death Comes for the Archbishop*. It was hopeless to do a real job from such inadequate secondary sources, nor did I think that American readers would like Martin if they were asked to believe things so foreign to the hardening process they had unconsciously drawn from Puritanism and the Reformation. Three or four chapters got as far as a first draft and then I was con-

286

vinced that I was incapable of doing anything worth reading. I had never been in Peru. I had no knowledge or of feeling for background. You can't write a book without mentioning a tree or flower or gateway. So, placidly putting the poor pages in the department of things someone else better do, I went my way and let Martin go his.

Seven or eight years ago, Father Norbert Georges, a Dominican who lived next to me at St. Vincent's and operated the Blessed Martin Guild, came into my room and said "Why don't you write a play about Blessed Martin?" I asked him "Why?" because that's always a good first question, and he said that schools were frequently asking for such material. I told him I didn't know how to write school plays and didn't have any material, anyhow. He said he had the entire "Process" for Martin's beatification and that it would be available to me. But there were other pressing things and we dropped the matter again.

When *Lady of Fatima* was finished, we at Black-friars were rather happy about the spiritual effects the play had and naturally we looked for something of the same pattern for the following Lent. We might bow to professional criticism during the year, but Lent was ours. And the problem of scripts seemed no nearer a solution than it had been the previous year. So we talked about many things and Martin was one of them.

There was pressure—gentle pressure—but pressure reminding me of *Fatima*. I agreed to look at Father Georges' colored slides of Lima and came out of that session with half a page of notes, mainly geographical references of the old city. Then I received the eight-hundred pages of crowded handwriting which was the translation of the "Process." This was the testimony of hundreds of witnesses who under oath told an ecclesiastical court the most striking events of Martin's life.

It took a week to put things in order, and then I started to read, still not convinced that there was what we call a play in the enormous amount of material. That was because the testimony was taken in 1660 and 1664—twenty and twenty-four years after the holy man had died. Consequenly, most of the first-hand witnesses were old and knew Martin when he was coming toward the end of his life. And there wasn't a bit of conflict there. Crystallized in good, Martin went his way helping people quietly—and that isn't drama. What made him do it? Wasn't there some conflict in his own soul? No doubt there had been, but over the years he had beaten it out.

That's one of the problems of writing about saints. Their emotions are not on the surface and the playwright needs ready laughter and tears.

Another point which caused me to forgive the Spanish writers and the subsequent writers in English for their lack of chronology was that the original sources had none. People just groped back from memory and told stories. No dates. Well, you could figure a sort of internal time schedule if you analyzed the age of each witness and tried to correlate the relationship with one another and with Martin.

I put all sorts of inconsequential and random notes on file cards until I knew who married whom in Lima in 1620 and who stole from whom and all that. But I didn't have a conflict nor a story line for a play.

The documents were finished by the beginning of September and then the cross-filing began. About a hundred episodes were lined up on paper and still no angles, as they say in the trade. All that reading gave me only two angles—the unwanted child whose father deserted him and the mulatto in a white man's world.

When scenes and acts were outlined and thrown away time after time, I announced at Blackfriars that I was beaten again. I couldn't get a story out of primary sources and so thought we ought to think of another play. But that was a little late. Mrs. Tyne had been selling houses on Blessed Martin. I was caught in Martin's real story and couldn't deviate—Well, I'd try but I wouldn't promise anything. There wasn't any second-act curtain, no crisis—unless such be found in his childhood, and the documents said little about that.

Preoccupations came with *The Minstrel Boy,* but finally, in November, a working draft of the script was ready for our readers. They were strangely enough divided—all liking parts but few liking all. Most of the women who read it first thought that the childhood of Martin and his mother's scenes were good theatre but that the monastery scenes were just talk. Men on the other hand weren't sure about the melodrama at the start but thought the adult Martin would play. Since they couldn't agree, they got it pretty much as it stood and we began the difficult task of casting, because it was far from actor-proof.

David Reppa, whose sets for *Fatima* and *Minstrel Boy* manifested a maturity, had gone to the coast, but Floyd Allen caught the spirit and came up with designs

289

which we thought just right. Irene Griffin dove into the sixteenth century and had the place full of sketches for costumes.

The matter of a title was intriguing, too. To call it "Blessed Martin" would scare away those who feared to be preached to in the theatre. "Martin" would mean nothing to many, too. There was no title at hand which expressed what the play was about. So we settled on the name of his city. In 1535, Pizarro founded his new capital and dedicated it to the three Kings of the Epiphany on that feast day, calling it "Ciudad de los Reyes."

The new name "Lima" is obviously a corruption of the name of the river "Rimac." I haven't been able to find out if the name was ever officially changed. At least the Peruvian Consulate had no answer, nor did the Lima Library at Catholic University, nor the map-makers, nor the air-lines, nor the Public Library nor the better-known information centers. With a production coming up, we had no time to go further into this little research matter. So, by dropping the articles, the title became *City of Kings*.

Casting was not easy. Actually, for the past couple of years, casting had not been easy, because we had been rather unintentionally tending toward plays of simple people and most of our actors trained in stock or drama schools seemed most adept at drawing-room comedy. They were frequently good in the media they knew, but we didn't want that style and they weren't seasoned enough to change. *Hoboes* was Flemish and earthy; *Fire* was elemental enough; *Fatima* was the story of Portuguese peasants; *Minstrel Boy* was drawing room enough, but it demanded first Irish and English accents; and *Kings* was frontier stuff.

So we read and reread people until they must have been tired of the grilling. It paid off, however, because most critics—official and otherwise—assured us it was our best cast to date. I'm so conscious of the help of that cast in making the script play that I must deliberately hold myself in check to avoid going off in tributes to nearly all of them. Let me settle with one symbol. Elwood Smith, who did Martin, underplayed so brilliantly that theatre-goers and non-theatre-goers simply think of him as Martin. And when his mother's illness called him to New Orleans, Julian Mayfield stepped in on short notice and was accepted completely.

The production was put together with all the fears and tensions of our more successful plays. But in this case they seemed rolled into one and hung about my neck. I was on the spot. Those who claimed that New York Blackfriars was quietly coming round to a stage for self-exploitation—and there were some and they spoke aloud—didn't know the effort we made to find scripts, nor the difficulties involved in satisfying enough people to remain solvent and keep actors interested, nor the reluctance with which we doubled the work of our undermanned staff while I crept away to do a historical play. But their lack of knowledge on the subject merely made the fear of failure greater.

We had a big advance sale, we had a good cast, we had a great cause. Did we have a play? It's a responsibility—even in theatre. I didn't want to face opening night.

There were episodes which lightened the tension. There always were. But at best they were moments of escape and forgetfulness. I began to dream of Peru, even though we laughed our way into the production on the surface.

One of the Negro actors brought a statue of Blessed Martin home. His roommate, who was not a Catholic, asked who the "gent" was. When he heard it was Martin he grunted, but the little statuette fascinated him and he asked, "What is the address of Blackfriars?" His informant said, "316 West 57th St."

The next day he brought home $540.00 from playing 316 in the "numbers" game and now treats Martin with respect approaching awe.

The play opens with Martin as a child and, after getting an actor as good as Herbert Coleman for the job, we began to look around for understudies. St. Mark's School sent down three lads one Friday morning and I worked them until after their lunch hour. So we sent them across the street to a restaurant of the counter-and-stool type for something to eat. They lined up and practically astounded the establishment and its habitues by saying grace before meals in public. Then they completed the staggering effect by ordering three hamburgers on Friday.

Martin died during the singing of the "*Credo.*" So I dug up an old plain-chant "Credo" from the Dominican liturgical books, taught it to the cast and took their wire-recording to a studio to have some records made. The engineer heard it several times and, as he was labeling the last record, he was humming it. I asked him if he liked it and he said, "Yeah! It's catchy. Did you write it?"

Overheard in the lobby opening night were two representatives of the Negro press. One said, in effect, "There's one thing I can't understand. That Italian woman, Mother Cabrini, was canonized shortly after she died and Martin has waited three hundred years. That's discrimination."

And so the stories went. But we did open to a subdued audience. We still didn't know what the reaction was during the one intermission—because nobody said much. Even the final curtain wasn't reassuring. But the curtain calls did it and the next morning we knew the entire press wasn't a typographical error. I won't quote this time. Martin came to New York and people welcomed him. The *Times* even glowed.

Tickets sold naturally but there was a more important series of intangible results. Stories came in—haltingly and diffidently—of people going back to the practice of their religion. Both in offering acceptable theatre and in helping people in more important matters we had struck a formula and Blackfriars was coming of age.

XXII: THE MASQUE IS OFF

IN THAT SUMMER OF '49, THE CATHOLIC THEATRE
Conference held a convention in Hollywood. The organization had come of age and was answering the
questions and supplying the needs of close to 500 members. On the way to the coast I read newspapers more
thoroughly than usual. Having been compelled to read
news services and national magazines during the years
when I was attempting to edit *The Holy Name Journal,*
I went through a period of reaction when I chose to let
newspapers pretty much alone. But they do reward one
from time to time and on this occasion the report on a
single day of the Foley Square trial of eleven communists was the best high comedy I had seen in months.

The United States of America actually had the
courage—and the permission—to say what many of us
had been saying for years. We dared echo the Soviet
assertions of years that they intended to overthrow our
government by force and violence. Our newspapers
were actually printing what everybody knew. Something of staggering importance had happened. Some
lid was off. The few thousand who had led us around
by the nose actually heard a few small voices of protest
coming from the millions of victims. So, instead of the
inevitable slavery which seemed to be in the cards,
there was hope of resistance and freedom.

Such a release could easily induce hysteria. We might

be saved. That's why I dare call it high comedy. It was the first real indication that the imminent tragedy —perhaps the greatest in history—might be averted. We could talk back. Maybe we could fight back. The transcript of the trial itself was the most fabulous collection of barefaced lies, easily sprung traps, childish filibustering and magnificent human patience that our legal customs might be preserved in the history of court procedure. That statement seems a good risk, because I feel certain that never before were sane men allowed to appear before a tribunal daily and contort justice for a whole year.

That was obviously our next show. People couldn't appear daily in the small Federal Court in Manhattan to watch it, but we could pick out some of the highlights. And this was not make believe. This was so real as to chill us. I wrote Bob Healey and asked him if he would run through the daily reporting and see what line the story might take. I'd be back soon and we'd open with it if it could be bent, twisted or jammed into a story line.

It never became a play of which the formalists could approve. It was rather a juxtaposition of communist words, taken in most cases verbatim from the witnesses and defendants, with well-known communist practice. That little device can pack a punch. Healey picked six episodes. When the witnesses and defendants asserted— sometimes shouting—that Kremlin-inspired democracy was to help the Negro, we just gave them the Scottsboro case from the records of those who were there. When they told of the advantages for women in Russia, we re-enacted the Kasenkina case in which the teacher leaped in panic out of the Russian Embassy window rather than return home. When our labor practices were ridiculed, we gave the story behind a famous Allys Chalmers strike. Then there were the Canadian spy case, and the unbelievable switch of the *Daily Worker* when Germany attacked Russia. For the final impact we quoted their criticisms of American justice and presented a section of the trial of Cardinal Mindszenty. That was all. Just recall the routine Soviet practice and then read the testimony of that amazing trial. It makes quite a show.

Remember, however, that our emancipation was not complete. It is not complete yet. This trial was merely a harbinger that freedom might again be ours. The "transmission belt" of school, press and entertainment field had been markedly infiltrated and a sort of undefined reign of terror had been going on. I'm not witch hunting or saying, "Didn't we have an awful time?"—building it much blacker the while. I'm reporting simply that during the last ten years, when too many of the active members of Equity's Council were said to be members of from one to nineteen communist fronts, many actors were afraid to make a statement which might be interpreted as unfriendly to Soviet Russia—the enemy of the world, the enemy of human dignity and the avowed enemy of God.

One statistical report I can make. In twenty-nine shows, we averaged about one actor or technician per show quitting before opening. A job came up, sickness struck, money ran out or they were called home for one of many reasons which were none of our business. Many left us after opening because they got paying jobs, but over the years, practically everybody opened, because they liked being seen at Blackfriars by agents and critics.

In *Shake Hands with the Devil*—the name Bob Healey and I gave this documentary—forty-two actors and technicians walked out between the time they got their final assignments and opening night. I'm sure they were not all communists or frontists. I haven't much right to say that, because we never investigated our actors. But I knew some of them; they had worked with us before; some of them were good actors and those I knew were good people. But forty-two phoned, sent cards, or just disappeared. Those who contacted us said they had just received a telegram (that night) confirming a coveted job, there was illness in the family on the West Coast, they were suddenly too exhausted to do another play, and so on down the line.

How many were telling the simple truth I shall never know or seek to know. But I want to point out that actors were terrorized two years ago and that the recent exhausting investigating committees and "witch-hunts" which annoy so many people are giving them the first breath of fresh air they have had since it became fashionable in theatrical circles to discuss liberals and reactionaries without, of course, defining terms.

That we have police and Federal agents in the audience opening night was requested by some of the actors who had the courage to buck the trend. Having grown in the knowledge of the American theatre, we took the necessary precautions.

I said once in these pages—and somewhat softly—there is more to opening a theatre in New York than meets the eye. We weren't bothered. We weren't important enough to be bothered. But the terrorism was there and that is a bother or worse in America.

A more terrifying matter from a producer's viewpoint is that a spokesman for the government thought we shouldn't open until the trial was closed, lest it should be used in the expected appeal as a prejudicial incident. We might use the episodes of communist activities but we were asked not to portray the easily identifiable trial with its direct quotes. So we prepared another frame. It never reached the actors, but I still have some of the script. The trial seemed headed for conclusion on time, but small delays made it touch and go. In the announcement to the religious of the area, I asked for special prayers and we wound up in a photo finish. Sentence was passed on Saturday morning; at least, that is when it reached the newspapers. Saturday noontime, the Sisters began arriving for their first dress rehearsal. I told a few that we had been worried and they brushed it aside with a casual, "There wasn't any doubt. We had the children praying."

The American press liked it; the anti-American press lashed out with attacks persisting in calling black white. Most satisfying comment came from one who had a major part in the trial in the words, "You caught the diabolicalism in the whole thing."

Lent was coming up and we had no scripts. After much discussion, it was agreed that I should try a play on the life of St. Paul. It was much too big to handle but we faced a kind of pressure which was becoming routine. Again a good play might be written on one episode, but the last Apostle has given us an autobiography with material for a serial which would put old thrillers to shame. My outline called for twenty-four scenes. Shades of DeMille, Lavery, McCleery! Another problem was that while I had one of the two copies in the country of the "Process" for Blessed Martin and thus could pose as an authority, genuine Pauline scholars are legion, and reconciling the opinions of various schools of thought down the centuries makes it bold indeed to say "This is what happened." There is a North Galatian theory and a South Galatian theory; there are those who say St. Luke came from Antioch in Syria and others from Antioch in Pisidia; there are those who say Paul went far west of Rome between the two imprisonments and others who say he never left Rome; and the dogmatic implications of the controversy with St. Peter mount into many volumes.

But we cast the forty-seven characters, put them in formalized costumes in front of stylized sets, cut two scenes including the dramatic climax before opening (and four more scenes after the first night) and faced our public. Mr. Gurney said that we couldn't print the usual synopsis of scenes because people would get up and go home, so we turned the cover of the programme into a map of the journeys of our hero.

The press was eminently fair, pointing out that the play was just too big in scope to develop character sufficiently. The one liberty I took in quotations apparently confused one of our customers. For fluidity in acting, I chose here and there between the Douay version of the Bible, the Confraternity edition of the New Testament and Monsignor Knox's translation. For example, I preferred the Knox "echoing bronze" to the better known "sounding brass." The lady in question wrote in to ask for copies for her study club of "the author's" magnificent treatise on charity which begins, "If I speak with the tongues of men and of angels and have not charity . . . . " St. Paul helped in devious ways.

Summer brought its usual share of problems, but the one which gave us the most concern was a dispossess notice stuck on the office door with Scotch tape. That's an unadvertised use for that very serviceable article. No communication by letter or phone from the new owner of the building; no expressed complaints about the past; no discussion about an increase in rent—just "Get out."

The Doctor wasn't around at all that summer, so Mrs. Tyne and I had the dubious pleasure of looking for a new theatre. The infant industry of television had grown so rapidly in a few years that all the ailing movie houses, all the dark theatres, some offices, lofts, warehouses and garages had new names like Studio 74 of one chain or another. Some day, television will build with a definite plan and dump these inadequate makeshifts back on the market; some day, theatres may rise again in New York when certain restrictions in building laws are changed; but at this point in time there was nothing available except in outlying districts. We had to be central to hold our Northern Jersey, Long Island and Westchester trade. After talking to people about warehouses on the North River, we investigated the possibility of converting a former Russian church. The quest was so hopeless that reputable real estate agencies stopped answering our letters or returning our phone calls. Television, which has been known to spend

$100,000 for a show, has picked the city clean and is looking for more.

We had been saved from falling off precipices so often that I had a deep-down feeling that something would happen, but I didn't know what it might be. Talking to the new owner would have been futile; that possibility was checked. One church made the offer of a well-equipped theatre, but there was the likelihood that its whole plant would lose its tax exemption because we sold tickets, so that knowledge kept us away from all churches. An experimental theatre was for sale. It would cost three times our recent income to maintain and it had even fewer seats. We couldn't hold casts in conscience or, in fact, for longer runs. So we couldn't afford it. I was getting to know the financial condition of all the little movie-house owners in Manhattan. What all this has to with a theatre of ideas, I don't know, but theatre has ramifications.

Late in the summer (we managed a brief extension by promising to go quietly and without benefit of a court action which we couldn't win), a Mr. Franklin Hauser walked into the office. He walked in because he was curious about the notice which I left stuck on the door. It was such a complete and unexpected insult that it drew to itself a characteristic of untouchability. Somebody with that kind of power put it there; we read it; now let it stay there as a symbol of that power until the tape fell off. Mr. Hauser passed it every day going to his office, which was just down the corridor, and he walked gingerly one day, wondering (I presume) why we didn't take it down, make a fight or get out.

He probably knew as little about our operation as we knew about his, but a few conversations taught us that he and Mr. John Gilbert ran the School of Radio Technique which had branches in New York, Chicago and Hollywood and a television department in our aging building. We had vaguely feared that this outfit would some day need a theatre and ours was in their building but the issue was never raised. Mr. Hauser became indignant that we were to be so summarily expelled. He and Mr. Gilbert had been offered the theatre at more than three times what we had been paying. So they took it, not knowing just what they would do with it in their last-gasp expansion before the GI Bill went out of effect and invited us to play our full schedules at our old rent. It happened again. The hero arrived just as the villain was about to foreclose the mortgage and we could sail along as sub-tenants.

When that excitement was passed, we announced as our next play *Angel with Red Hair.* Ted Farah, a local Associated Press man, born in eastern Canada, though not of French extraction, brought us a French-Canadian story with much charm, with one set (after we wrote out a second) and nine characters. Such a combination is a great joy to a producer who is used to mobs of North Galatians, Peruvians or Portuguese, not because of prejudice against any nationality but rather against mobs. If it were a much worse play we'd probably have worked on it, but it happened to be a good play.

Set in the bucolic background of a sleepy Canadian village, it pitted the reforming forces of modernity against the spirit of Brother Hilaire who, although he

302

was dead for hundreds of years, in his own way watched over the fortunes of and even influenced the actions of those who remembered him. Peggy Ann McCay as the ingenue (if that word is still in good usage) gave the play a big lift and the press, by and large, agreed with that opinion of ours. It is difficult, as always, to single out performances, because the whole cast came off well. Brother Hilaire, who doesn't appear, merely laughs at the final curtain, and Dennis Gurney got an old friend of his, Edward Arnold, to make the record of Hilaire's laugh which shook the rafters of the theatre.

During the play-doctoring days, Mr. Farah asked if we'd mind having a lamb brought onstage. It helped two sequences and it should be easy to manage. Having gone through the experience of Rainbow, various cats, dogs and mice, I couldn't see how a little lamb would be a problem, so it was left in. You can make the same mistake over and over again! New York meat packers offered so many problems because of departments that we decided to look elsewhere. It seems that if a lamb comes to New York, labeled for the table, you must have a law passed to borrow him for an actor. New Jersey doesn't ask so many questions. So I contacted a meat man in the Jersey City stock-yards and was told that the right sort might be bought for fifteen dollars. That seemed a reasonable expense for a good effect. I bundled him—Hector was his name in the script—into a car and started him out on the stairway to stardom. The policeman whose booth I passed in the Holland Tunnel looked at me, looked at Hector, and looked back at me, but held his peace. Perhaps they see strange things in the Holland Tunnel.

Arriving at the theatre—and this is a few days before opening—Hector and I agreed that he couldn't live there happily. The housing problem again. All actors seem to face it. Since there are no pleasant farms in the forties of fifties, we called veterinarians and dog and cat hospitals in the area. We found one in the sixties which would board a lamb for three dollars a day. He was installed in a private room, but the doctor—after a thorough psychiatric analysis—reported that he was lonesome. He must have a companion or he would go into a decline. Another lamb, much more violent, was secured from the stockyards, and this time the policeman closed his eyes in pain. He firmly believes that I always have a lamb in the back seat.

As Hector was no good at finding his way around New York alone, we had to hire a keeper to take him to and from the theatre. Then the psychiatric vet warned us that he couldn't walk the few blocks because he was emotionally disturbed by crowds, automobiles, dogs and New York in general, so he made the nightly trip by taxicab. The nightly five-minute appearance of Hector cost us five hundred dollars.

Let's close the episode by saying that in the next play we shifted from the problem of lambs to the problem of singers. You may decide which is more difficult. Dennis Gurney started the whole thing by advocating that we get into the operatic field. His reasons were that we had to be different and truly experimental. We had done an increasing number of "audience" shows and the newer critics weren't challenged by such as *Fatima* and *Armor of Light*. They weren't condescending, but they were dropping us into

for their opposite number in the double-cast system; or they announce flatly that they won't be in next week.

Still, I thought I was going to be a tenor once, and perhaps I understand them. For, when a cast was checked in for the night, they gave all the audiences could have hoped for. Good singers at work are a pleasure.

The press was a bit confused, but the final score was in our favor. Drama critics said that the music department should have covered it, and vice versa. Audiences, as at opera, ballet and modern dance, were bewildered enough to go home satisfied. Joan Scardon's costumes were the best we had done; Floyd Allan's sets were unimpeachable; Joan Tyne's lighting was right. Those things I understood. The press and audience went away happy. I can do no less. But for my own peace of mind, perhaps I should stick to my field.

It was our thirty-first production in New York and the Voice of America in a German broadcast pointed out that it was the first opera ever written on a New Testament subject. Under the musical direction of Herbert Garber, *Open the Gates*—for that was the name of the piece—must go down as an artistic success.

That's more or less the story. Maybe it has no dramatic conclusion such as have a Hollywood extravaganza, a big downtown production, professional in every way, or a television series which would bring our ideas to millions. And maybe it holds all these possibilities. Hollywood has said, "Come on out and work on Fatima"; conferences are going on about a commercial

Broadway production which should play to larger audiences; the School of Radio Technique has talked at length of working with us to do just the right kind of television programmes.

This is, however, a story of the last twenty years—the struggling years—and not speculation on an uncertain future. It's been a try—maybe even a good try—which will serve its immediate purpose and be forgotten. Yeats and the Abbey Players ran their tempestuous course battling casts and audiences. But Yeats was the conscious artist and the rules he tried to impose were not always accepted by all. Gheon in France is more understandable. He casually broke all the unimportant rules, yet in his little plays he gets something said and hits with some of the impact of St. Luke.

Blackfriars' Guild has adhered to a definite set of standards in play selection and that is perhaps its justification. If it has stumbled in production standards or in pleasing all of the great diversity of people who came to watch, the reasons are obvious enough and need little apology. Whether it is destined for a period of success on its own will be left to the future.

At least, many of its plays have been popular with a fast-growing and fast-improving Catholic theatre throughout the country. *Lady of Fatima,* which was written and rewritten in production and which had the benefit of New York critics—professional and otherwise, has played between 750 and 1,000 performances in the "provinces" and *City of Kings* has had at least nine productions in Ireland. We have whittled and polished to the best of our ability a few plays a year and have offered them to those who were looking for the

308

things we had sought twenty years ago. Maybe that is our contribution. And I've always felt that anyone who succeeded in building a theatre like Blackfriars in New York or anywhere else would profit by knowing what I have seen throughout the years.

Remember, too, that this is a book about the Blackfriars' Guild, so it is about a group activity. If I have mixed up my reporting with theories, it's because I knew what I was thinking and couldn't know what others were thinking unless they told me. If my part grows into undue importance, it is because I couldn't possibly give due credit to the thousands who made it possible. It's not a one- or two-man job, but a complete sharing among many. If I've neglected hundreds who should have a part in this report, I know they'll understand. If I've laughed at those who have worked closest to me, it's because I wanted you to know that there was fun in it and that we weren't being tragic. And if I've never had time or opportunity to explain to patient religious superiors, thousands of actors, hundreds of playwrights and legions of friends, let me now offer them, along with all who wish to hear, what one experiment in theatre looks like from behind the masque.